KINGS & PROPHETS

KINGS & PROPHETS

Monarchic Power,

Inspired Leadership,

& Sacred Text in

Biblical Narrative

Cristiano Grottanelli

New York   Oxford

Oxford University Press

1999

Oxford University Press

Oxford   New York

Athens   Auckland   Bangkok   Bogota   Buenos Aires   Calcutta
Cape Town   Chennai   Dar es Salaam   Delhi   Florence   Hong Kong   Istanbul
Karachi   Kuala Lumpur   Madrid   Melbourne   Mexico City   Mumbai
Nairobi   Paris   São Paulo   Singapore   Taipei   Tokyo   Toronto   Warsaw

and associated companies in

Berlin   Ibadan

Copyright © 1999 by Cristiano Grottanelli

Published by Oxford University Press, Inc.
198 Madison Avenue, New York, New York 10016

Oxford is a registered trademark of Oxford University Press

Chapter 2, 5, 6, and 9 translated by Lesley Antonelli Sullivan

Library of Congress Cataloging-in-Publication Data
Grottanelli, C. (Cristiano)
Kings and prophets : monarchic power, inspired leadership, and
sacred text in biblical narrative / by Cristiano Grottanelli.
    p.   cm.
Includes bibliographical references and index.
ISBN 0-19-507196-4
1. Kings and rulers—Biblical teaching.   2. Religion and state—
Israel—History.   3. Religion and state—Middle East—History.
4. Religion and state—Mediterranean Region—History.   5. Israel—
Kings and rulers—Religious aspects.   6. Middle East—Kings and
rulers—Religious aspects.   7. Mediterranean Region—Kings and
rulers—Religious aspects.   8. Prophets.   9. Bible. O.T.—
Criticism, interpretation, etc.   I. Title.
BS1199.K5G76   1998
221.9'5—dc21   97-7851

9 8 7 6 5 4 3 2 1

Printed in the United States of America
on acid-free paper

ACKNOWLEDGMENTS

Though the introduction was written in 1996 especially for this volume, this book is a collection of essays published between 1977 and 1993.

Chapter 1 appeared as *The King's Grace and the Helpless Woman: A Comparative Study of the Stories of Ruth, Charila, Sītā*: History of Religions 22 (1982), pp. 1–24.

Chapter 2 was published as *Dal re al profeta: distribuzione di cereali e ideale religioso nella Bibbia ebraica*, in Rita Dolce and Carlo Zaccagnini (eds.), *Il pane del re. Accumulo e distribuzione dei cereali nell'Oriente antico*, Clueb, Bologna 1989, pp. 117–135.

Chapter 3 appeared as *The Enemy King Is a Monster: A Biblical Equation*: Studi Storico-Religiosi 3 (1979), pp. 5–36.

Chapter 4 appeared as *The Story of Deborah and Baraq: A Comparative Approach*: Studi e Materiali di Storia delle Religioni 53 (1987), pp. 149–164.

Chapter 5 appeared as *Possessione carismatica e razionalizzazione statale nella Bibbia ebraica*: Studi Storico-Religiosi I (1977), pp. 263–288.

Chapter 6 was published as *Specialisti del soprannaturale e potere nella Bibbia ebraica: appunti e spunti*, in Frederick Mario Fales, Cristiano Grottanelli (eds.), *Soprannaturale e potere nel modo antico e nelle società tradizionali*, Franco Angeli, Milan 1985, pp. 119–140.

Chapter 7 was published as *Healers and Saviours of the Ancient Mediterranean in Pre-Classical Times* in Ugo Bianchi (ed.), *La soteriologia dei culti orientali nell'Impero Romano*, Brill, Leiden 1982, pp. 649–670.

Chapter 8 appeared as *Biblical Narrative and the Ancient Novel*: Quaderni Urbinati di Cultura Classica 27 (1987), pp. 7–34.

Chapter 9 was published as *Profezia e scrittura nel Vicino Oriente*: La Ricerca Folklorica 5 (1982), pp. 57–62.

Chapter 10 appeared as *Making Room for the Written Law*: History of Religions 34 (1994), pp. 246–264.

Though I have corrected some mistakes, the essays collected in this volume have not been modified. Even the notes have remained as they were (for bibliographical abbreviations, see the list on page ix).I have not attempted to alter

VI   ACKNOWLEDGMENTS

their contents or to update the bibliography—not even when other scholars had discussed my work in print (Walter Burkert, Ioan Culianu, Giovanni Garbini, Jan Alberto Soggin, Carlo Zaccagnini) or in personal communications (Mario Liverani, William Malandra, Lucio Milano, Jonathan Paradise, Morton Smith). Bruce Lincoln, Wendy Doniger, and Lawrence Sullivan helped me to put the essays together; Leslie Antonelli Sullivan patiently translated my Italian texts, and Bruce Lincoln kindly revised my English. Cynthia Read and Robert Milks provided invaluable assistance with the preparation of this manuscript. I am grateful to all these friends, as well as to Giovanna, Lorenzo, Ruggero, and Chiara Angelica, who kept me alive from 1977 to 1997.

CONTENTS

ABBREVIATIONS

Am. Journ. Philol.	*American Journal of Philology*
Am. Journ. of Semitic Lit.	*American Journal of Semitic Literature*
ANET	*Ancient Near Eastern Texts Relating to the Old Testament*
AOAT	*Alter Orient und Altes Testament*
BASOR	*Bulletin of the American Schools of Oriental Research*
BWANT	*Beiträge zur Wissenschaft von Alten und Neuen Testament*
CAH	*Cambridge Ancient History*
Catholic Bibl. Quart.	*Catholic Biblical Quarterly*
Class. Quart.	*Classical Quarterly*
Dialoghi archeol.	*Dialoghi di Archeologia*
Hist. of Relig.	*History of Religions*
IEJ	*Israel Exploration Journal*
JAOS or Journ. Am. Orient. Soc.	*Journal of the American Oriental Society*
JBL or Journ. Bibl. Lit.	*Journal of Biblical Literature*
Journ. Jewish Stud.	*Journal of Jewish Studies*
JSS	*Journal of Semitic Studies*
KAI	H. Donner and W. Röllig, *Kanaanäische und aramäische Inschriften*, 1–3, Wiesbaden, 1969–1971
KBo.	*Keilschrifttexte aus Boghazköi*
KTU	M. Dietrich, O. Lorentz, and J. Sanmartin, *Die keilalphabetischen Texte aus Ugarit*, Neukirchen, 1976 (2nd. ed., Münster, 1995)
KUB	*Keilschrifturkunden aus Boghazköi*
Mitt. Orient. Samml.	*Mittheilungen aus den Orientalischen Sammlungen*
Opus. Intern. Journ. for Soc. and Econom. Hist. of Antiquity	*Opus. International Journal for Social and Economic History of Antiquity*
Oriens Ant.	*Oriens Antiquus*
Quad. Urb.	*Quaderni Urbinati di Cultura Classica*
RAI	*Rencontre Assyriologique Internationale*
Rec. archéol. orient.	*Recueil d'archéologie orientale*
Rev. Ét. Gr.	*Revue des Études Greques*
Rev. hist. et philos. relig.	*Revue d'Histoire et de Philosophie Religieuses*
Rev. sciences relig.	*Revue de sciences religieuses*
RSO	*Rivista degli Studi Orientali*

SSR	*Studi Storico-Religiosi*
St. BoT	*Studien zu den Boghazköy-Texten*
UT	C. H. Gordon, *Ugaritic textbook*, Rome, 1965
VT	*Vetus Testamentum*
Yale Class. Stud.	*Yale Classical Studies*
ZAW or Zeitschr. f.	*Zeitschrift für die Alttestamentliche*
Alttestamentliche Wissens.	*Wissenschaft*

KINGS & PROPHETS

INTRODUCTION

I

In this book, the unifying themes are two institutions, kingship and prophecy, as they appear in the Hebrew Bible and elsewhere. In order to understand this duality it is necessary to envisage the great longevity of monarchic systems. For since the beginning of the state, it is only in short periods of time and in small geographic areas that societies have been organized in state forms different from monarchy; and the most famous nonmonarchic organizations of societies that were successful before the age of modern revolutions were the ancient Greek polis and the mediaeval and early modern republics of Europe—small communities ruled by a minority of peers and surrounded by an ocean of monarchies. This lasting success of monarchic institutions was based in good part upon the ideological strategy we have been used to call sacred or divine kingship; or, in other words, upon monarchy's deceptively simple symbolic structure, which contrasted, and in different ways identified, the whole social body with only one other body—the body of the king.

I have described this stragegy elsewhere;[1] and in this book a few aspects of the ideology of kingship are discussed. But the essays collected here deal with the first historical *crisis* of monarchy in the East Mediterranean basin—a crisis most clearly identified by Fritz M. Heichelheim in the first volume of his work *An Ancient Economic History*[2]—which was connected with profound changes in technology (with the introduction of iron), in the structure of international exchange and politics, and in writing systems (with the spread of simpler, syllabic or alphabetical scripts). That crisis marked the first centuries of the first millennium B.C.E.; another aspect of that same crisis, or rather its final outcome, to be dated around the middle of that millennium, is the series of innovations described as the Axial Age by scholars such as Karl Jaspers and Arnaldo Momigliano.[3]

The new prophetic literature and the new narrative texts about nonroyal healers and saviors, discussed in this volume, are a product of that dangerous moment of change; but before one turns to them one should be aware of the monarchic outcome of that crisis of kingship in the Eastern Mediterranean: the institutional continuity tying the Neo-Babylonian hegemony to the Persian imperial system. But even in the Greek world, where the palace system did not outlive the critical period (the "dark" ages), and was replaced by the polis,

3

monarchy was back again in different forms after a few centuries, when marginal and backward Macedonia conquered and attempted to rule.

This institutional recreation of monarchy marked a victory of kingship; but the crisis had produced—or at least made possible—cultural and religious innovations that could not be removed. The rise of nonmonarchic ideologies around the middle of the first millennium B.C.E. had shaped a whole series of texts that were to mark the future history of the Mediterranean world and the destiny of three continents. In particular, it has produced literatures recorded in the new consonantic or alphabetic scripts by two societies organized as nonmonarchic communities for a part of their histories, and more specifically at the time of the redaction of the first bodies of (Greek and Hebrew) texts not created by scribal bureaucracies centered upon palaces.

2

In Greece, the new alphabetic literature shared and expressed the complexities—and the contradictions—of the polis system, though its most archaic forms were shaped by poetics of divine inspiration and of oral performance that had much in common with the ideologies of prophetic utterance attested further east. But the new literature of the exilic and postexilic Jewish communities marked the victory of prophecy in spite of, and contextually with, the institutional victory of universal kingship, because the central theme—and the ideological core—of that body of texts was precisely the direct communication between the national deity and a nonroyal member of the nation, chosen by the godhead as the correct mediator between the divine sphere and the human level.

Just as I have stressed the paradox of the monarchic outcome of the crisis of kingship during the first half of the first millennium B.C.E., I must also point to the further paradox of the correlation between the institutional victory of universal kingship and the rise of the biblical prophetic model around the middle of that millennium. Indeed, it was the victory of universal kingship that allowed the new, prophetic literature to emerge, because it was precisely the universal monarchic power of the Achaemenid empire that created the preconditions for the organization of nonmonarchic, hierocratic communities of Jews both in Palestine and in other parts of the imperial territories; and in turn such communities made a new coherent body of prophetic texts in Hebrew both possible and necessary. This new literature presented as based upon divine inspiration and prophetic mediation prepared two innovations that were logical corollaries, if not necessary implications, of the prophetic model. The first of these was the idea of a canon of sacred texts directly stemming from divine revelation; the second was a tendency toward monolatry, if not actually toward monotheism, modeled upon the exclusive quality of nation and canon, but also upon the universalistic implications of imperial monarchy. As the new texts that were to become the core of the Hebrew Bible were being written or reorganized, both canon and monotheism lay in a distant future; but canon and monotheism were implicit in the new textual facies, shaped by the crisis of kingship and hosted in the interstices of universal monarchy.

3

None of the essays collected in this volume presents precisely such a picture. The preceding pages are the summary of the lesson I have learned from the data studied in the essays collected here, and the result of further research and discussion. Moreover, the earliest pieces I have chosen to include in this volume go back to a time when I was aware of few—if any—of the problems and perspectives I have addressed above. Yet from the very beginning I was guided by the desire to achieve a better understanding and a clearer definition of three main topics: the form and meaning of the narrative part of the Hebrew Bible; the structure of powers, roles, and functions presented in those texts; and the complex discourse strategies involved in the construction of such powers, roles, and functions by way of such narratives. The need to confront these problems led me to question many of my own too obvious assumptions and opened up new horizons as it became clear to me, for instance, that biblical narratives were neither historicized myths nor mythicized historical events; or that the ways in which kingship was presented by some of those texts could not be explained just by imagining a special type of monarchic power, different from all other known types attested in the Near East, and characteristic of Israel and Judah.

As I have rearranged them here, my essays form a unit that has some degree of coherence while also reflecting the diachronical differentiation one must expect in a production extending from 1977 to 1993. They are organized in five pairs: in each pair the first essay is older than the second by several years, so that the two essays coupled together are two slightly different ways of treating similar or connected themes as well as two stages in an ongoing process of research and often of revision.

4

The first two couples of essays deal with two different aspects of kingship: (1) the ideology of redistribution, whereby the centralized economy of the monarchic state, based upon taxation, was presented as kingly generosity toward the needy, and (2) the symmetrical ideology of tribute, representing foreign kings, or usurpers, as oppressive monsters exploiting the cosmos and withholding wealth, energy, and life. Both themes are traditional aspects of the political ideology of the Fertile Crescent, and both are expressed in the mythologies and in the ritual behaviors of the Near Eastern and Egyptian state systems. In the biblical context, both themes acquire new meanings because they are treated in new ways. In my essays, I point to two main innovations. First of all, the generous redistribution theme is separated from kingship and attributed to nonroyal figures, only one of which is the ancestor of a royal lineage, while the tribute theme is constantly connected with foreign kings envisaged as gods by their peoples and presented as the enemies not only of Israel, but also—indeed, more prominently—of Yahweh. Second, heroes who are not kings but faithful servants of the national deity are given the central role in the new narratives, both as generous distributors and as leaders in the fight against greedy and monstrous oppressors; and in two cases (studied respectively in the second essay of each pair) the nonroyal figures are presented as prophetic: Deborah, who takes the lead in the fight against the enemy kings and their champion Sisera; and Elijah/Elisha, who offer their Israelite followers a miraculous distribution of cereal food.

5

Biblical texts also deal with the theme of kingly taxation in more direct ways, as in the story of King Rehoboam who "added to the yoke" his father Solomon had made heavy for the Israelites, and lost the bigger part of his kingdom, while Adoniram, the king's tribute collector, was stoned to death by the people (I Kings 12). Another such theme is the story of the institution of monarchy by Samuel which I discuss here in chapter 5: the general message of this narrative is the idea that the Israelites, though they have been warned of its drawbacks, have accepted monarchy once, and later they shall have to bear its burden. Whatever happens is their fault: the refusal of direct rule by Yahweh is an original sin that implies punishment. In chapter 5 I compare this biblical story to an Aesopic fable commonly known as the *Fable of the Frogs Who Asked for a King*. The frogs have enough of anarchy (*anarkhia*): so they ask Zeus, the king of the gods, to send them a king, and Zeus throws a stick into their pond. When the frogs protest that their king is too lazy, the ruler of the gods sends them a water snake, who catches them and devours them. In spite of the rationalizing conclusion ("It is better to be ruled by a lazy than by a wicked ruler"), the fable is obviously about the stupidity of the frogs who insist upon having an active ruler, while they can only choose between a good-for-nothing monarch and a greedy tyrant.

Many fables are about kings, and some refer to tribute; but here it is important to quote only one futher example, because it helps to understand the biblical attitude to kings. When in Judges 9 the Shechemites made Abimelek king, Jotham, the youngest son of Jerubbaal, and the only one of his brothers Abimelek had not killed, climbed to the top of Mount Gerizim overlooking Shechem and told his fellow townsmen the tale of the trees who wanted to anoint a king over themselves. The fig tree and the vine refused to leave their productive occupations in order to become kings, but the useless bramble, when its turn came to be chosen, told the other trees: "If in truth you anoint me king over you, then come and put your trust in my shadow; and if not, let fire come out of the bramble and devour the cedars of Lebanon." In this fable the king is thus both useless (his protective shadow being no larger than the shadow of a bramble-bush) and a devouring menace. Jotham, whose name means "orphan," had to escape and hide in a cistern;[4] but Abimelek was rejected by the Shechemites and, when he laid siege to the city, was killed by a woman, who hit the top of his head with a millstone. The fable, it seems, had been effective.

6

In most of these texts dealing more explicitly with kings and taxes, criticism is directed against a type of king rather than against kingship per se; but in a few of them the attack upon kings and taxes is more radical and becomes an attack against kingship. More specifically, the Aesopic fable of the frogs and the biblical tale of the trees choosing a ruler, told by the only surviving brother of a kingly murderer, convey the idea that kings are either useless or obnoxious or both. A further narrative of the same series—the story of how monarchy began in Israel at the time of the prophet Samuel—is discussed in the third pair of essays collected in this book.

The two essays in question, chapters 5 and 6, examine the biblical presentation of kings and prophets not only in connection with taxes—though the economic cost of both institutions is discussed—but in their relationship with their respective function as mediators between the divine and the human sphere. The most direct and powerful form of such mediation—divine possession—is examined in both chapters to show that the biblical narratives present it as the appanage of prophets. When kings are described as possessed, as in the case of Saul, discussed in chapter 5, problems are shown to arise; and a positive situation can only be established by "inventing" a different kind of king. But such a solution has its own problems, as shown in chapter 6, where I deal with the conflict between the authority of charismatic figures, such as the n^{e}bi'im raised by Yahweh from among the people, and that of the ruler, seen as the head of one specific form of the social organization that is not the only possible form. As I wrote those two essays, I was not aware of the possible solution of the dilemma they presented, which seems to me now almost obvious: the postmonarchic dating of those biblical texts, and thus the connection between the message they convey and the construction of a model centered upon figures such as Moses, Samuel, and their prophetic successors.

7

But how were such figures constructed? This question is important if one realizes that for the first time since the beginning of writing—for the first time in history—the biblical texts and the contemporary Greek literature presented protagonists who were not kings, priests, or scribes and attributed to those protagonists the heroic actions and functions of temple and state: mediating between men and gods, saving the people, destroying greedy monsters. These nonkingly healers and saviors are examined in chapter 7, and the contemporary rise of such figures in Greece and in the "anti-Oriental" body of biblical narrative texts is the central object of that chapter. The following piece (chapter 8) is less focused upon the specific figures invented during the first millennium B.C.E. in Greece and Palestine as well as in some parts of the early diaspora, and more concerned with some narrative forms and strategies of the same literatures, as well as in later texts belonging to the same tradition. In those chapters I speak of a Mediterranean common ground as the locus for the origin of literary, ideological, and religious forms and types. The use of this term has caused some misunderstandings; but the context in which chapter 7 is now presented is sufficient to make it clear that the term in question referred not to a presumed archaic Mediterranean substratum, but to the common monarchic traditions underlying the cultures of Greece and Israel as well as to the nonmonarchic ideologies attested by the two innovative consonantic or alphabetic literatures.

8

This book is about kings and prophets; but the real object of my inquiry is a series of texts; indeed, kings and prophets are in a way mere actors in the complex play whereby the texts in question construed their specific discourse. This is implicit in most of this book; but the last pair of articles collected here (chapters 9 and 10) treat this problem explicitly.

Chapter 9 is about the formation of prophetic texts; or, more precisely, about the gradual liberation of prophetic utterance from the bonds of oral performance by way of the creation of prophetic writing. Chapter 10 is about the formation of an ideology of the written text within the written narrative of the Bible. Together, the two chapters account both for the rise of the prophetic texts themselves and for the ideological validation of such texts, and thus for two different aspects of biblical textuality. In this discussion, kingship is marginal, because the central issue is one of divine inspiration—and the possible royal claims to direct divine inspiration through possession trance, discussed in chapter 5, are dismissed as absurd by biblical narratives, while other forms of direct contact between godhead and monarch, such as Solomon's dream, are rare and not unproblematic. Prophet and text face each other; but the confrontation is a complex one, because the text (including the Pentateuch, envisaged as inspired by the deity and written by Moses) stems from the words of the inspired prophet, while an inspired prophetess can be asked to evaluate the inspired quality of a newly found text. Though kingship is not central in this interplay between the authority of the sacred text and the authority of the living prophet, it remains present in various ways. The confrontation between king and text may take the shape of a comparison (as in the narratives about the finding of a true king in the Jerusalem Temple, so similar in structure to the narratives about the discovery of a true holy text in that same temple), or of a direct relationship (as in the relationship between king and text dictated by Deuteronomy). But in all cases the text is presented as superior to the monarch. This further assessment of the limited value of one of the two institutions discussed in this book is but another aspect of my general theme: kingship is both criticized and played down in the "inspired" consonantic literature that was written by scribes of a new type in the context of a nonmonarchic community. Such texts are both a part of the future biblical canon and the expression of a religiosity that prepared the very idea of a canon. In describing the confrontation between king and holy text, they are validating themselves as the true guides for Israel's journey in time. They are lifting the crown from the king's head, in order to place it above the sacred scroll written by an inspired, prophetic figure.

NOTES

1. Cristiano Grottanelli, *Kingship: An Overview*, in *The Encyclopedia of Religion* (Macmillan: New York, 1987), volume 8, pp. 312–322; C. Grottanelli and S. Bertelli (eds.), *Gli occhi di Alessandro. Potere Sovrano e Sacralità del Corpo da Alessandro Magno a Ceausescu*, Ponte alle Grazie (Firenze, 1990).

2. F. M. Heichelheim, *An Ancient Economic History*, volume 1 (Leiden, 1964) (quoted in chapter 7, note 5).

3. Karl Jaspers, *Vom Ursprung und Ziel der Geschichte*, 1949; A. Momigliano, *Alien Wisdom. The Limits of Hellenization* (Cambridge University Press: Cambridge, 1975) (chapter 1).

4. This, I think, is the real meaning of the mysterious Be'er of Judges 9:21, on which see J. A. Soggin, *Judges: A Commentary*, Old Testament Library (SCM Press: London, 1981), pp. 171–173. Jotham "hid out" from Abimelek on a previous occasion (Judg. 9:5).

THE KING'S GRACE AND
THE HELPLESS WOMAN

Ruth, Charila, Sītā

To the very dear memory of Roland Barthes,
mythologue

I

The biblical story of Ruth contained in the postexilic Book of Ruth, the Delphic myth of Charila preserved by Plutarch, and the story of Rāma and Sītā told by the Rāmāyaṇa, which I shall henceforward call the story of Sītā for the sake of brevity and of symmetry, are stories about a woman or girl and her male counterpart, a kingly figure. The kingly quality of the male protagonist is obvious in the stories of Charila and of Sītā; in the story of Ruth that quality is signified by the final genealogy that shows Ruth's benefactor to be an ancestor of King David, the prototypical monarch of Israel, and of his line from which the kingly Messiah shall rise.[1]

In spite of this, it is immediately obvious that the three stories differ greatly in many respects. Indeed, they are bound to differ, for the story of Ruth is contained in a short booklet that is part of the Holy Scripture of the Jewish and Christian religions and one of the five *Megillôth*;[2] the story of Charila is told by an erudite writer in a late gloss of about a dozen lines;[3] and the story of Sītā, popular in ancient and modern India and the subject of many traditions, is transmitted mainly by the thousands of verses of the Rāmāyaṇa. As for their distance in time, the Book of Ruth is dated by most scholars after the sixth century B.C.E. and is probably not earlier than the fourth—but the story is probably older;[4] Charila's story we know from Plutarch's *Moralia*, but of course the narrative itself may be much older, for it is a myth of the Greek sanctuary of Delphi and connected to an archaic festival of that sanctuary that was important, and then central, in Mediterranean culture and politics from the seventh century B.C.E. onward.[5] As for the Rāmāyaṇa, the central period of its formation ranges roughly from the last two centuries B.C.E. to the first one or two centuries of the Christian era.[6] It is unnecessary to stress that these differences in context, space, and time mean that the three stories are the very different products of three very different cultures.

Yet, far from being diverging variations on similar subjects, the three stories—as becomes clear if we inspect them more closely—have a common structure, common themes, and common motifs—motifs that are important keys for understanding the stories. So we shall study them together: we shall look at the structure first, then deal with the common themes and motifs. This analysis, combined with a brief look at the context of the stories, will enable us to attempt a reconstruction of some important meanings and functions of the narratives—meanings and functions, as we shall see, once again common or at least similar.

2

The common structure can be summed up in the following sequence: an initial crisis is solved, but the rejection of a helpless female causes a further crisis that ends only in a final comprehensive solution. However, this structure needs to be examined in detail in each of the three narratives. To do so, we shall avail ourselves both of a scheme (table 1-1) that permits us to visualize the comparative analysis synoptically and of the following verbal description. For the sake of clarity, it is advisable to consult the scheme while reading the description, so that one may shed light on the other.

In the story of Ruth, the initial crisis consists of a famine in the Judahite city of Bethlehem (significantly meaning "house of bread") that causes the exile of the family of Elimelek to the land of Moab, where the two sons of Elimelek and Naomi marry two Moabite women and die without offspring a short time after their father's death. In the story of Charila the initial crisis is simply famine in Delphi, while the initial crisis in the story of Rāma and Sītā is threefold like that of the story of Ruth—involving dynastic disorder; the ensuing exile of the heir to the throne, Rāma, with his wife Sītā; and the kidnapping of Sītā by Rāvana. In the three stories, the response to the crisis is one of fidelity and trust on the part of the inferior members of the community. In the story of Ruth, the group is a patriarchal family of the tribe of Judah; the heroine, Ruth, is faithful to Naomi, her mother-in-law: though Naomi begs her to return to her country and to her gods, she remains with the old woman. In the story of Charila, the Delphic community, headed by its king, is involved; the people, including the helpless orphan girl whose name is not yet known to be Charila, go to the king and make supplications (ἱκέτευον) for barley and legumes. In the story of Sītā, the royal family is involved; the royal heir is faithful to the word he has given to his father, and his brother and wife are faithful to him and follow him in his forest exile. Sītā in particular is praised by all for her faithfulness, especially by her mother-in-law, who calls her her daughter.[7]

The solution of the initial crisis follows. In the story of Ruth, the sequence is (1) end of the famine, (2) return from exile, and (3) solution of the food problem through the generosity of Boaz, the kinsman of Elimelek, who lets the helpless widow Ruth glean in his field for the helpless widow Naomi. This sequence corresponds well to the threefold sequence of the crisis (famine, exile,

TABLE 1-1

		Narrative Content		
Structural Elements	Story of Ruth	Story of Charila	Story of Sītā	
Crisis	1. Famine 2. Exile in Moab 3. Death of husbands	Famine	1. Dynastic disorder 2. Exile in forest 3. Loss of protagonist's wife, Sītā	
Response from inferiors	Ruth faithfully follows mother-in-law in spite of Naomi's pressures	The people trustfully turn to the king	Sītā and Lakṣmaṇa faithfully follow Rāma; Sītā remains faithful to Rāma in spite of Rāvaṇa's pressures	
Solution	1. End of famine: barley harvest 2. Return from exile 3. Generosity of Boaz, a good provider	Distribution of barley and legumes by "real" king to nobles	3. Sītā reconquered 2. Return from exile 1. Right king on throne: offering of aśvamedha	
Rejection	a) No husbands for Ruth b) Nearest go'el refuses to marry Ruth; takes off his sandal	1. No barley and legumes for anonymous orphan girl (Charila) 2. The king hits her with his sandal	I. Rāma rejects Sītā II. Rāma rejects Sītā again, then imposes a new ordeal	
Lament/protest	Naomi laments; she should be called Mara ("bitter"), for Yahweh has made her empty	Charila protests by hanging herself with her own belt	I. Sītā weeps, protests, suicide by fire—ordeal by fire II. "Ordeal by Earth"—final return to Mother Earth	
New crisis	No progeny for the dead men; no master for field or Ruth	Famine and disease (no burial for Charila)	I. Risk; queen lost again; no heirs II. Queen lost for good; king back in heaven	
Final solution	Ruth accepted as wife by Boaz; a child, Obed, ancestor of King David, born; Naomi rejoices	Charila's body named, found, and buried; ritual king distributes barley and legumes to all; Charila myth reenacted	I. Reconciliation; happy reign II. Sītā (= Lakṣmī) back to the Earth; Rāma (= Viṣṇu) back in heaven; twin heirs	

death of the male providers) and follows the same order. The solution of the Delphic crisis in the story of Charila is as simple as the crisis itself and consists of food distributions on the part of the king. In the story of Sītā, the solution is threefold like the crisis, just as in the story of Ruth, but the order is reversed, the last problem being dealt with first: (3) Sītā is reconquered and Rāvaṇa killed by Rāma, (2) the royal exiles return to their palace, and (1) the dynastic disorder is removed and the correct heir is finally placed on the throne.

But the solution of the crisis is not complete: problems are left open, so the stories can and must continue. In the story of Ruth, the male members of the family are replaced by Boaz only as providers. The family remains without off-spring, which means that Elimelek's field is unowned and uncultivated, that the dead receive no ritual care, and that Ruth is also abandoned: like the field, she receives no seed; like the dead, she receives no attention.[8] In the story of Charila, the barley and legumes distributed by the king are enough only for some of the Delphians: of course, for the most powerful (τοῖς γνωριμωτέροις αὐτῶν). In the story of Sītā, the abducted wife of King Rāma is regained only in part: the recaptured woman, who has sat on the lap of foul Rāvaṇa, is now the object of rumor; and things will never be the same again.[9]

The incomplete solution of the initial crisis leaves an opening for further crisis, and in the three stories the further crisis is caused by the rejection of the heroine. In the story of Ruth, the rejection is twofold: first, a more general situation: no near kinsman or go'el turns up to claim, to redeem—g'l—and marry Ruth, to take possession of Elimelek's field, and to raise on it a progeny for the dead males, so the line of Elimelek has no offspring. This causes Naomi's lament. Then, a more specific rejection: the nearest go'el refuses to marry Ruth, to cultivate the field of Elimelek, and to raise offspring for his dead kinsman, and he signifies his rejection by taking off his sandal.[10] In the story of Charila, the rejection is simple: the king refuses to give barley and legumes to an unknown orphan girl, who is poverty stricken and without pro-tectors (πενιχρά τις οὖσα καὶ ἔρημος), then takes off his sandal, strikes her with it, and casts it in her face (ἐρράπισεν αὐτὴν ὑποδήματι καὶ τῷ προσώπῳ τὸ ὑπόδημα προσέρριψεν). In the Rāmāyaṇa, the rejection of Sītā is repeated twice, in two different textual passages surely to be dated to different periods. In the sixth book, Rāma rejects Sītā because he cares more about the prestige of his illustrious family and about public opinion than about the happiness of himself and his wife.[11] In the seventh book, Rāma rejects Sītā once more, and she takes refuge in the forest, where she gives birth to twin sons of Rāma. Later, the twins, who have learned the Rāmāyaṇa from the poet Vālmīki, at-tend the great aśvamedha festival of Rāma, who is distributing kingly gifts to all and especially to helpless widows and poor orphans, and sing the whole poem to their father. Rāma, who has offered the aśvamedha accompanied by a golden image of Sītā, recognizes his sons, calls for Vālmīki, and agrees to take Sītā back if she successfully undergoes an ordeal.

The rejection provokes a reaction in each of the stories, ranging from lament to protest or combining both. In the story of Ruth, as we have seen, the

general situation represented by the lack of marriage proposals for Ruth, causing the lack of male providers and of offspring, is to be read as a generalized
and implicit rejection, and provokes the lament of Naomi. On the other hand,
the explicit rejection of Ruth by the nearest possible go'el causes no lament
and no protest, for the very simple reason that the rich, righteous, marrying
go'el has already been found in the person of Boaz, and the negative, "un-
shod" relative is harmless in the new situation, or rather necessary as a dialectic counterpart to the good go'el. The rejection of Charila arouses no lament,
but causes the terrible protest of that not ignoble child (οὐκ ἀγεννὴ δὲ τὸ
ἦθος), who hangs herself, causing a further crisis. Sītā's reaction involves both
lament and protest: in the episode of the sixth book she weeps desperately and
begs for confidence; then she criticizes Rāma ("Tiger among men, by giving
way to anger like a trivial man you have made womankind preferable"); finally, she has a pyre built and climbs on it to die ("That is the medicine for this
calamity"), arguing that as she is abandoned before an assembly of people by
her husband, who is no longer pleased with her virtues, the only thing for her
to do is to enter the oblation-eater. But this suicide soon turns into an ordeal by
fire;[12] and the second reaction of Sītā to a distrustful Rāma, who in the seventh book of the Rāmāyaṇa asks for a further ordeal, consists of turning the ordeal into a suicide, or rather into a permanent exit, by asking her mother, the
Earth, to engulf her forever if she be innocent.[13]

In each of the three stories, the rejection of the heroine and her reaction
cause a further crisis. In Elimelek's family, as we have already seen, sterility,
lack of male providers and of land, as well as loss of status within the community, are the consequences of the lack of a husband for Ruth. For the community as a whole, this means a serious gap in the social cohesion, waste of land,
and the necessity of caring for two unattached females, for there is no seed for
the dead and no master for the women or the field. At Delphi, the famine does
not cease; indeed, the death and the unburied state of the young orphan girl
causes disease to break out. In the story of Sītā, the queen, who has been regained with Rāma's honor through many emphatic lines of heroic fighting, is
lost again for the sake of her spouse's kingly prestige. In the episode of the sixth
book of the Rāmāyaṇa, she ascends the pyre ready to enter the oblation-eater,
and the king risks being left alone without his queen and without any heirs; in
the seventh book, the loss is permanent and soon followed by the symmetrical
exit of the king in the opposite direction.

So a new solution is needed for the new crisis. In all three cases, the solution
is somehow provided by the dual quality of the male protagonist. We have two
male figures in the story of Ruth, a mythical and a ritual king in the story of
Charila, and a kingly figure endowed, so to speak, with a double nature in the
Rāmāyaṇa. In the story of Ruth, the anonymous, egoistical nearest go'el refuses
Ruth, but the generous next go'el, Boaz, marries her; and a child is born and
placed on the knees of Naomi, who exults and praises the Lord Yahweh. So in
the story of Ruth the solution is found within the narrative—is, we may say,
mythical; in the story of Charila the solution is ritual, for when the Delphians

had discovered with some difficulty that [Charila, whom the prophetic priestess had ordered the king to appease] was the name of the girl who had been struck, they performed a certain sacrificial rite combined with purification, which even now they continue to perform every eight years. For the king sits in state and gives a portion of barley meal and legumes to every one, alien and citizen alike, and a doll-image of Charila is brought thither. When, accordingly, all have received their portion, the king strikes the image with his sandal. The leader of the Thyad [priestesses] picks up the image and bears it to a certain place which is full of chasms; there they tie a rope round the neck of the image and bury it in the place where they buried Charila after she hanged herself.[14]

So it is clear that the ritual king of the eighth-year ceremony founded on the Charila myth is to the king of Delphi in that myth what Boaz is to the anonymous nearest kinsman in the story of Ruth: a positive counterpart, founding the solution of the crisis and correct behavior. Boaz lets the foreign, defenseless widow Ruth glean in his barley field and then marries her, solving the crisis for good. The ritual king in the Delphic festival distributes barley and legumes to all, including defenseless aliens; then the myth is reenacted, culminating in the burial of the Charila doll-image just where the poor helpless orphan was buried to solve the crisis in the myth.

Containing two different rejections, the story of Sītā in the Rāmāyaṇa has two different final solutions. In the sixth book, Sītā is proved by the fire to be pure; Rāma takes her back and they live happily ever after. This fairytale solution is somewhat complicated by the fact that during this episode Rāma's true nature as *avatāra* of the god Viṣṇu is revealed to him and used as an argument against his trivial, blind attitude to Sītā, which stems from a selfish and narrow conception of honor and is unworthy of a god.[15]

The *avatāra* nature of Rāma is central in the final solution presented by the seventh book of the Rāmāyaṇa, for, after Sītā has disappeared into the bosom of her mother the Earth, Rāma symmetrically leaves his throne to his heirs and returns to the sky as the god Viṣṇu. This final solution differs from the "simple" final solutions of the story of Ruth (marriage with offspring) and of the story of Sītā in the sixth book of the Rāmāyaṇa (happy reunion of the couple), but also from the more complex final solution of the story of Charila (appeasing of the wronged girl, end of the famine and disease, foundation of the ritual); for apparently it has nothing of the "happy ending." Since we know that "the story of Rāma the mortal king was certainly known in India centuries before Rāma was elevated to the status of an avatar of Viṣṇu,"[16] we can envisage it as a late addition prepared by Rāma's self-discovery in the corresponding episode of the sixth book; but this would be no excuse for not explaining it. I propose to read it as a final solution based not, like the others, on the removal of a critical contradiction between the helpless woman and the powerful king but on the acceptance of that contradiction. Rāma the human and godly king is freed from his human status and returns to the sky of the gods because of the desperate gesture of his queen, caused by his common, unjust, ungrateful attitude. Sītā regains her real nature, that of an Earth figure (to this we shall return), because she is offended by Rāma, and this allows or forces Rāma to return to the skies. The cosmogonic flavor of this epic separation of heaven and earth, whereby male and female remain bound by their complementarity in separation, and its connection with the Indian marriage ideology and ritual, enhance my suggested interpretation.[17]

On a note that is significantly cosmogonical, we have completed our comparative analysis of what should now be clearly recognized as the common structure of the three tales. In the next section we shall continue our search, and look for the common themes—common themes expressed by that common structure or, better still, common themes that caused the common structure.

3

One common theme that is easy to recognize is fertility involving agriculture (more specifically, the cultivation of cereals and precisely of barley), the seasonal pattern and the risks of that economy, and the symbolic connections of such a pattern with sex and reproduction. The story of Ruth moves from famine to cereal food, and along a parallel path from lack of offspring to marriage and birth. The exiles return to the House of Bread "at the beginning of the barley harvest," Ruth gleans during the harvest in the field of Boaz, and, during a dark night of the harvest period, secretly joins Boaz on the threshing floor where he is sleeping at the end of the heap of corn, uncovers his feet, and lies down by him. The two spend the night together. Boaz promises to marry Ruth and sends her away in the morning laden with six measures of barley he has poured into the veil that she holds out. Ruth takes the good news and the barley to Naomi, and when she tells her that Boaz has said to her "Go not empty (*ryqm*) to your mother-in-law," the echo of Naomi's lament ("I have left Bethlehem full, and Yahweh has taken me back empty [*ryqm*]"), where "empty" means not "devoid of barley" but "devoid of offspring," is loud and clear. And in fact Boaz, who has given Ruth the barley for Naomi, soon gives her seed to bear a son, who is taken by Naomi, laid in her bosom, and nursed by her, while the women of Bethlehem declare that a son is born unto Naomi.

The story of Charila, too, is about a famine, the distribution of barley, and the protraction of that famine because of the king's denial of barley to the yet unnamed orphan girl. When Charila is buried and a correct ritual involving barley and legumes is founded, the sown seed produces food again and the famine is over. As for the story of Sītā, it is clearly no fertility myth; but no feat of interpretation is necessary to see Sītā as "la terre ensemencée," for the name Sītā means "furrow." Sītā is born from the furrow traced by King Janaka while plowing the ground to prepare it for a sacrifice to obtain progeny, and returns to the Earth, her mother, at the end of one story. It is true that both this birth and this exit of Sītā appear in parts of the Rāmāyaṇa usually considered to be later textual additions;[18] but Rig Veda 4.57 already mentions a figure by the name Furrow (Sītā), imploring it to be fruitful, in the context of a prayer for plowing, and D. Dubuisson has provided many arguments in favor of the "furrow" quality of Sītā.[19] So the possible late redactional date of the two episodes in question seems to be nothing but proof of the continuity of that quality.

To all this I should add that the three stories have in common not only a fertility theme but also a connection with rituals of fertility and with seasonal or periodic festivals tied to agriculture. This connection should be envisaged, in the context of the most recent speculation on relationships between myths and rituals, as an extremely delicate and complex affair. As we did in the case of the common structure of the three narratives, to express it we shall avail ourselves of a scheme (table 1-2) and of a verbal description: the reader should use both together.

As we have seen, the crucial period in the story of Ruth is the period from the beginning of the barley harvest ot the winnowing and threshing of the barley and the hoarding of cereals. Now, this period corresponds to the "fifty" days between the beginning of the barley harvest and the end of the wheat harvest, that is, to the period between the biblical, agrarian feast of *maṣṣôt* and that of *bikkurîm* or *šabu'ôt*. Because the seduction of Boaz takes place toward the end of the barley harvest and on a threshing floor full of cereals, this important episode, at least, should be placed in the neighborhood of the feast of *bikkurîm-šabu'ôt*. This feast of "firstfruits" or of "weeks," the second great feast of the biblical Israelite calendar, is the feast of the end of the harvest—marked by cereal offerings to Yahweh (including two loaves of bread made with the new flour, baked with leaven) and connected with the gleaning activities of the poor and aliens, as well as with cereal distributions (Lev. 23:22; Kings 4:42–44).[20] Since the fifth century C.E. if not earlier, the Book of Ruth has been recited in synagogues throughout the world on the day of *šabu'ôt*, thus confirming and enhancing the connection we have noted.[21] I shall add that the spirit of the fiftieth day of *šabu'ôt* resembles that of the biblical Jubilee, marking the square of the seventh year or sabbatical period, the "fiftieth year" (Lev. 25:8–55), for the first rule of the Jubilee, the avoidance of agricultural labor, meant that the (spontaneous?) produce of the fields should be left at the disposal of the poor (notably of widows, orphans, and foreign residents), while the second rule, "liberty throughout the land unto all the inhabitants thereof," involving the freeing of enslaved debtors, the redeeming of clan property sold in periods of crisis, and so forth, clearly aimed at maintaining the property rights of the extended family, just as the *ge'ullah* did, and indirectly favored the increase of agricultural production that was yearly celebrated on the day of *šabu'ôt*.[22] The connections between the story of Ruth and those festivals of the archaic agrarian calendar of Palestine, *šabu'ôt* and the Jubilee year, are thus both direct and indirect, and extremely clear.

As for the Charila myth, we have already dealt with the ritual to which it was connected. We should add now that the ritual in question took place on the third day of a great Delphic feast held every eight years, that is, in the intercalary year of an archaic calendar system that may be compared to the sab-

TABLE 1-2

Festival and Season

	šābūʿōt (End of Wheat Harvest, 50 Days after maṣṣōt)	Jubilee (Every 50 Years)	Delphic Year (Every 8 Years)	Attic Festivals (Plowing-Sowing [Pyanepsion]; Harvest [Thargelia])	Dussehra (End of Rainy Season)	Diwali (Autumn Plowing and Sowing)
Celebration of mythical victory, liberation, return	(Later connected to the giving of the Torah during the Exodus)	(Liberation of "Hebrew slaves" in memory of Exodus)	Killing of Python, *anagoge* of the Herois	(Connections with the Theseus myth)	Victory of Durga over buffalo-demon; of Rāma over Rāvaṇa (reenacted)	Liberation of Lakṣmī, Sītā, etc.
Purification and atonement	(Back to normal bread after unleavened bread: first leavened loaves)	(Normal cultivation interrupted)	Fast and purification for killing of Python; atonement for sin against Charila	Chasing away of *pharmakoi* (Thargelia); plague and atonement (Pyanepsion)	...	Whitewashing and cleaning of houses; new clothes; new lights
Concentration of cereals	Cereal firstfruits and two loaves of "new" bread offered to Yahweh	Negative: Cultivation and hoarding interrupted	...	Cereal offerings, storing in Eleusis (Pyanepsion); offering of a loaf (Thargelia)	...	...
(Re)distribution of cereal and other goods	Festive rejoicing for the orphans, widows, etc. miraculous distribution	Poor glean freely in the uncultivated fields	Distribution of barley and legumes	*Eiresione*, gifts to boys carrying and offering boughs (Pyanepsion)	Gifts to persons carrying and offering *noratras* (barley shoots)	Gifts of sweets; gambling
Direct connection with the stories	Book of Ruth is read aloud on šābūʿōt	...	Story of Charila reenacted	...	Rāmāyaṇa read aloud; episodes reenacted	Return of Rāma and Sītā celebrated

batical and Jubilee year system.[23] On the first day of that festival, Septerion or Stepterion, the Delphians celebrated "a representation of Apollo's fight with Python and of the flight to (the valley of) Tempê and pursuit that followed the battle": the feast included a ritual reenacting of the deed. A group of young men of the local aristocracy, led by the *kouros amphithalés*, an adolescent both of whose parents were alive, entered suddenly upon a circular esplanade in the sanctuary of Apollo, put fire to a wooden construction similar to a theater scene representing a royal palace, overturned a table, and then fled and left Delphi to undergo a number of ritual ordeals: wandering, "serving," fasting, and total purification in the valley of Tempê, where Apollo had expiated the murder of Python during a whole Great Year or eight-year cycle. After having offered a sacrifice and broken the fast, the young men returned to Delphi, adorned with laurel wreaths and playing flutes. The "palace" they had destroyed was said by some to be Python's lair, by others the house of Priam in Troy. About the feast celebrated on the second day, Herois ("the feast of the heroine"), we have few data: Plutarch writes that it has a secret import only the priestesses knew, but "from the portions of the rites that are performed in public one might conjecture that it represents the return [ἀναγωγὴ] of Semele,"[24] and Georges Roux notes that Semele, the mother of Dionysos, was an Earth figure whose hair, according to Pindar's fourth Dithyramb, was richly adorned with flower wreaths in the spring:[25] her son was said to have rescued her from the netherworld, and she became an Olympian goddess under the name of Thyone. But Plutarch's identification of the Heroine with Semele does not seem to have convinced all scholars, for Jeanmaire writes that the Heroine was probably none other than Charila, "whose death was lamented on another occasion":[26] and indeed, as the Charila ritual I have described took place on the following day, the third and last of the Delphic Great Year festival, the temptation to see a connection between the two figures is strong.

This is the specific ritual context of the story of Charila, but a look at the Attic seasonal festivals and especially at the ones connected with harvesting (e.g., the Attic Thargelia) and with plowing and sowing (e.g., the Attic Proerosia-Pyanepsia-Thesmophoria of the month Pyanepsion) suggests that many mythical and ritual elements of the Delphic Great Year festival and more specifically of the Charila complex were common Greek agricultural mythical and ritual motifs.[27] The founding myth of the Thargelia is a story of sin, pollution, and atonement through a Delphic oracle, and its ritual consists of purification and cereal offerings, including a loaf of bread (θάργελος), in view of a good reaping, while the preplowing and plowing-sowing complex of festivals in the month Pyanepsion includes the concentration of cereals in the "royal" sanctuary of Eleusis, followed, significantly, by a distribution of food offerings to ritual beggars carrying a bough of olive (the usual sign of the suppliant) wreathed with wool. The *eiresione*, the bough that gave the procession its name, was left at the house of the generous giver and set up at the door, where it exercised its beneficial influence for the year.[28] In this more general context, the story of Charila regains its fertility significance beyond all possible doubt.

As for the ritual connections of the story of Sītā, the ritual contexts of the birth of the heroine in the first book of the Rāmāyaṇa and of her return to the Earth in the seventh book (respectively, ritual plowing in preparation for a kingly sacrifice and the *aśvamedha*) are highly significant, but I shall not dwell on them here. I prefer to deal briefly with the fact that the story of Sītā is in modern India connected to two archaic agricultural autumn festivals,[29] just as the story of Ruth is connected today with *šabu'ôt*, the agricultural traits of which are significantly being rediscovered in modern Israel. During Dussehra, a festival celebrated all over India at the end of the rainy season in the month of Aśvina (September–October) and mainly centered on the victory of the goddess Durga over the buffalo demon, of Rāma over Rāvaṇa, and in general on the killing of a chaotic monster, the Rāmāyaṇa is read aloud at large gatherings. In many villages and towns of Northern India, including Delhi, the story of Rāma and Sītā is enacted in plays; and on the last day of the festival an arrow shot by the actor portraying Rāma sets fire to a huge ten-headed effigy of Rāvaṇa.[30] Dussehra is concluded by an *eiresione*-like quest: as Brijendra Sharma puts it in his work on the festivals of India, "poor persons and the middle-class brahmanas carrying *noratras* (small fresh shoots of barley plants, which are sowed in every house on the first day of the festival) go to wealthy people to offer them the stalks of *noratras* and get alms in return."[31] Diwāli, occurring somewhat later in the autumn, in the month Kartika (October–November) during the sowing of the winter crops, is a festival of purification and of the liberation and return of a goddess of abundance, or of Rāma and Sītā, or even of a Sikh *guru*, and is also connected with the defeat of a daemonic enemy. Diwāli is celebrated by the whitewashing of houses, the donning of new clothes, the distribution of greetings and gifts, gambling, and the lighting of the lamps that give the feast its name.[32]

By going into further detail I could clarify this delicate point more; but the data presented so far permit me to state that, in view of the obvious connections to fertility and agriculture of the story content (Ruth, Charila), the quality of the heroine (Sītā), and the ritual context of the narrative traditions (Ruth, Charila, Sītā), there can be no doubt about the importance of a common agricultural fertility theme in the three stories. Nor should one be astonished to discover that, especially in the 1930s when this type of interpretation was lavishly applied, all three stories have been interpreted, independently for each other, as so-called fertility myths.

The fertility-myth interpretation of the story of Ruth, well represented by Staples's article in the 1937 issue of the *American Journal of Semitic Languages*,[33] stresses the agrarian connotations of the story and even goes as far as identifying Ruth with the Mesopotamian goddess Ištar or, with a tale-telling generation shift, Naomi with Astarte and Boaz with the god Baal himself. It is wrong to push this type of interpretation to these ridiculous extremes, precisely because the agrarian and seasonal value of the story of Ruth is immediately obvious and need not—so should not—be stressed: the story of Ruth is in a certain sense also a fertility myth, as indicated, among other things, by the presence of the typical weeping-and-laughter motif; but it is also much else. Moreover, there is absolutely no need to look for underlying gods, goddesses, and myths to understand the actual and intrinsic mythical and agrarian qualities of the narrative.

As for the story of Charila, since myths about goddesses and heroines hanging themselves or being hanged are frequent in Greek mythology, the hanging of Charila has been projected against this background and a naive suggestion made, originally, if I am not mistaken, by Charles Picard in 1928,[34] that these traditions arose from the actual presence of small divine statuettes and emblems hanging from trees and boughs in a fertility-cult context. But things are much more complex, and the "hanging-goddess" motif itself is not a compact entity. Moreover, I think that, though one should accept the general and widespread "fertilistic" interpretation of the feasts and myths of the Delphic Great Year system, one should on the whole refrain from imagining archaic lost festivals, cults, and traditions behind the data. One need not, therefore, discuss the unwarranted hypothesis attributed by Roux to Plutarch himself,[35] of an original different meaning of the Septerion/Stepterion ritual happenings or, for the Charila ritual, the useless explanation offered by Roux that "when a god's attention is requested, some violence is often exerted on its statue," or yet the still older, simplistic, Mannhardian view that the buried heroine is the eight-year cycle coming to a just end. Any interpretation based on the unwarranted assumption that the ritual is "older" than the "corresponding" myth (or, to quote Roux, that "without doubt an ancient magical ritual is hidden beneath the romantic story") and must be explained without it is bound to be unsatisfactory, because it will only account for part of the evidence. Myth and ritual, when, as in the case of Charila, they appear not only connected but tightly interwoven in our very sources, must be explained together.

Finally, the fertility-myth interpretation of the story of Sītā is a peculiar one, for the story of Sītā has been studied by specialists who were often trained in comparative Indo-European linguistics and mythologies; and it has been usefully compared to other Indo-European myths and traditional tales. This is the way followed by A. H. Krappe in 1931:[36] that author compares the Sītā story to the Celtic myth of Lancelot and Guenevere—involving a married woman stolen by deceit by an enemy (who nevertheless does not succeed in having intercourse with her) and then recovered by her husband—and thus to the similar Greek myths of Alkestis and Helen. According to Krappe, these myths were about the disappearance and recovery of a vegetation goddess, ravished by a winter death demon and reconquered by spring. Now, on the one hand, we have seen that there are other and more correct approaches to the fertilistic quality of the story of Sītā, and, on the other hand, other widespread mythical themes could be compared.[37] Yet Krappe's intuition is a fruitful one and acquires new meaning if in its light we compare, as shown in table 1-3, the suggested structure of the story of Sītā—killing of the monster, recovery of the Earth figure, rejection and reaction of that figure—to the structure of the Great Year Festival in Delphi—Septerion/Stepterion (killing of the monster),

TABLE 1-3

Structure of Story of Sītā	Structure of Festivals	
	Delphic Great Year	Dussehra/Diwali
1. Rāma kills Rāvaṇa	1. On first day, Apollo kills Python with bow and arrow; with a torch, fire is set to a structure representing Python's den (or Priam's palace)	1. On last day of Dussehra, killing of Rāvaṇa by Rāma is reenacted by setting fire with an arrow to an image of Rāvaṇa
2. Sītā, Earth-figure, liberated	2. On second day, the return of the Heroine (Semele?), an Earth-figure, celebrated	2. On Diwali, the freeing of Lakṣmī, or return of Rāma and Sītā, celebrated
	3. On last day, barley distributed to all by the king	3. On last day of Dussehra, gifts given to people carrying and giving *noratras* (barley shoots) (Dussehra is a "royal" festival)
4. Sītā rejected by Rāma	4. On last day, the rejection of Charila is reenacted	

Herois (return of Semele?), Charila (cereal distribution, rejection of the un-named orphan girl, pollution, and expiation)—or to that of Dussehra and Diwāli, involving the slaying of a monster, the freeing of a female figure, and the distribution of alms and gifts.

So the old fertility-myth theories about the three stories provide us with new hints and with new material for the reconstruction of what we have called the agricultural (or better, cereal) fertility theme in the narrative and in their contexts. Yet we cannot accept their basic assumption, not only for the specific reasons I have mentioned case by case, but also, or better, especially because though most if not all ancient myths are (also) about agricultural fertility, there is no such thing as a "fertility myth" *stricto sensu*, for no myth is only about fertility, and agricultural fertility, being the consequence of social cohesion, is never "alone."

4

Another great theme common to the three stories, and much more specific than fertility, is that of the mistreating of a helpless woman by a powerful male, which follows the solution of a crisis but determines a new critical situation. The second crisis is solved only when the wronged female is somehow ap-peased or repaid. This theme is often directly connected to the fertility theme, for the crisis caused by the sin against the helpless woman is mostly of an agricultural nature (a famine, the abandoning of a field, and so on), yet in other cases the calamities provoked by that sin are of a different nature, which shows that the fertility theme, though it is always present, need not be central.

The nature of the heroines, their relation to the males who reject them, and the quality of the offense and of the wronged females' reaction vary in the three stories; but one may safely state that there are a limited number of motifs in the narratives, combined in different ways to form different, yet basically similar, patterns. Ruth in her first encounter with Boaz and Charila in her relationship to the king of Delphi are clearly presented as suppliants begging for cereal food. Charila's suppliant quality is paradoxically revealed by her suicide, that is, the typical suppliant's suicide of Greek myth and tragedy.[38] That suicide also reveals her as being "not ignoble" and thus resembles the noble suicide of the offended wife Sītā, who orders the pyre to be built while reproaching Rāma for a deed unworthy of his noble nature. We have already seen that Sītā's speech in the sixth book of the Rāmāyaṇa contains both a lament that we can compare to the lamentation of Naomi and a protest that is similar to the silent protest of Charila's suicide. We shall note that Ruth is first accepted as a suppliant, in a situation similar to that of Charila; and that she is then refused but finally accepted by Boaz as a wife, just as Sītā is first conquered, then rejected, and finally accepted as a wife by Rāma, only to be rejected again in the seventh book of the Rāmāyaṇa. So Ruth's first "risk" (that of being rejected by Boaz when, as a suppliant, she "fell on her face, and bowed herself to the ground, and said unto him, Why have I found grace [ḥn] in thine eyes that thou shouldest take knowledge of me, seeing I am a stranger?") corresponds precisely to the rejection of the suppliant Charila, while Ruth's second "risk," that of finding no husband, corresponds to Sītā's repeated loss of her husband.

While the motifs are variously combined, there seems to be a profound symmetry between the paradoxical situations caused in the three stories by the mistreating of the helpless females. In the story of Ruth, an Israelite man is unfaithful to the laws of Israel, while a foreign woman upholds them as a real champion of the ge'ullah. In the story of Charila, the king is unable to perform his duty as a provider, while a mere girl who is no member of the nobility is shown to be not ignoble and nobly dies. In the story of Sītā, a king who is in reality a god behaves in such a way that a woman may reproach him and declare to Rāma: "By giving way to anger like a trivial man you have made womankind preferable."[39]

The structure of the paradox clearly reveals that the three stories are about social relationships of unequal status and power in their connections to ethical behavior. Since we have shown the royal quality of the three narratives, we should state that they are about royal generosity; and since generosity is a duty for him who is master of all, royal "grace" or mercy should not be distinguished from royal "justice." In this perspective, the well-known agricultural connections of royal justice, studied already by the pioneers of the history of religions,[40] should be quoted to account for the coexistence of the royal grace-

and-justice theme and of the fertility theme in our stories. But more precise links are provided by the stories themselves and by their ritual context: the distribution motif, recurring both in the stories (the gleaning of Ruth, the kingly distributions in the story of Charila, the gifts distributed by Rāma during the crucial *aśvamedha*) and in the festivals (*šabuʿôt*, Charila, Dussehra), and the Earth-figure quality of the rejected females (whether direct, as in the case of Sītā, or mediated by other female figures, as in that of Charila, or expressed by the connection between the ownership of the woman and the ownership of the land, as in the cases of Sītā and of Ruth) connect the generosity of the male protagonist to agricultural fertility. In this new context we should consider both the fact that Naomi and Charila bear names derived from terms (*nʿm, charis*) meaning "grace" in the sense of "pleasantness" and "benignity, favor" and the fact that in the stories of Ruth and Charila the rejection of the helpless female is indicated by the removal of a sandal,[41] signifying the withdrawal of the protagonist from the soil he will not govern and till (in the story of Ruth) and from the woman he will not protect (Charila), own, and fecundate (Ruth). These facts suggest that the rejection of the helpless female is in reality the rejection of the land: in other words, that the master who is not generous toward the helpless offends the land, pollutes it, and ends by losing it. And the rather different use of the same motifs in the Rāmāyaṇa, where the name meaning "charming, graceful" is born by the king and the monarch's sandals are placed on his throne during his temporary absence, shows that the same symbolic language is used there to convey a message that is similar but not identical.

So the same basic theme, the sin of a powerful male against a helpless female, takes on different shapes in the different stories: and the same is true, as we have seen, of the final solutions that form the dialectic counterpart of that theme. In the story of Ruth, the tribesman who is most faithful to the divine commandments that rule Israelite society (and becomes a champion of agriculture as well as of sexual reproduction within the clan) gives a posterity to the dead and is chosen to produce—and to be—an ancestor of the messianic king David: kingship is in the future. In the story of Charila, a king of myth proves to be a bad provider for his subjects and insults a suppliant; but a ritual king periodically distributes barley to all, and presides over the ritual expiation of the mythical crime: kingship is in the time of myth and in ritual fiction. In India, kingship is present and the solution is either in a reconciliation between the king and the Earth figure he has rejected, granted by the gods and leading to a happy reign, indeed, to heaven on earth (*Rāmarājya*),[42] or else in the recognition of the divine quality of the mythical king, who is a god in spite of his faults and unknown to himself, and only ceases to function as a king in order to begin functioning both as a god and as an example of kingly and manly honor.

So the stories comment on kingship. At the same time, they uphold an economy based, first of all, on the preservation of the property of the extended family and of the extended family itself in its village and on its soil where it tills the fields, then on the centralization through tribute and periodical redistribution, or redistribution in case of need, of cereal and other agricultural produce. It is the economy of kingship, in which redistribution, that is, kingly generosity, plays a central role.[43] But in examining the connection of the three stories with kingship, we can and should be more specific. In particular, the special stress that all three narratives put on the problem of kingly grace and on the disastrous consequences of a sinful lack of generosity may lead us to envisage the myths we have studied so far as a product of that tendency to reform or to criticize kingship, indeed of that crisis of kingship, that took place in so many different societies around the so-called *Achsenzeit* and later, in the second half of the first millennium B.C.E.[44] The connection between kingly justice and agriculture, a very archaic feature in many societies, was there already, fit to be used by the great culture-shaping and innovating entities such as the international sanctuaries (Delphi), the national sacred books (the Bible), and the national epic traditions (the Rāmāyaṇa). Once the heroine with her transparent name had become, like Hesiod's suppliant Dike,[45] a protagonist, wronged by kings but immediately rescued or avenged by the gods because of her virtue, the story was ready to communicate a new critical message: power is nothing without generosity; indeed, it is nothing compared to generosity. The way to the paradoxes of the great founded religions was open.[46]

NOTES

1. This interpretation is criticized by authors who believe that the connection of the story of Ruth and Boaz with David is late, secondary, and fictitious, because they see the genealogy appended to the Book of Ruth as an artificial addition (see, e.g., Otto Eissfeldt, *The Old Testament: An Introduction*, trans. P. R. Ackroyd [Oxford: Basil Blackwell, 1965], pp. 477–483, esp. pp. 479–481). However, the arguments for considering the genealogy as a secondary addition are not cogent, especially not the argument based on the giving of the name Obed to a "son" of Naomi (see Eissfeldt, pp. 479–480: the "original" name "should" have been *ben-noʿam*). In Northwest Semitic cultures the two roots *nʿm* and *ʿbd* are often connected, as in Ugaritic, where they both refer to the mythical king Keret as being a gracious servant of the god El. Even if the arguments were valid, one would still have to explain why the Book of Ruth is concerned not only with the tribe of King David, but also (*a*) with the town where that king's family originated according to all biblical traditions and (*b*) with the only biblical figure of those placed in premonarchical times (and apart, of course, from the kingly figures Melchizedek and Abimelek) that bears a name compunded with the Hebrew word for "king." Surely these are not all late additions!

2. Eissfeldt, p. 570.

3. Plutarch, *Moralia* 293B–F; G. S. Kirk (*Myth, Its Meaning and Functions in Ancient and Other Cultures* [Cambridge and Berkeley: Cambridge University Press and University of California Press, 1970], pp. 16–17), treats the myth disappointingly but gives some bibliography.

4. Eissfeldt, p. 483.

5. On the Delphic santuary see the monograph by George Roux, *Delphes: Son oracle et ses dieux* (Paris: Belles Lettres, 1976).

6. A somewhat earlier date was accepted at the beginning of this century: see A. A. Macdonnell, A *History of Sanscrit Literature* (London: 1905), pp. 305–307. But one should accept the dates established by A. D. Pusalker (*Studies in the Epics and Puranas* [Bombay: Bharatiya Vidya Bhawan, 1963]), Morris Winternitz (A *History of Indian Literature*, trans. S. Ketkar, 2d ed. [Calcutta: University of Calcutta, 1959]), and others, while for the *terminus post quem non* one should take into consideration the argument offered by V. Pisani and L. P. Mishra, *Le letterature dell'India* (Milan: Sansoni, 1970), pp. 89–90: "Aśvaghosa presupposes Valmiki, and the former belongs to the time of Kaniska, that is, at the beginning of the second century after Christ, so that it is appropriate to conclude that the Rāmāyaṇa was composed, at the very latest, in the first century of the common era." The Rāmāyaṇa should now be read according to the critical ed. published by the Oriental Institute, Baroda, 1960–1975.

7. Sītā and her in-laws: Rāmāyaṇa 2.29.25; Rāmāyaṇa 7.44.21.

8. On this complex in ancient Israel, see the excellent article by H. Chanan Brichto, "Kin, Cult, Land and Afterlife—a Biblical Complex," *Hebrew Union College Annual* 44 (1973): 1–54.

9. See Rāmāyaṇa 6.95–96.

10. On the importance of the redemption motif, see Eissfeldt, pp. 482–483.

11. I quote here the very words of W. Doniger O'Flaherty, *Hindu Myths: A Sourcebook Translated from the Sanskrit* (Harmondsworth: Penguin Books, 1975), pp. 197–198. See also R. Sharma, *A Socio-Political Study of the Vālmīki Rāmāyaṇa* (Delhi: Motilal Banarsidass, 1971), pp. 80–81: "When it came to choose between 'honour (public popularity to say it correctly) and wife' the latter was ruthlessly cast away. Rāma expressly told his brothers: 'Even the celestials speak ill of bad name— whereas fame is adored in all regions. Therefore the high souled ones exert their best to acquire reputation.'"

12. Most scholars have concentrated on the ordeal by fire (*agni-parkīshā*), often forgetting that this was originally the suicide of a wronged, desperate, protesting woman (see E. W. Burlingame, "The Act of Truth," *Journal of the Royal Asiatic Society* [1917], pp. 429–467; W. Norman Brown, "The Basis for the Hindu Act of Truth," *Review of Religion* 5 [1940]: 36–45; "The Metaphysics of the Truth Act," *Mélanges d'Indianisme à la mémoire de L. Renou* [Paris, 1978], pp. 171–178).

13. See the naively severe judgement of Sharma, A *Socio-Political Study of the Vālmīki Rāmāyaṇa*, p. 81: "The callousness with which the husbands could treat their wives is further shown by the mean suggestion that Sītā should again submit herself to some purificatory ordeal . . . to convince the people of her purity. We call it mean because . . . now when [Rāma] was perhaps tempted to own her sons Kuśi and Lava, he threw that suggestion. It was worthy of the self-respecting Sītā that she proved the purity of her character but did not suffer a situation in which she would have been compelled to live once again, as the wife of such a husband."

14. Plutarch, *Moralia* 293 E–F.

15. On this aspect of the episode, see the shrewd comments of O'Flaherty, pp. 197–198.

16. Ibid., p. 198.

17. I owe part of this last sentence to Bruce Lincoln, who reminded me that in

the traditional Indian marriage the husband is identified with the sky and the wife with the earth. On Hindu marriage in central India today, see Tom Selwyn, "Images of Reproduction: An Analysis of a Hindu Marriage Ceremony," *Man* 14 (1979): 684–698.

18. On this problem see Camille Bulcke, "La Naissance de Sītā," *Bulletin de l'Ecole française d'extrème orient* 46 (1952): 107–117.

19. Daniel Dubuisson, "La Déesse chevelue et la reine coiffeuse," *Journal Asiatique* 266 (1978): 291–310.

20. Roland De Vaux, *Ancient Israel, Its Life and Institutions*, trans. J. McHugh (London: Darton, Longman & Todd, 1973), pp. 485–495.

21. Eissfeldt, p. 570.

22. Robert North, *Sociology of the Biblical Jubilee* (Rome: Pontificio Istituto Biblico, 1954).

23. On this festival, see Roux, pp. 164–171, and Joseph Fontenrose, *Python: A Study of the Delphic Myth and Its Origins* (1959; reprint ed., Berkeley: University of California Press, 1980).

24. Plutarch, *Moralia* 293D.

25. Roux, pp. 169–171.

26. Henri Jeanmaire, *Dionysos: Histoire du culte de Bacchus* (Paris: Payot, 1970), p. 223.

27. On these festivals see the comprehensive and sound book by H. W. Parke, *Festivals of the Athenians*, Aspects of Greek and Roman Life, ed. H. H. Scullard (London: Thames & Hudson, 1977).

28. On the *eiresione* and its connection with myths about the disappearing and return of an angry deity, see W. Burkert, *Structure and History in Greek Mythology and Ritual* (Berkeley: University of California Press, 1979), pp. 123–142.

29. Not only agricultural, of course, as shown, e.g., for Diwāli by Alf Hiltebeitel, "Nahuṣa in the Skies: A Human King of Heaven," *History of Religions* 16 (1977): 341–347 (Diwāli as an autumn feast of the Dead, quoting B. A. Gupte, "Divali-folklore," *Indian Antiquary* 32 [1903]: 237–239) and Johann Jacob Meyer (*Trilogie Altindischer Mächte und Feste der Vegetation* [Zurich: Max Niehaus, 1937], pt. 2, Bali).

30. B. Sharma, *Festivals of India* (New Delhi, 1978), pp. 109–112.

31. Ibid., p. 112.

32. Ibid., pp. 118–119; see also the bibliography in Hiltebeitel, p. 341, n. 50, esp. B. A. Gupte.

33. O. Staples, "The Book of Ruth," *American Journal of Semitic Languages* 53 (1936–1937): 145–157.

34. Charles Picard, "Phèdre à la balançoire et le symbolisme des pendaisons," *Revue archéologique*, 5th ser., 28 (1928): 48–64.

35. Roux, pp. 167–168.

36. A. H. Krappe, "Lancelot et Guenièvre," *Revue celtique* 48 (1931): 92–123.

37. I think in particular of the Urvaśi-Mélusine motif (see the excellent article by J. Le Goff, "Mélusine maternelle et défricheuse," *Annales-économies, sociétés, civilisations* 51 [1971]: 587–622) or of the motif of the mating of the sky god with an earth figure.

38. On this theme see B. Vickers, *Toward Greek Tragedy: Drama, Myth, Society* (London: Longman, 1973), pp. 467–489: "[Aeschylus' Suppliant Maidens] resolve that if gods and men do not give help they will exploit the suppliant's ultimate

pressure-point by committing suicide, so putting the guilt on those concerned."
See also M. Delcourt, "Les suicides par vengeance dans l'antiquité grecque,"
Revue de l'histoire des religions 60 (1939): 154–171; M. Mauss, "Sur un texte de Posi-
donius: Le suicide, contreprestation suprème," *Revue celtique* 42 (1925): 324–329;
and C. Grottanelli, "Encore un regard sur les bûchers d'Amilcar et d'Elissa," in
Proceedings of the First International Congress on Phoenician and Punic Studies
(Rome, 1979).

39. I follow here the translation of O'Flaherty, p. 198.

40. I refer especially to A. M. Hocart, *Kingship* (1927; reprint ed., Oxford: Oxford University Press, 1969), but also, of course, to Frazer and others.

41. On this motif in the story of Ruth see Calum M. Carmichael, "'Treading'
in the Book of Ruth," *Zeitschrift für die Alttestamentliche Wissenschaft* 92 (1980):
248–266, and "A Ceremonial Crux: Removing a Man's Sandal as a Female Gesture
of Contempt," *Journal of Biblical Literature* 96 (1977): 321–336.

42. On Rāmarājya and the Rāmāyaṇa, see Sharma, *A Sociopolitical Study of
the Vālmīki Rāmāyaṇa*, pp. 446–447, who concludes his book by quoting the description of Rāma's reign (Rāmāyaṇa 6.110.2–9) and by adding: "It is the Rāmarājya which has through the ages been the dream and aspiration of the Indian people."

43. On the ideology pertaining to this economic organization, see, for the Near
East, M. Liverani, "La Struttura politica," in *L'Alba della civiltà: Società, economia
e pensiero nel vicino oriente antico*, ed. S. Moscati (Turin: Unione Tipografico-
Editrice Torinese, 1976), vol. 1, chap. 3, pp. 292–324; J. De Fraine, *L'Aspect religieux de la royauté Israelite* (Rome: Pontificio Istituto Biblico, 1954), pp. 370–386,
specifically for ancient Israel; for India, esp. the Arthaśāstra, D. D. Kosambi, *The
Culture and Civilization of Ancient India in Historical Outline* (London: Rout-
ledge & Kegan Paul, 1965), pp. 141–165; and, for the ancient Greek world, the first
chapters of A. R. Hands, *Charities and Social Aid in Greece and Rome*, Aspects of
Greek and Roman Life, ed. H. H. Scullard (London: Thames & Hudson, 1968),
pp. 1–115. On the subject more generally the basic texts are three very different
works: M. Mauss, *The Gift: Forms and Functions of Exchange in Archaic Societies*
(New York: W. W. Norton & Co., 1967) (originally: "Essai sur le don," *L'Année
sociologique*, vol. 2, no. 1 [1925]); M. D. Sahlins, "On the Sociology of Primitive
Exchange," in *The Relevance of Models for Social Anthropology*, ed. M. Banton
(London: Tavistock, 1966), with much on reciprocity but something on redistribution; and K. A. Wittfogel, *Oriental Despotism. A Comparative Study of Total Power*
(New Haven, Conn.: Yale University Press, 1957), with practically no attention to
redistribution.

44. For the *Achsenzeit* see A. Momigliano, *Alien Wisdom: The Limits of Hellenization* (Cambridge: Cambridge University Press, 1975), pp. 1–20, quoting
K. Jaspers (*Vom Ursprung und Ziel der Geschichte*, 1949). This is the period covered by M. Eliade, *Histoire des croyances et des idées religieuses*, vol. 2 (Paris: Payot,
1978), ranging from the rise of Buddhism to the rise of Christianity. In Eliade the
correspondence between religious innovations in the Indian, Iranian, Hebrew, and
Greek worlds during this period is always clear, though not always explicit.

45. Hesiod, *Works and Days*, verses 248–264 ("Virgin *Dikē*, the daughter of
Zeus, is honoured and revered among the Gods who dwell on Olympus, and
whenever anyone hurts her with lying slander, she sits [like a suppliant] beside her
father, Zeus the son of Cronos, and tells him of men's wicked heart, until the peo-

ple pay for the mad folly of their princes who, evilly minded, pervert judgement and give sentence unjustly").

46. I dealt with the connection between the crisis of monarchy and the rise of the new soteriological religiosity around the middle of the first millennium B.C.E. in my essay "Healers and Saviours of the Eastern Mediterranean in Pre-Classical Times," in *Proceedings of the International Colloquium on the Soteriology of the Oriental Cults in the Roman Empire, Rome, September 1979*, ed. U. Bianchi (Leiden: E. J. Brill, 1982), now republished as chapter 7 in this volume.

RELIGIOUS IDEALS AND THE DISTRIBUTION OF CEREAL GRAINS IN THE HEBREW BIBLE

1. Storage and Redistribution in the Hebrew Bible

The storage and the (re)distribution of cereal grains in the Ancient Near East were administered by centralized organizations (temple or, more often, palace) in the context of social structures that were decidedly hierarchical and centralized. To the political centralization in such structures, there corresponded an economic centralization of the conservation, distribution, and consumption of foodstuffs. In fact, one centralization appears as a function of the other, in a system that is both coherent and complex.

Within this framework, which is variable but fairly consistent as well, I would like to juxtapose the testimony of certain biblical texts. Some of these biblical verses appear to be consonant with that framework, while others appear profoundly different. This diversity is most revealing. It is made possible by the fact that in these texts, for the first time in the Near East, we encounter voices emerging from contexts other than the traditional ones: the scribal contexts of palaces and temples. The authors (that is, the "redactors") of the Hebrew Bible are, in fact, the militant ideologues of a national and monolatrous religiosity. They were the heirs of the message of the great prophets, a message that, if not completely revolutionary, was certainly a rival alternative to the royal ideology. The Hebrew Bible as we know it was formed in a national community that had no king of its own. Instead, it was centered around a cult that saw itself as exclusive in postexilic Palestine. While it is true that the dates of the Books of Ruth and of the Chronicles, which I will examine here, are justifiably set within the postexilic period, the dating of the other biblical passages I will examine is controversial. These are usually dated to a much more ancient time (incorrectly, it seems to me). In any case, however, all agree that the definitive redaction even of texts like Genesis and the books of Samuel and Kings is not earlier than the sixth century B.C.E.[1]

2. David (II Samuel 6 and I Chronicles 16)

An explicit and relatively ancient mention of the distribution of cereal foods by a reigning king to his people is found in the passage II Samuel 6:19, and the parallel passage I Chronicles 16:3. There exists only one other biblical story of an analogous distribution in II Chronicles 31. I will return to the second episode toward the end of this essay. For the moment, I will take up the distribution of bread by David to his people in II Samuel 6 and I Chronicles 16.

The passage presents some problems. The current translation reads "David [when he had finished offering sacrifice on the occasion of the arrival of the ark in Jerusalem] distributed among all the people, to each man and each woman in the entire multitude of Israel, a loaf of bread, a cut of roast meat, and a raisin cake."[2] The Masoretic text indicates those things given to each Israelite with the terms *ḥlt lḥm*, *'špr* and *'šyš(h)*. The first term indicates certain cereal food (*lḥm* is "bread" or "gruel" of wheat or barley or other grains). The third term refers certainly to some sort of (leavened) cereal food. The term *'špr* is a hapax legomenon, which is sometimes translated "loaves with dates." More specifically, Hertzberg 1960 (2d ed.) denies that there are elements that would indicate the presence of meat.[3] The Greek of the Septuagint (*kollurida artou, eskharitēn, laganon apo tēganou*) seems in fact to indicate "bread cooked in the hearth" or some such expression for *'špr*, given that this seems precisely the meaning of *eskharitēn*. *Laganon*, on the other hand, means "loaf" or "layered pastry" (compare *lagaros* meaning "soft, flexible, tight, narrow"); and *teganon* means "pan."

Whatever may be the meaning of *'špr*, the first and the third foods distributed by King David to the people are, respectively, "bread" and "loaf." Of note is the festive context (the celebration of the transfer of the ark to Jerusalem, where Solomon, David's son and successor, would build the Temple to house it). The festival context is, moreover, specifically sacrificial. David (verse 13) had just sacrificed an ox and a fattened calf. He then (verses 14–17) accompanied the ark, dancing while it proceeded to the sound of music. Finally (verse 18), he offered holocausts and peaceful sacrifices and blessed the people. The distribution of cereal foods by the king to the people (with or without meat) is, therefore, part of the cult offered to Yahweh and is described as a great sacrificial meal.[4] Ideologically, the emphasis is placed not on the distribution of bread to a hungry people, but on the festival and its sacrifices, tied to the holy ark of the god and celebrated by the people and by the prototypical king.

3. Joseph (Genesis 41 and 47)

In contrast to David, the patriarch Joseph distributes grain to the hungry. Chapter 41 of Genesis recounts how Joseph, who after interpreting the dreams of the Egyptian Pharaoh that foretold seven years of abundance followed by seven years of famine, was placed by Pharaoh at the head of his household and his people. He ordered each city to store one-fifth of all the foodstuffs gathered from the surrounding countryside for the entire duration of the seven years of abundance. So it was that "Joseph garnered grain (*br*) in quantities like the sands of the sea so vast that at last he stopped measuring it, for it was beyond measure" (Gen. 41:49). When the famine arrived, the people cried to Pharaoh to have bread (*lḥm*) and Pharaoh "directed all the Egyptians to go to Joseph and do whatever he told them. When the famine had spread throughout the land, Joseph opened all the cities that had grain and rationed it to the Egyptians, since the famine had gripped the land of Egypt. In fact, all the world came to Joseph to obtain rations of grain, for famine had gripped the whole world" (Gen. 41:55–57).

The fact that foreigners would buy Egyptian grain is of interest in the biblical text to explain why Jacob and his sons came down into Egypt. But with regard to the sale of grain to the Egyptians, chapter 47 tells that they first paid for their grain in silver (*ksp, argurion*). When the silver was spent, they gave in exchange their livestock—horses, sheep, oxen, and asses.

> When that year had ended, they came to him in the following one and said: "We cannot hide from my Lord that, with our money spent and our livestock made over to my Lord, there is nothing left to put at my Lord's disposal except our bodies and our farmlands. Why should we and our lands perish before your very eyes? Take us and our land in exchange for food (*lḥm*), and we will become Pharaoh's slaves and our land his property; only give us seed, that we may survive and not perish, and that our land may not turn into a waste." Thus Joseph acquired all the farmland of Egypt for Pharaoh, since the famine forced every Egyptian to sell his field. So the land passed over to Pharaoh, and the people moved into the cities, from one end of Egypt's territory to the other [Here the Masoretic text, which is probably corrupt, and also the Greek of the Septuagint, states something much stronger: "They were reduced to slavery."]. Only the priests' lands Joseph did not take over. Since the priests had a fixed allowance from Pharaoh and lived off that allowance, they did not have to sell their lands. Joseph told the people: "Now that I have acquired you and your land for Pharaoh, here is your seed for sowing the land. When the harvest is in, you must give a fifth of it to Pharaoh while you keep four-fifths as seed for your fields and as food for yourselves and your families [and as food for your children]." "You have saved our lives!" they answered. "We are grateful to my Lord that we can be Pharaoh's slaves." Thus Joseph made it a law for the land in Egypt, which is still in force, that a fifth of its produce should go to Pharaoh. Only the land of the priests did not pass over to Pharaoh. (Gen. 47:18–26)

The meanings of this account are varied and complex. First of all, one reads there startled admiration of the redactors for a perfectly constructed and powerful state mechanism. This mechanism typifies the social and political tradition of Egypt, which, for the Hebrews, was so near and yet so different. In the second place, one can also find a prideful reversal of that more complex and powerful foreign model. This reversal consists of the mythical attribution of the invention of this very model to a son of Israel, a son who is, moreover, a slave. This second aspect is certainly tied to the traditional theme of the patriarch who tricks the Egyptians, which appears elsewhere in Genesis (see Gen. 12:10–20). The fundamental meaning of the account in Genesis 47, however, must be seen as a *reversal* of the leitmotif of royal ideology that is expressed by the public distribution of grains to the people by the palace—rather than as the foundation myth of any specific Egyptian reality. This is confirmed by the fact that the picture described by Genesis 47 does not correspond to any attested Egyptian social and political reality.[5] The point of reference and the central problem addressed by the narrative of Genesis 47:18–26 is most probably the indebtedness of Palestinian peasants and their consequent loss of land, and even of children and personal freedom, especially in times of famine or failed harvests.

Although the endemic possibilites of indebtedness, loss of land, enslavement for debt, in the entire scope of the history of the Near East have been often stressed, some interpreters have pointed out certain convergences between the framework presented by the story of Joseph and some elements inferred from Egyptian and Syro-Palestinian texts of the late Bronze Age.

In my opinion, there is no substantial reason for referring Genesis 47 to the Bronze Age. First of all, it is important to stress that the framework in question existed for millennia in substantially analogous forms within the Syro-Palestinian area.[6] But obviously the biblical texts would have had as their reference and principal target the social and political reality of the Palestine of the first millennium B.C.E. In particular, a framework of the type here discussed has been recognized as conspicuously present in the prophetic book attributed to Amos (eighth century B.C.E.?). B. Lang has traced an interesting outline of the phenomenon, as reconstructed from Amos and other biblical texts. The usurious loaning of grains, the mechanisms of surety, the enslavement of insolvent debtors, all appear frequently also in wisdom literature from Proverbs to Ben Sirach.[7] In all of the biblical attestations of this topos, sympathy rests with the poor debtors. The rich who exploit them and accumulate property are condemned. Beyond that, there are specific important commandments in the apodictic books, which aim to control and mitigate this problem.[8]

In light of these facts, it is clear that the intention of the protagonist in Genesis 41 and 47 is not to save or give life to his people, even though they may claim in a stereotypical way to owe him their lives (*hhytnw*; the Greek of the Septuagint has *sesōkas hēmas*; and the Egyptian name given to Joseph probably has a meaning connected with this traditional concept).[9] His intention is, rather, to procure for the palace, which he serves, total dominion and total ownership over the land and the people (with the notable exception of the lands of the priests and the priests themselves). At the hands of this protagonist and through the perverse mechanism of debt, the palace amasses all the silver, all the livestock, and all the land (except that of the priests). Finally, the palace takes possession of the people, "reducing them to slavery," or, in an alternative reading, "deporting farmers to the urban centers." Clearly, the concentration and control of grains serves here to acquire the control and concentration of every economic and human reality. In light of this ruthless process, even the prophet Samuel's much celebrated denunciation of the arrogance of kings grows pale (I Sam. 8:1–22). The comparison of these two passages demonstrates the same ideological atmosphere and the same intention of unmasking the monarchic institution, which is only apparently beneficent. In addition, a series of precise juxtapositions lends itself to a synoptic reading of the texts.[10]

It is noteworthy, however, that the king in this passage is not the king of Israel, as in I Samuel 8:10–22, but a foreigner. The reality that is both founded and, if my reading is correct, criticized in these passages from Genesis is described as a foreign reality. This is so even if, from all evidence, the criticism is aimed at problems internal to the society of Israel. What is the function of this displacement of a "Palestinian" problematic to the land of Egypt? The answer to this question is probably complex. At the level of pure narrative logic, however, it is noteworthy that the presence of a Jew in the Egyptian court is the only means by which it is possible for the book of the primordium, the book of Genesis, to treat a large centralized state, instead of patriarchal family units dedicated to pastoralism and occasional cultivation of grain.[11] If the dating I find most convincing for the biblical story of Joseph is correct, the situation of a Jew in charge of a foreign palace bureaucracy is similar to those described in the postexilic books of Daniel and of Esther, and in the Aramaic romance of Aḥiqar, found at Elephantine in Egypt and dated to the fifth century B.C.E.[12]

4. Boaz (Ruth 2 and 3)

The Book of Ruth, which is certainly postexilic, narrates an exemplary story set in the time of the Judges. The Hebrew sons of the Hebrew woman Naomi marry Moabite women in the land of Moab. They die young, with no offspring. The widowed Naomi returns poor and desperate to her native land of Palestine, which she had abandoned with her sons at the time of a famine. The famine is now over, but, in the homeland, in the absence of males, no one can claim the inheritance (the land) which is due to the family. This can be remedied only if a relative marries a widow of one of the deceased, thereby producing, according to the law of the levirate, a son that could stand as heir to the deceased: coming into possession of his goods, taking charge of the women in the family, and celebrating the funeral rites (regarding this threefold complex—continuation of the line, ownership of land, funerary rites—see Chanan Brichto's article of 1973).[13] The situation is resolved by the Moabite Ruth who, rather than remain in her own country, follows her mother-in-law and finds a relative willing to marry her. From their union, Obed is born, who is the ancestor of David and Solomon. The relative who champions the levirate and marries Ruth is Boaz, a rich land owner. In doing so he saves the family from dispersion and becomes, through Obed, the ancestor of kings.

Some read the Book of Ruth as a declaration of family and religious piety (ḥsd) or as a celebration of mixed marriages in contrast to the obligatory endogamy of the postexilic times. Others (among them especially Angelo Penna) consider it a text illustrating the royal genealogy of David from whom would spring the Messiah, according to the most ancient messianic expectation of the Jews (but, among others, Eissfeldt denies the antiquity of the "genealogical" ending). Still others (Haller and, more recently, Wright) recognize here the traces of ancient fertility rites in connection with the fact that, from the first centuries of our era, the text is the liturgical reading for the feast known as *Shavu'ot* or Pentecost, marking the close of the harvest season, particularly the harvest of grain.[14] In reality, all of these readings can be justified. The Book of Ruth is the book of the levirate, that is, of an institutional mechanism that is typically (but not exclusively) biblical, designed to ensure the continuity of the line and its ownership of the soil, which is the central function of that continuity.

Now Boaz, the ancestor of the king, appears in the story as the protector of the weak (in this specific case of two widows, a mother-in-law and a daughter-in-law). In addition, he is shown to be a generous distributor of cereal grains. In fact, he first meets Ruth when she comes to glean in his fields, following the harvesters working for him. Boaz seeks information about her. Having gotten it, he invites her to continue gleaning in his fields:

> "Listen, my daughter! Do not go to glean in anyone else's field; you are not to leave here. Stay here with my women servants. Watch to see which field is to be harvested, and follow them; I have commanded the young men to do you no harm. When you are thirsty, you may go and drink from the vessels the young men have filled." Casting herself prostrate upon the ground, she said to him, "Why should I, a foreigner, be favored with your notice?" Boaz answered her: "I have had a complete account of what you have done for your mother-in-law after your husband's death. . . . May Yahweh reward what you have done! May you receive a full reward from Yahweh, the God of Israel, under whose wings you have come for refuge." She said, "May I prove worthy of your kindness, my Lord: you have comforted me, your servant, with your consoling words; would indeed that I were a servant of yours!" At meal time, Boaz said to her, "Come here and have some food; dip your bread in the sauce." Then as she sat near the reapers, he handed her some roasted grain and she ate her fill and had some left over. She rose to glean and Boaz instructed his servants to let her glean among the sheaves themselves without scolding her, and even to let drop some handfuls and leave them for her to glean without being rebuked. She gleaned in the field until evening, and when she beat out what she had gleaned it came to about an ephah of barley, which she took into the city and showed to her mother-in-law. Next she brought out and gave her what she had left over from lunch. (Ruth 2:1–18)

Naomi explained to her daughter-in-law that Boaz, a relative of their deceased husbands, is among those that, according to the custom of the levirate, can marry her and produce a son for the continuation of the line. She encourages her to go to him that evening, joining him on the threshing floor where he spent the day sifting barley. Ruth takes up her suggestion and spends the night with Boaz near the pile of sifted barley. The following morning, Boaz dismisses her in secret before dawn, and bids her: "'Take off your cloak and hold it out.' When she did so, he poured out six measures of barley, helped her lift the bundle, and left for the city. Ruth went home to her mother-in-law . . . So she told her all the man had done for her, and concluded, 'He gave me these six measures of barley because he did not wish me to come back to my mother-in-law empty-handed!' " (Ruth 3:15–17). The outcome of the encounter is the one sought by the two women, because Boaz marries Ruth and from their union is born Obed, future ancestor of Jesse, ancestor of David.

We have in this passage a royal ancestor who lets the widow Ruth glean in his fields, and then offers barley in abundance for her and her mother-in-law. The connection with the ideological theme of the generous king who bestows grain seems quite clear. Nevertheless, a series of specific circumstances qualifies the ideological message of the text in a quite special way. First of all, it is an obligation for every Israelite farmer to allow the disinherited to glean in their fields, as Leviticus (19:9–10; 23:22) and Deuteronomy (24:19) assure us. Second, the "royal" aspect of the text is qualified by the fact that the story of Ruth is dated to a period in which Israel did not have a king. It is also qualified by the fact that the story is attributed by its author to a time, that of the Judges, in which "there was no king in Israel." The kingship is, therefore, in the future with respect to the period in which the events unfold, and in the past with respect to the time in which the book was edited. (One might also say that it is a kingship of the future, taking into consideration the messianic overtones of the text.) It is not a king but an ancestor of David who distributes cereals generously. With one important exception, to which I will return, never again does a Hebrew king other than David distribute cereal grains in the biblical text. Finally, and here is the most distinctive feature, the generous donor of cereals is, at the same time, the hero of the levirate and of the ge'ullah, that is the man who, by marrying the widow and procreating a son for the deceased relative, allows the line to continue and keeps the land of the line from being dispersed for lack of heirs. The just king from of old descends, therefore, from a rich landowner of cereal grain fields who, acting with piety, defends the family ownership of the soil. He is diametrically opposed to Pharaoh who deprives the Egyptians of their fields with the aid of his wise minister Joseph. Like Joseph, he receives the homage of an inferior (here Ruth, there the Egyptians) who calls him "my Lord" and declares him/herself his slave. Like Joseph, he distributes cereals, but, unlike Joseph, he is a champion of land ownership on the part of the lineage of peasants.[15]

This reading of the text is indirectly confirmed by the double meaning of the term go'el, which in the Book of Ruth qualifies Boaz as a relative of Ruth's deceased husband. The go'el is one who has the right and obligation to marry the widow in a levirate marriage. Elsewhere in the Bible (Gen. 38; Lev. 25:25) the go'el is the relative who has the right to recover lands which have been given up by an Israelite through dire necessity. As Leviticus affirms (25:23) this right derives from the principle that the land cannot be sold irrevocably.

5. Elisha (II Kings 4)

In the Books of Kings, Ahab is the prototype of the wicked king. The gravest sin that Ahab commits, and which eventually causes the end of his dynasty, is the forced expropriation of the vineyards of Nabot (I Kings 21), who had refused to sell them to the king: "The Lord forbid that I should give you my ancestral heritage." The prophets Elijah and Elisha, defenders of Yahwism, directly oppose Ahab (and his wicked son and successor as well) as an enemy of family land ownership sanctioned by Yahweh.[16] Among the many miracles attributed to Elisha in II Kings is a miraculous distribution of cereal grains in a time of famine.[17] After having miraculously sweetened a bitter stew made of flour and wild gourds, Elisha receives from a man of Baal-shalisha "twenty barley loaves made from the first fruits, and fresh grain in the ear. 'Give it to the people to eat,' Elisha said. But his servant objected, 'How can I set this before a hundred men?' 'Give it to the people to eat,' Elisha insisted. For thus says Yahweh, 'They shall eat and there shall be some left over.' And when they had eaten, there was some left over, as Yahweh had said" (II Kings 4:42–44).

In line with what we have seen thus far, in this passage the distribution of cereals in time of famine is attributed to a defender of family ownership of the soil. In this case, however, he who defends is not a royal ancestor, but a prophet who opposes the king. Other elements enrich the picture, including the story of the end of the siege of Samaria; the easy conquest of the provisions of the enemy (after the conquest, as foreseen by Elisha, two seahs of barley cost a shekel, and one seah of fine flour also cost a shekel) (II Kings 7); and the defense of the woman from Sunem who took refuge in the land of the Philistines during a famine and, upon her return, through the intercession of Elisha, regained possession of her fields from the king (II Kings 8).

The link between the situations of famine and the loss of ownership of the land on the part of Israelite families is no less strong in these passages than in the Book of Ruth. And even here, the abundant yield and the distribution of cereals are linked with the defense or reappropriation of family property. The prophets are the guarantors of abundance (II Kings 4) and defenders of property (II Kings 8), while the kings threaten property (I Kings 21) and are incapable of guaranteeing abundance (II Kings 6:25–27): "Because of the siege the famine in Samaria was so severe that an ass's head sold for eighty pieces of silver and a fourth of a *kab* of doves' dung for five pieces of silver. One day, as the king of Israel was walking on the city wall, a woman cried out to him, 'Help, my Lord king!' 'No,' he replied, 'Yahweh help you! Where could I find help for you: from the threshing floor or the winepress?' "[18]

6. Hezekiah (II Chronicles 31)

As I stated above, besides David in II Samuel 6 and I Chronicles 16:3, there exists one other king who accumulates and redistributes cereals and other edible goods in the Hebrew Bible. This is Hezekiah, king of Judah, who in II Chronicles 31:4–10 gathered together the tithes of the children of Israel and of Judah. "As soon as the order was promulgated, the Israelites brought, in great quantities, the best of their grain, wine, oil and honey, and all the produce of the fields; they gave a generous tithe of everything . . . and things that had been consecrated to the Lord, their God; these they brought in and set out in heaps. It was in the third month that they began to establish these heaps, and they completed them in the seventh month" (II Chronicles 31:5–7). As the text makes immediately clear, the tithe is the part belonging to the priests and the Levites. When Hezekiah, after having blessed Yahweh for the abundance, questioned the priests and the Levites regarding the heaps, the head priest Azariah of the house of Zadok answered him: "since they began to bring the offerings to the house of Yahweh, we have eaten to the full and have had much left over, for Yahweh has blessed his people. This great supply is what was left over" (II Chronicles 31:8–10).

Numerous issues induce us to read this text as a foundation story for the tithe which was owed to the priests and Levites in the postexilic age. Among them are the importance of the temple in Jerusalem as the place of distribution of harvested foodstuffs, the generally accepted dates of the Books of Chronicles (fourth through third centuries B.C.E.), and the correspondence with an analogous passage in the Book of Nehemiah (10:32–39). The role of the king should thus be questioned, together with the documentary value of the account.[19] As is true in general of the Books of Chronicles, what is of central importance to the redactors here is the status of Yahweh's priesthood, in particular the priesthood of Jerusalem.[20] The theme of the king who concentrates and distributes cereal grains and other goods is, by now, the pretext for the transmission of other ideological messages, intended to sanction quite different realities.

Conclusions

The complex ideological message of these biblical passages that relate to the distribution of grain is clear. The positive values are the abundance of the harvest and, strictly tied to it, both as cause and as effect, the social and territorial order based on land ownership by the extended family approved of by the deity. The theme of the concentration and distribution of cereal grains, one so important in the ideology of the palace societies of the ancient Near East, is redeployed to support these values characteristic of a quite different milieu. In some cases, the link between the centralization of the product and centralization of the means of production is clearly evident. In such cases, the concentration and redistribution of grain are presented with critical overtones, if not with outright negative comments. In other cases, distribution is entrusted to positive figures, who are at the same time champions of the inalienable family property. Where they are not outright enemies of centralizing kings, such figures are mythic ancestors of royal dynasties who symbolize the happy times in which Israel was united and powerful on its own territory and also, perhaps, promise a messianic restoration. Finally, the theme reappears, much altered, in discussions of a nonmonarchic institution: the tithe owed to the priests in postexilic Israel.[21]

There is no doubt that a similar original conception owes much to the ideology peculiar to the Israel that returned to Canaan from exile: a people without a king, which centered its identity on the cult of the national god and on its (re)acquired relation to the land of its fathers. But this conception may have deeper roots. It may well arise from the distinctive character, different from other palace-governed states in the ancient Near East, that distinguished the Palestinian monarchy of the first millennium—at least insofar as we can reconstruct it.[22] Some day we may see just how deep these roots actually go. But that day will come only when there is more clarity about dating those texts, including the ones examined in this study, which are traditionally considered the most ancient.

NOTES

1. For an outline of the problem of dating the biblical books in the traditional manner see J. A. Soggin, *Introduzione all'Antico Testamento* (Brescia, 1974), especially pp. 23–222, which contains a rich bibliography. For a traditional approach to the Pentateuch, see the excellent synthesis by Henri Cazelles and J.-P. Bouhot, *Pentateuque*, in *Dictionnaire de la Bible. Supplément* (Paris, 1963 and 1964). For a position that is strongly critical, but still working within the same logic, see studies such as H. H. Schmid, *Der sogenannte Jahwist* (Zürich, 1976), and R. Rendtorff, *Das überlieferungsgeschichtliche Problem des Pentateuchs* (Berlin and New York, 1977). Jan Van Seters, *In Search of History* (New Haven and London, 1983), comes close to a real discussion of "source criticism": this book has been reviewed by Giovanni Garbini ("Rivista degli Studi Orientali" 56, 1982 [but published in 1985], pp. 193–194), and by Mario Liverani (in "Oriens Antiquus" 24, 1985, pp. 307–310). More recent and potentially revolutionary approaches address the problem of the comparative study of the Masoretic text, the Greek translations, and the Qumran fragments. Such approaches show how complex and intricate is the history of the formation of the Hebrew text as we know it today. The work of Morton Smith, *Palestinian Parties and Politics That Shaped the Old Testament* (New York, 1971), on the context and background of the formation of the biblical texts, is fundamentally correct and original, but much too optimistic in its reconstruction. The work of Giovanni Garbini, *Storia e ideologia dell'Israele antico* (Brescia, 1986), offers numerous openings for a new approach to the texts as well as arguments for a global rethinking of their dating (as synthesized on p. 36: "The texts are all considered to be more ancient than they are in reality").

2. This translation of the biblical passage was taken by the translator of the Italian text from the *New American Bible*, 1974–75 edition, and was slightly modified by me.

3. H. W. Hertzberg, *Die Samuelbücher (Das Alte Testament Deutsch* 10) (Göt-

tingen, 1960, 2d ed.). Note, however, that the translation of the Vulgate (*assaturam bubulae carnis*) indicates a portion of (sacrificial) meat. The context, which is sacrificial, encourages such an interpretation. It might be, however, that it is precisely the context that guided the Latin translation of a rare and already obscure term.

4. Regarding banquets and sacrifices in the ancient world, see volume 9 (1985) of the journal *L'Uomo*, which contains the presentations made at the International Conference on Sacrifice held in Siena, Italy, in September 1983. See also the volume edited by Cristiano Grottanelli and Nicola F. Parise, *Sacrificio e società nel mondo antico* (Rome-Bari, 1988), with contributions by Cristiano Grottanelli, Maria Giulia Guzzo Amadasi, Lucio Milano, and Carlo Zaccagnini. Regarding the Ugaritic text about the banquet of the god Il, KTU 1.114, see Cristiano Grottanelli, *Ancora sull'ebbrezza del dio El (KTU 1.114)*: "Vicino Oriente" 7 (1988), pp. 177–188.

5. With regard to this problem, see the treatment by D. B. Redford, *A Study of the Biblical Story of Joseph (Genesis 35–70)* (Leiden, 1970), pp. 236–241. According to Redford, all the elements are generic or, at least, difficult to attribute with precision, with the exception of the favorable treatment of the priests. This would be indicative of a late period, from the Saitic Dynasty forward (exemption from taxes), or perhaps only from the Ptolemaic (royal subsidy—*syntaxis*—to the priests). See, however, the important review by A. Kitchen in "Oriens Antiquus" 12 (1973), pp. 233–242. Regarding the restrictive rather than "generous" politics of the Achaemenids pertaining to Egyptian sanctuaries and on the dietary obligations expected at the Egyptian temples during the Persian era, see, in addition, the observations of M. Dandamaev, *Temple and State in Late Babylonia*: "Vestnik drevnej istorii" (1966/4), pp. 17–39. See also the general treatment by R. F. Gyles, *Pharaonic Policies and Administration, 663 to 323 B.C.* (Chapel Hill, 1959). Most of the bibliography mentioned in this note is owed to a long discussion with C. Zaccagnini on this point.

6. See Mario Liverani, "Sydyk e Mysor," in *Studi E. Volterra*, VI (Rome, 1969), pp. 55–64, for an original reading of the subject in question and its long history (in particular, the ideology of justice as the canceling of debts). I will not hazard into the intricate forest that is the evidence and the discussion on this topic. One should see J. Ennew, *Debt Bondage: A Survey* (London, 1981), for a complete overview (not only on the ancient Near East). For ancient Israel, see F. Steiner, *Enslavement and the Early Hebrew Lineage System*: "Man" 54 (1954), pp. 73–75; H. G. Kippenberg, *Die Entlassung aus Schuldknechtschaft in antiken Judäa*, in G. Kehrer (ed.), *Vor Gott sind Alle gleich* (Düsseldorf, 1983), pp. 74–104 (canceling of debts); Innocenzo Cardellini, *Die biblischen "Sklaven"-Gesetze im Lichte des keilinschriftlichen Sklavenrechts* (Bonn, 1981) (comparison with Mesopotamian sources). See Jeremiah 34:8–22 for a classic biblical text concerning the liberation of the "Hebrew slaves" (here understood as Israelite peasants who were insolvent debtors). The liberation is decreed but not effected by King Zedekiah and the palace aristocracy (*kl-hšrym*), and unheeded even by the people (*wkl-h'm*). Through the mouth of the prophet, Yahweh announces that the punishment will consist of the destruction of Jerusalem and the other cities of Judah by the king of Babylon.

7. In Proverbs and in Job the problem discussed is the behavior of the rich individual (usurer or creditor) toward the poor. For example, Proverbs 11:15 (loans, surety, forfeiture); 11:26 (cornering the market and the sale of grains); 20:16 (a gar-

ment as surety); 27:13 (again, a garment as surety); 28:8 (usury and interest at the expense of the poor); 29:13–14 (the usurer, the poor man, and the just king). Thus, the impious man of Job 20 "stole a patrimony he had not built up" and "oppressed the poor." In compensation his sons would have to "seek out the favor of the poor." The admonition of ben Sirach is, on the other hand, totally different. It concerns those who are too quick to ask for loans or to post surety, perhaps only to throw banquets (it is clear that the texts do not refer to the poor in these instances). Regarding Proverbs, see R. N. Whybray, *Wisdom in Proverbs* (London, 1965), and M. J. Dahood, *Proverbs and North-West Semitic Philology* (Rome, 1963), but these two books pay little attention to our theme and accept a too-ancient date for Proverbs, which is very much a composite. M. V. Fox, *Aspects of the Religion of the Book of Proverbs:* "Hebrew Union College Annual" 39 (1968), pp. 55–69, is more attentive to the ethical aspects of Proverbs. In studies on Job, the portrait of the usurer in chapter 20 has seldom been drawn in high relief. Mesopotamian parallels have been detailed by A. Kuschke, "Theologische Literaturzeitung" 81 (1956), pp. 55–69. On the ethics of Wisdom literature, see W. Richter, *Recht und Ethos* (Munich, 1966).

8. See Bernhardt Lang, *Sklaven und Unfreie bei Amos:* "Vetus Testamentum" 31 (1981), pp. 482–488. As B. Lang shows in his book *Monotheism and the Prophetic Minority* (Sheffield, 1983), p. 168, note 253, the passages (Deut. 23:20, Lev. 25:36, and Ezek. 18:17) that absolutely prohibit the gaining of interest on loans made by one Hebrew to another are definitely postexilic, and make appeal to a strong sense of national solidarity. Exodus 22:24, perhaps being more ancient, was, according to Lang, different in that it did not originally prohibit the taking of interest. This prohibition (as already proposed by G. Beer, *Exodus* [Tübingen, 1939], p. 117) could be a later redactional addition. In any case, other passages referring to biblical legislation, such as the regulations of the sabbatical year (Exod. 23:10, Lev. 25:1–7, Deut. 15:1–6), with the remission of debt, the rules for the jubilee, those regarding the "Hebrew slave" (Exod. 21:11), those regarding the inheritance of women (Num. 36 and 27:1–11), those on the levirate (Deut. 25:5–10) and others. All of these regulations point in the same direction, that is, the continuity of family land property and the concomitant freedom of the Israelite peasant. On this issue see Robert North, *Sociology of the Biblican Jubilee*, Analecta Biblica 4 (Rome, 1954), is useful, as is the older treatment by H. Schaeffer, *Hebrew Tribal Economy and the Jubilee as Illustrated by Semitic and Indo-European Village Communities* (Leipzig, 1922), when stripped of its "primitivist" tendencies. On the theme of debts, slavery for debts, and liberation, see, in addition to the texts cited in n. 6 above, Nehemiah 5:1–3 (indebtedness in order to pay taxes to the Achaemenid king).

9. Regarding the Egyptian name of Joseph, see H. F. Lutz, *The Egyptian Archetype of Saph^eneath Pa^eneah* (Los Angeles, 1945). On the Egyptian theme of the Pharaoh who gives life, see the clear formulation by Henri Frankfort, *Kingship and the Gods* (Chicago, 1948), pp. 51–60 ("The king 'produced barley' not merely in an indirect way, for instance by caring for the farmers or furthering agriculture, but through his own actions—by maintaining Maat, the right order which allowed nature to function unimpaired for the benefit of man"; p. 57). On the Akkadian "translation" (and Syrian interpretation) of this and similar Egyptian concepts in the Amarna epistolography, see Mario Liverani, *Le lettere del Faraone a Rib-Adda:* "Oriens Antiquus" 10 (1971), pp. 253–268; idem, *Rib-Adda, giusto sofferente:* "Altorientalische Forschungen" 11 (1974), pp. 182–187; idem, *Stereotipi della lingua 'altra'*

nell'Asia anteriore antica: "Vicino Oriente" 3 (1980), pp. 15–31, as well as the article by Carlo Zaccagnini, *L'ambiente palestinese nella documentazione extrabiblica del Tardo Bronzo:* "Rivista Biblica Italiana" 32 (1984), pp. 13–27.

10. On I Samuel 8, see I. Mendelsohn, *Samuel's Denunciation of Kingship in the Light of the Akkadian Documents from Ugarit:* "Bulletin of the American Schools of Oriental Research" 143 (1956), pp. 17–22, with the important criticism by Zaccagnini, "Rivista Biblica Italiana" 32 (quoted in note 9), p. 18: "In reality, I Samuel 8:10–18 offers a testimony that, insofar as it is generic and allusive, can refer to practically any epoch or any area of the ancient Near East. In its specifics, it is referable to the neo-Assyrian organization, in its more mature epoch, that is, approximately half a millennium after the supposed epoch of Samuel." As to the relationship between Genesis 41 and 47 and I Samuel 8, which I discussed at length with Zaccagnini, I am struck in particular not only by the more general comparisons, but by the more specific points of contact, for example, the chariot of the king or vizier (*mrkbt*) before which (*lpny*) hurry along the heralds (Genesis 41:43 and I Samuel 8:11. For the position of Zaccagnini, which differs from mine both in the interpretation of Genesis 41 and 47 and in the relationship between the passages of Genesis and I Samuel 8, see Zaccagnini, *Note sulla redistribuzione dei cereali nel Vicino Oriente del II e del I millennio,* in Rita Dolce and Carlo Zaccagnini (eds.), *Il pane del re. Accumulo e distribuzione dei cereali nell'Oriente antico* (Bologna, 1989), pp. 101–116.

11. Regarding the grain cultivation of the patriarchs see Genesis 26:12. "Isaac sowed a crop in that region and reaped a hundred fold the same year. Since the lord blessed him. . . ." It is noteworthy that the entire orientation of Genesis seems to be, contrary to the *opinio communis*, strictly agricultural and, in particular, geared toward the cultivation of grains, rather than pastoral and seminomadic. Note here the frequent mentions of bread (*lehem*) or dough to make small loaves (18:5–6; 25:34; 28:20, etc.), more frequently mentioned than the consumption of meat and dairy products; oil and wine (for example, 28:18; 35:14; 19:32–33); the acquisition of fields as silver security (but for use in burials or the like); but, above all, the strictly agricultural and cerealicultural blessing of Jacob (27:27–28: dew, fertility, fruit, must, the fragrance of a field that has been blessed) and the cerealicultural dream of Joseph (37:5–8: "There we were biding sheaves in the field when suddenly my sheaf rose to an upright position, and your sheaves formed a ring around my sheaf and bowed down to it"). Livestock and metals were a measure of portable riches (see, for example, 24:35), as in Homer and in the Hittite story of Appu (on which see Cristiano Grottanelli, *Observation sur L'histoire d'Appou:* "Revue Hittite et Asianique" 36 [1978], pp. 49–57, especially p. 57, where I incorrectly describe this circumstance in the story of Appu and in Genesis as typical of a "pastoral" economy). In addition, the episode of Ruben in the fields at the time of the harvest in Genesis 30:14 shows, at the very least, a familiarity with cereal grain agriculture. The frequent relocations of the Patriarchs across vast stretches of space, which are often ascribed to famines (as in Genesis 26:1–4 and, of course, in Genesis 46), do not seem to be "seminomadic" at all, but should be interpreted along the lines indicated by T. L. Thompson, *The Historicity of Patriarchal Narratives* (Berlin and New York, 1974), pp. 308–314 (above all in the section "Some Notes on the Structure of Genealogies and Sagas in Antiquity"), by this book's chapter 6, and by the other contributions by Liverani and Grottanelli quoted in that chapter. The interpretation of Jacob's movement in space in the

light of pastoral transhumance proposed by de Pury, *Promesse divine et légende cultuelle dans le Cycle de Jacob* (Lausanne, 1975), is interesting but not convincing (see my review in "Oriens Antiquus" 18 [1979], pp. 357–362).

12. On the dating of the story of Joseph to the postexilic period (seventh to fifth century B.C.E.) see the arguments presented by Daniel B. Redford, *A Study of the Biblical Story of Joseph (Genesis 35–70)* (Leiden, 1970), and the above-cited review by Kitchen in "Oriens Antiquus" 12 (1973). Regarding the comparison between the story of Joseph and the narrative traditions of the Persian period discussed here, see J. J. Collins, *The Court Tales in Daniel and the Development of Apocalyptic*: "Journal of Biblical Literature" 94 (1975), pp. 218–234; A. Meinholdt, *Die Gattung der Josephgeschichte und der Estherbuches. Diasporanovelle I*: "Zeitschrift für die Alttestamentliche Wissenschaft" 87 (1975), pp. 307–324; idem, *Die Gattung . . . Diasporanovelle II*: "Zeitschrift für die Alttestamentliche Wissenschaft" 88 (1976), pp. 72–93; and chapter 8 in this book. On the central theme of the "court tale" narrative, see S. Niditch, R. Doran, *The Success Story of the Wise Courtier: A Formal Approach*: "Journal of Biblical Literature" 96 (1977), pp. 179–193, and F. C. Fensham, *The Change of Situation of a Person in Ancient Near Eastern and in Biblical Wisdom Literature*: "Annali dell'Istituto Orientale di Napoli" 31 (1971), pp. 155–164. For a dating in the Solomonic Age, see G. W. Coats, *From Canaan to Egypt: Structural and Theological Context of the Joseph Story* (Washington, 1976) (with my review, in "Studi e Materiali di Storia delle Religioni" 49 [1983], pp. 445–450.

13. See H. Chanan Brichto, *Kin, Cult and Afterlife: A Biblical Complex*: "Hebrew Union College Annual" 44 (1973), pp. 1–54.

14. On various aspects of the Book of Ruth see Angelo Penna, *Giudici e Rut* (Turin, 1963); O. Eissfeldt, *Einleitung in das Alten Testament* (Tübingen, 1964), pp. 645–654; G.R.H. Wright, *The Mother-Maid at Bethlehem*: "Zeitschrift für die Alttestamentliche Wissenschaft" 98 (1986), pp. 56–72; and, already, M. Haller, "Ruth," in the volume by various authors, *Die fünf Megilloth* (Tübingen, 1940). In Penna's book there is a good bibliography (see especially p. 264) regarding the juridical problems of the book: the levirate, *ge'ullah*, adoption. For an attempt at a more articulate reading see Oswald Loretz, *The Theme of the Ruth Story*: "Catholic Biblical Quarterly" 22 (1960), pp. 391–399, and this book's chapter 1. Finally, it is important to keep in mind the interpretation proposed by Edmund Leach, "The Legitimacy of Solomon," in his book *Genesis as Myth and Other Essays* (London, 1971), pp. 25–83.

15. Regarding the symbolic value of the name Boaz ("strength"), see J. A. Soggin, *Introduzione all'Antico Testamento* (Brescia, 1974), p. 515. On the social and ethical value of Boaz's action, see the juridical studies quoted by Penna in his book (see above, note 14), and more importantly chapter 1 in this book.

16. Two distinct traditions are at work in the Books of Kings: the traditional narratives about the prophet Elijah (I Kings 17–19 and 21; II Kings 1–2) and those on the prophet Elisha (I Kings 19:19–21; II Kings 2:4–10). They are usually dated around the ninth through eighth centuries B.C.E. See J. A. Soggin, *Introduzione all'Antico Testamento* (quoted above, note 15), pp. 277–279, and R. P. Carroll, *The Elijah-Elisha Sagas*: "Vetus Testamentum" 19 (1969), pp. 400–415, for the *opinio communis* on these traditions. The tendency among scholars is to doubt neither the historicity of the characters nor the accounts themselves: see, e.g., John Bright, *A History of Israel* (London, 1972, 2d ed.), pp. 242–249, and O. G. Fohrer, *Geschichte der Israelitischen Religion* (Berlin, 1968), chapter 3, section 18. Most scholars are

not concerned with the contradictions present in the biblical texts, as seen, for example, in Hosea 1 (which, as Soggin observed in his *Introduzione all'Antico Testamento*, p. 278, is not easily reconciled with the account of Elisha's actions). If Hosea 1:1–5 is indeed ancient, it is possible that the traditions on Elijah and Elisha (and not only those regarding Elisha, as Eissfeldt thought) may be less so. They may reelaborate in a "Yahwistic" fashion the coup d'état staged by Yehu, which was condemned by "Hosea."

17. It is clear that this miracle is the prototype for the New Testament miracle known as "the multiplication of the loaves and fishes." This is one of the many traces that indicate the importance of the figures of Elijah and Elisha in the culture of Christian origins.

18. Regarding the success of the prophets and the failure of the kings in the Bible, in this typically "royal" field of agrarian well-being, see chapter 1 in this book, and G. Garbini, *Storia e ideologia nell-Israele antico* (quoted above, note 1), pp. 124–128.

19. John Bright, *A History of Israel* (quoted above, note 16), p. 281, does not doubt the historical value of this account. Hezekiah, he suggests, attempted to gather around the Jerusalem Temple not only his Judahite subjects, but even the inhabitants of the former kingdom of Israel. But Bright cannot deny that here one encounters the Chronicler's characteristic handling of the material in treating the northern Israelites as if they were the later Samaritans. Regarding Hezekiah's "reforms" as tied to his anti-Assyrian politics, see Bright's pp. 281–282; and on the preparations for the Assyrian siege of Jerusalem, his p. 283. For a radical historical criticism of the biblical account of this siege, see G. Garbini, *Storia e ideologia nell'Israele antico*, pp. 72–76.

20. J. A. Soggin, *Introduzione all'Antico Testamento* (quoted above, note 15), p. 534: "For the *Chronicles* the center of the history of Israel is found in the Temple and in its cult, in its priesthood, even in its lesser personnel."

21. Regarding this problem, see the discussion in Alfred Cody, *A History of Old Testament Priesthood*, Analecta Biblica 35 (Rome, 1969), pp. 175–190, which is carried out with a fair degree of naivete. See also the older, stimulating (but at times quite fantastic) account by Gerhardt von Rad, "Die Levitische Predigt in den Bücher der Chronik," in *Festschrift Otto Proksch* (Leipzig, 1934), pp. 113–124, and the discussion on Aaron's economic dependance upon the people in A. Cody, *A History of Old Testament Priesthood*, pp. 194–195 (attested by ben Sirach 45:6–25).

22. Giorgio Buccellati, *Cities and Nations of Ancient Syria*, Rome, 1967.

THE ENEMY KING IS A MONSTER

A Biblical Equation

1. An Introduction: The Golden Calf

1.1. The Golden Calf and Mot

In her 1973 study,[1] M. K. Wakeman looked at the well-known motif of "the God's battle with the monster" as it appears in the Bible, aiming to show through such a specific research "that the antimythological attitude of the Bible is not only the self-conscious polemic of the priestly authors of the first chapter of Genesis, but can better be described as the outcome of a more generalized change of attitude that required new forms of expression."[2] In fact, she has duly shown that a "new language" was gradually created out of the traditional mythical material in order to express the new cosmological (and, I should add, political) realities of the yahwistic faith.[3]

A good example of such a process is the similarity between Anat's treatment of Mot in the Ugaritic myth and Moses' treatment of the golden calf, which is also burned (*tšrpnn*, cf. Exod. 32:20: *wayyiśrōp*), ground (*tṭḥnn*, cf. Exod. 32:20: *wayyiṭḥan*), and scattered on the water (*drʿ bym*, cf. *wayyizer ʿal-pᵉnê hammayim*).[4] As S. E. Löwenstamm[5] has shown, "the biblical description of the Golden Calf constitutes an Israelite development of an early literary pattern that was employed in Canaan to describe the total annihilation of a detested enemy"[6]: but we should speak of a mythical, not just of a "literary" pattern. This, of course, means that Anat's treatment of the monster has nothing to do with the fate of the "corn spirit" (or of any other entity connected with fertility), as it appears in folklore and mythology.[7] Its value is more broadly cosmological, and consists in the complete destruction of a dangerous and chaotic being whose very presence is an obstacle in the construction of a correct world order.[8] In the similar episode of the golden calf the correct order that has to be founded and requires the annihilation of the "monster" is Israel's relationship to its god Yahweh, which is the very core and foundation of that new community's existence.

But M. K. Wakeman's interpretation goes further than this, for she proposes that "Mot and the calf are not only related as enemies but are one and the same enemy."[9] The existence of a monster called *arš* in Ugaritic tradition is attested by the parallel "*bym·arš·wtnn*" (UT, 62:50); and the synonymity of Mot (who, like the tannin, is a swallower) and *arṣ* is established elsewhere in Wakeman's essay.[10] To this one must add the fact that Ugaritic *ar[š]*, in ʿnt III 40–41, has been restored as *ar[s]*, "earth," by Virolleaud.[11] Wakeman[12] agrees with Gaster's[13] and Driver's[14] criticism of Virolleaud's restoration, but proposes to regard *arš* as an alternate form of *arṣ* on the basis of a parallel with the alternance between *mḫš* and *mḫṣ* in Ugaritic studied by M. Held.[15] If this is correct, then "the identity of the calf and Mot suggested by their similar fates finds confirmation in the parallel between *arṣ* and *ʿgl* in ʿnt III: 40–41"[16] (a list of monsters defeated by ʿAnat). *ʿgl* could then well be "an appellative of Mot-Ereṣ-arṣ in the same manner that *naḥaš* is an appellative of Rahab."[17]

Though this suggestion may not be accepted,[18] we have to consider that both the golden calf and its Ugaritic homonym *ʿgl . il . ʿtk* are "monsters" that have to be, and actually are, destroyed, and that the accounts of Moses' and Anat's actions against their respective enemies stem from a common mythological background and share the common function of preparing the conditions for the construction of a correct cosmic (or religious and social) order. If we bear in mind that, as we have shown, the same can be said of the story of Mot and of its annihilation, we shall conclude that the typological and functional identity of the golden calf, the Ugaritic *ʿgl . il,* and Mot, is securely acquired as a basis for further research.

Moreover, a mention of "calves" as monsters that have to be "cursed," and thus vanquished or destroyed, by Yahweh is found in Ps. 68:31 (*gᵉʿar ḥayyat qāneh ʿadat ʾabbîrîm bᵉʿegᵉlê ʿammîm:* "curse the beasts of the reeds, the herd of bulls with the calves of the people"). It is true that Gunkel[19] has suggested that the term *ʿegᵉlê* is wrongly used here by the scribe as a parallel for *ʾabbîrîm* ("mighty ones"), mistakenly interpreted by him as "bulls"; yet the very possibility of such an ambiguity is significant, showing as it does that bulls and calves could well be mentioned as Yahweh's enemies in such a "cosmic battle" context.[20] This gives us an instance of a direct conflict between calf-monsters and the divine being himself, and allows us to sketch this diagram of a fourfold cosmic battle:

Ugarit: Anat vs. Mot (UT, 49:v)	The Bible: Yahweh vs. *ʿegᵉlê ʿammim* (Ps. 68:31)
Anat vs. *ʿgl. il* (ʿnt III: 40–41)	Moses vs. golden calf (Exod. 32:20)

1.2. Two Narrative Traditions about the Creation of Israel

Though it is clear by now that both the episode related in Exod. 30 and the conflict alluded to in Ps. 68:31 are outcomes of one single mythical motif attested also by the Ugaritic texts we have quoted, it is equally evident that the two passages differ greatly in many respects. In Ps. 68:31 we have a reference to a battle between Yahweh and his cosmic counterparts that is exactly of the same nature as the two Ugaritic mythical conflicts I have compared it to; but in Exod. 30 the setting and implications of the narrative are of a completely different quality. In this last case we have to do not with a battle between God and monster, clearly set in a mythical past, but with an important episode of the (sacred) "history" of a *historical* social and ethnic entity (Israel) and with the conflict between a *human* protagonist (who is Israel's leader and its true god's "prophet") and a false god that is in reality a manufactured object to which a cultic worship is unduly tributed.[21] We can well say then that while the form of this episode is provided by the mythical tradition of the battle against the (calf-) monster, its contents are new ones, i.e., two typical biblical motifs: the polemic against "manufactured gods" and the rejection of "false" deities. This is clearly a case of the use of a very archaic traditional mythological material to express the new realities of the yahwistic faith. Since there is no reason to believe that the golden calf episode is in any way a "historical" fact, we have here not a real event reshaped by mythical thought, but the reinterpretation of a mythical tradition in order to convey a new religious message: the myth is modified and inserted into the continuous biblical narrative that accounts for the origin of the yahwistic faith. The very form and basic structure of the myth make of it, as we have seen, the story of the removal of an obstacle that endangers the cosmic order, and so, in a way, a "creation myth"[22]: and this is exactly the value it retains in the new setting. But, of course, the new order that must triumph over the golden calf is not the macrocosmic order of the Ugaritic mythology that has to be freed of the monsters and ruled by Baal: it is the relationship between Israel and Yahweh and the religious and social order that stems from that relationship.

We could express the nature of this new use of the monster myth by quoting what G. Dumézil says in discussing the absence in ancient Rome of a divine mythology and the presence, in the most archaic Roman "historical" tradition, of narrative motives and episodes that are supposedly typical of "Indo-European" mythology: "The myths have been transferred from that great (macrocosmic or divine) world to this (Roman) world, and the protagonists are no longer the gods but great men of Rome who have taken on their characteristic traits."[23] To conclude, the episode of Moses and the golden calf is a development of the monster battle myth that has been not so much "demythologized" as actualized and modified in order to express the removal of an obstacle to yahwism seen as a specific cosmic order.[24]

But, if the [supposedly historical event of] the destruction of the calf by Moses is really "mythical," on the other hand the clearly mythical combat between Yahweh and the "bulls and calves" in Ps. 68:31 is not without connections with the earthly national adventure of early Israel. M. Dahood writes that "this psalm may be fairly classified as a triumphal hymn (much like Exod. 15, the Song of Moses) which, in mythopoeic language and mythological motifs that are somewhat historicized, celebrates the defeat of the Egyptians and the deliverance of the Israelites (vss. 2–7), the escape into the wilderness and the theophany of Sinai (vss. 2–9), and finally the settlement in Canaan implied by the prayer for rain (vss. 10–15). The rest of the poem plays variations on these principal themes."[25] The whole psalm is *based* upon a correspondence between Egypt or its king and the monster defeated by Yahweh: Pharaoh for instance is identified with the serpent (Bašan) or with the deep sea (*mṣlwt ym*) that Yahweh has stifled or muzzled (vss. 22–23). As for the specific value of our verse 31, the same author adds: "vss. 25–28 describe a solemn procession into the assembly where the community, recalling the previous deliverance from Egypt, prays (vss. 29–31) for help against a new threat from Egypt, here termed 'the beast of the reed thicket'"[26]: according to such an interpretation, that is not alternative, but complementary, to the one I have accepted, the bulls and calves signify officers and soldiers, respectively, of the army headed by the *ḥayyat qāneh* monster, who might be not exactly "Egypt" but "the Pharaoh." The battle between Yahweh and the (calf) monster(s) is here strictly connected with another conflict that opposes Yahweh's people and the king of Egypt; yet we cannot simply affirm that the first is used as a (mythical) symbol of the second. The two conflicts really merge into one single cosmic battle, for even the fight against Egypt is really won by Yahweh, not by Israel.

Moreover, the tradition about the struggle against Egypt is thus in a way no less "mythical" than the story of Yahweh's struggle with the chaotic monster; and since Egyptian domination literally implies the impossibility of an orderly (yahwistic) Israelite microcosm in the Promised Land, whereby the covenant with the Patriarchs may be accomplished, the monstrous nature of Pharaoh and his people is not simply symbolic but is felt as a very profound and concrete reality.

On the basis of such observations, we can reach the tentative conclusion that in Exod. 32 as well as in Ps. 68 we have two similar Israelite traditional narratives about the Israelite past and the origin of the yahwistic faith that was the cement and core of that society and culture.

These narratives maintain the traditional form of the cosmic battle myth that in many ancient mythologies signified the conflict between chaos and the divine producer of cosmic order in the primeval time of creation, and, more specifically, develop a Canaanite narrative tradition of the conflict between a god or goddess and a calf-monster that is probably an aspect of the "earth" or "underworld." Yet, since the two similar (and connected) narratives have to do not with the foundation of the macrocosm, but rather with the birth of the microcosm Israel and of its special relationship with its god Yahweh, they oppose that god or its "prophet" and the leader of its people, Moses, to a false (calf-) god or to an enemy king, his people and his country. Finally, the similarity between the two tales will seem complete if we remember that that enemy king is a god to his people,[27] so that the tribute that is owed to that king but transferred to Yahweh (Ps. 68:32) corresponds to the worship that is unduly offered to the false god (Exod. 32), but later correctly tributed to Yahweh (see Exod. 33–40; Ps. 68:33–36). The implication is that, since Yahweh is king,[28] and the "foreign" kings are also false gods, fighting against those kings (e.g., against Pharaoh) is in itself a religious act, a way of establishing the correct order and a precise equivalent to the mythical cosmic battle against the monster.

2. Eglon and Agag

2.1. *The Killing of King Eglon of Moab*

That foreign kings, peoples and lands are monsters is not asserted only by the passages we have quoted so far: indeed, it is a biblical leitmotif. We are told that Pharaoh is the monster Tannin (Ezek. 29:3–6, 32:2–8); that Nebuchadnezzar the king of Babylon is that same monster (Jer. 51:34), who is a devourer and shall be devoured (Jer. 51:40); that Egypt is Rahab (Isa. 30:7); that Rahab can be mentioned in a list of enemy countries along with Babylon, Philistia, Tyre and Ethiopia (Ps. 87:4); that Babylon, like a mythical monster, is stilled by Yahweh and raises her voice while her waves roar like many waters (Jer. 51:55); that the Reed Sea is split open (*bqʿ*) just as happens to the chaotic monster in many myths.[29] In all these cases, the foreign king or country that is identified as a primeval monster is or shall be destroyed by Yahweh because it oppresses and exploits Israel. Yet we should notice that all the passages we have quoted are no more than short verses or groups of verses that merely hint at a mythical tradition and synthetically present the equation: Israel's enemy=mythical monster; so that we may well describe them as poetic allusions. Seemingly, the only explicit narrative account of the destruction of a being that is felt as chaotic and monstrous, and thus identical to a mythical enemy of the cosmic order, is the story of Moses and the Golden Calf.

Yet at least two important biblical narratives are precisely accounts of the elimination of an enemy king. In the book of Judges (3) the tale is told of Ehud's action against Eglon, king of Moab, who is killed by that fearless Benjaminite in the very heart of his residence; and I Sam. 15:1–35 recounts the capture and dismemberment of Agag the king of Amalek. There is nowhere any explicit suggestion that these tyrants who are so justly destroyed are similar or identical to mythical monsters; yet in the light of the data examined so far we feel entitled to suspect that such may be the case. To verify this hypothesis will be the scope of the following two sections: and to do so, we shall examine the two biblical narratives more closely.

We shall begin with Eglon. First of all, we cannot ignore that tyrant's name, which is nothing but the noun *ʿgl* plus the suffix *(w)n*. As R. G. Boling has recently confirmed,[30] this name means "young bull," or better "fat calf": this makes Eglon at least homonymous to the Golden Calf whose destruction by the hand of Moses I have discussed above, and to the chaotic monster *ʿgl*. As for the king's nature and aspect, he is "very fat" (vs. 17), so fat that when Ehud hits him with his sword "even the hilt went in after the blade, and the fat closed over the blade" (vs. 22). He is left dead by Ehud, who locks the doors of his room and flees by the emergency exit; so that when his servants come to him they think their king has shut himself up in the loo for some private need and wait so long that they become very embarrassed[31] (vss. 24–25). Moreover, one possible meaning of the expression *wyṣʾ hpršdnh* in vs. 22 (not translated by LXX) is that through the hole made by Ehud's dagger in the king's belly, excrements came out.[32] All this is not so much grossly satirical as rich in connotations of uncleanliness, so that the least we can say of King Eglon is that he is a disgusting figure and that he ends his life in an extremely filthy and squalid way; but probably the intimations of impurity contained in the text are to be interpreted as possessing a specific religious value, and convey the idea that Eglon is a foul and monstrous creature that fully deserves what it gets from the savior Yahweh has raised.

As for the narrative itself, Boling writes that it is "rhythmical in large parts"; and if we consider that "the story was simply incorporated [in the Book of Judges] without revision" and that it is "drawn directly from the corpus of Israelite saga," we may well interpret its rhythmical quality as a device to facilitate the reciting of a text. So I tend to agree with those authors[33] who see in the story of Ehud a Benjaminite tale, or a tradition of the Gilgal sanctuary, but I think the second hypothesis is the most convincing one, in view of the probable mythical quality of the tale.

In the First Italian Congress of Near Eastern Studies I read a paper on the biblical story of Ehud,[34] which compared the Ehud episode to the Roman traditional story about the heroic citizen and soldier Mucius Scaevola: in both stories a solitary and valiant warrior saves his people from the oppression of a foreign king by deceitfully entering the enemy camp and the abode of that monarch and by trying to kill the unsuspecting tyrant with a sword he has hidden under his clothes. In the Roman story the attempted murder is unsuccessful; yet the final scope of the dangerous act, i.e., the removal of oppression and the salvation of the nation from the foreign yoke, is attained in both tales. The resemblance between the two stories is indeed strong but, since the motif is a simple and frequent one, it may be purely accidental. What assures us that the similarity is no mere chance coincidence is the fact that both protagonists are not only left-handed (and Mucius is left-handed in his very name, Scaevola) but "restricted" in their right hands. Ehud is explicitly described as "restricted in his right hand" in vs. 15;[35] as for Scaevola, he burns his right hand in the king's brasier in order to persuade him, by this proof of heroism, that 300 young warriors, equally resolved, stand ready to repeat the attempt to murder him (which seems not to have been true, but rather a sudden contrivance on Mucius's part).[36]

To G. Dumézil[37] we owe the discovery that the story of Mucius is no historical or even "legendary" tale but the Roman version of a widespread myth. In fact, both the Scandinavian god Týr[38] and the Persian hero Jamshid, in a Parsi *rivayāt*[39] that has a strong avestic flavour, lose their right hand, which is devoured or contaminated by a monstrous enemy, in using it as the pledge of a deceitful promise; but in both cases the deceit, though it involves the loss of the protagonist's hand, permits that champion of the cosmic order to outwit and to vanquish the monster. In the Scandinavian myth, Týr's opponent is the wolf Fenrir, who will devour the gods: he is bound by Týr, who agrees to place his hand in the beast's mouth to warrant that the fetter is tied round Fenrir only as a sport: the hand is bitten off when the young wolf discovers that he has been imprisoned for good, but the gods are safe, until the end of time when "all the forces of evil will be liberated and will destroy the world and the gods with it." Jamshid's antagonist in the Persian mythical tradition is none other than the arch-enemy Ahriman, the chaotic being whose very nature is a menace to the Cosmos and to its "good" deity Ahura Mazda: the hero's brother, Taxmoruw, binds Ahriman and rides on his back, but the monster shakes him off and devours him; Jamshid promises Ahriman a homosexual coitus if only he will let him introduce his hand in his anus, and when the enemy grants him this he extracts his brother's body from the devourer's belly and flees without fulfilling his promise, whereupon his hand, polluted by the impure contact, is dried up and stinks.

As has been suggested in the paper I have quoted, the biblical story of Ehud and the three mythical narratives Dumézil has examined are all outcomes of a single mythical and symbolic complex in which the use of the left hand or the loss of the right hand are necessary to accomplish a *deceitful* deed that *saves* the cosmos or the social microcosm from the oppression of an impure enemy. In the Roman and biblical versions the mythical theme is, so to say, "actualized": the effort to classify correctly an ethically ambiguous behavior is transposed on the level of what we could term "military praxis," and, correspondingly, the enemy is not a cosmic monster, but a foreign king.[40] Yet what we have observed about Eglon's name and personality allows us to note here that in the story of Ehud that hostile monarch still displays much of his monstrous quality, and resembles the impure Ahriman very closely in his connection with the more unpleasant aspects of physical life. Eglon *is* a cosmic (calf-) monster as well as an enemy monarch, and the (mythical) account of his dispatch differs in no essential way from a proper cosmogonic battle myth. Of him we can say what we have said of the golden calf and of Pharaoh: it is by his defeat and destruction that Israel is created.

2.2. *The Monster Lusts after Tribute*

The concrete aspect of Eglon's oppressive power over Israel is the tribute he exacts from the Israelites. Ehud kills him in the very heart of his mansion; and he has reached that closely guarded spot as a tribute-bearer:

> (12) When the Israelites continued doing wrong in Yahweh's sight, Yahweh strengthened Eglon, king of Moab, against Israel, because they did evil in Yahweh's sight. (13) He enlisted as allies the Ammonites and Amalekites; they went out and defeated Israel, and gained control of Palm City. (14) The Israelites served Eglon, king of Moab, for eighteen years. (15) But the Israelites appealed to Yahweh and Yahweh raised a saviour for them, Ehud ben Gera, a Benjaminite, a man restricted in his right hand. The Israelites sent tribute to Eglon, king of Moab, by his hand. (16) Ehud made himself a short double-edged sword a foot and a half long and fastened it under his clothes on his right thigh. He presented the tribute to Eglon, king of Moab.

Now Eglon was an exceptionally fat man. (18) When he had finished presenting the tribute, he escorted the men who carried the tribute.[41]

Now, that they "lust after tribute" (in the expression b^erassê kāsep) is said of the enemies that must be destroyed by Yahweh in the passage Ps. 68:31 I have quoted in connection with the mythical calf-monster(s). M. K. Wakeman[42] follows Gunkel[43] in separating the final ym from ʿm in the preceding word ʿmym and reads yam mitrâppēs b^erassê kāsep (the befouling Yam that lusts after tribute) identifying the enemy that Yahweh should "rebuke" (gʿr) with Yam of the Ugaritic and biblical texts. This could be accepted; but we must bear in mind that the present text alludes to Pharaoh, and that the whole context is the following:

> Rebuke the beast of the reeds, the herd of wild bulls with its calves (or: the council of the mighty ones), the befouling Yam (?) who lusts after tribute, scatter the people who delight in war. Let the Egyptian tribute-counters (i.e. the Egyptian court that usually receives, and so must "count," tributes) bring blue cloth (as a tribute), Cush speed his wares to God. O kings of the earth, sing! O gods, sing praises to the Lord![44]

—conveying the message that the kings and/or monsters who have so far *received* tributes or paid them to Yam must from now on *offer* their tributes to the triumphing Yahweh.

M. K. Wakeman[45] is right in affirming that Gunkel's tentative recognition of Yam as the monster that lusts after tribute in Ps. 68:31 (and, we should add, Yam's implicit identification with Pharaoh) is now enhanced by the text UT, 137:37:

[wyʿn.]tr.abh.il.ʿbdk.bʿl.y ymm.ʿbdk.bʿl
[tpt.nhr]m bn.dgn.asrkm.hw.ybl.argmnk.kilm
[argmnk]ybl.wbn qdš.mnhyk

"And the Bull El his father answered: 'Baal is thy servant, o Yam, Baal is thy servant, [Judge Nahar], Dagan's son is thy bondsman. He himself shall be brought (as) thy (tribute of) purple when the gods bring [thy (tribute of) purple] and the holy ones thy gift.'"[46] Where argmn, "tribute of purple," corresponds precisely to "blue cloth" of Ps. 68, and the gods bring their tribute to Yam just as they sing the praises of Yahweh in that same Psalm. But another text that would greatly strengthen the value of Gunkel's hypothesis seems to have escaped Wakeman's attention.

An Egyptian tale of the eighteenth dynasty[47] recounts the mythical contrast between Yam and the other gods of the pantheon: Yam demands the tribute of the gods:

> The tribute is bought to him [. . .] or else he will make us prisoners [. . .] Renenet has already bought to him his tribute, that is silver and gold, lapislazuli and turquoise, filling the coffers! So they told the Ennaead: "Procure that [. . .] the tribunal of the god Yam, so that he may hear from us all the words of the earth and may be protected by his hand."

Astarte is then sent to speak to the tyrant, who seemingly (the text is very frag-
mentary) claims the hand of some goddess: if it is given to him, he will abstain
from fighting against the other gods (?). Astarte returns to the Ennaead and repeats what she has been told. Seth is then mentioned, and it has been sur-
mised that this god, who is often assimilated to the Syrian deity Baal, finally
fights and defeats Yam; but the last part of the text cannot be reconstructed
with certainty.

What we have here is in all probability the Egyptian version of some
Canaanite myth, extremely similar to the Ugaritic narratives about Baal and
his enemy Yam. As in the Ugaritic text we have quoted, but with more wealth
of detail, the monster Yam is presented as a tyrant demanding tribute from the
other gods. The mythical motif of the chaotic monster unduly receiving tribute from the subjects it terrorizes is thus attested both in Ugaritic and in Egyptian literature, and "silver" is mentioned as one of the riches that are brought
to him, which corresponds well to the "silver" in Ps. 68:31, just as "tribute (of
purple)" in UT 137 equals the "blue cloth" of that same biblical text. The oppression of the cosmos and of its gods by the chaotic usurper is expressed in
terms of the political oppression and exploitation exercised by the earthly
monarchs of the ancient East. Correspondingly, the oppression of the people
by the enemy king is easily identified with the violent tribute-demand of the
monsters of mythology.

In the face of this evidence, Gunkel's identification of Yam in Ps. 68:31
seems even more credible; yet at the same time such a hypothesis seems not
relevant for the solution of our main problem, for the correspondence between the enemy (Egyptian) monarch(s) who "lust after tribute" in Ps. 68 and
the mythological monster Yam is assured independently from such a hypothetical reading. We can thus sketch the following diagram, showing the presence of the tribute motif in the four narrative traditions we have examined:

Ugarit: Yam receives the tribute of the Gods—Yam is dispatched by Baal.
Egypt: Yam demands the tribute of the Gods—Yam is dispatched by
          Seth (?).
Ps. 68:   Yam (?) lusts for tribute—the enemy is "rebuked by Yahweh."
Jud. 3:   Eglon receives the tribute from Israel—he is dispatched by Ehud.

The presence of such a motif in mythical narratives as well as in the Ehud
episode of the Book of Judges is conclusive evidence for the recognition of that
episode as the "actualized" version of a mythical battle with the chaotic monster. If we bear in mind that Eglon is a "fat calf" or a "young bull" (Boling), we
cannot avoid being reminded of another similar mythical tradition. In Greek
mythology,[48] Minos is a foreign, enemy king who rules the seas (cf. Yam?) and
claims and receives tribute from the city of Athens; more precisely, he asks for
youths and maidens that are to be offered to his son, the bull-monster whose
tale-telling name is Minotauros. The hero Theseus, savior of his people,
comes to him with the tribute, reaches the abode of the monster, stabs him to
death and, with the help of Minos's daughter Ariadne, cunningly finds his way

out of the Labyrinth and away from Crete, escaping unharmed from the territory of the hateful tyrant. In this myth the fiendish king and the calf-monster
are two different figures, yet strictly connected by their father-son relationship
and by the very correspondence between their names: but that Minos is no
mere earthly tyrant is made clear by his role as a judge of the dead in the
Netherworld. The infernal nature of the foul enemy is no less clear in this tradition than in the Canaanite and biblical mythology of Mot, whom we have
seen to be similar (if not identical) to the Calf of ʿnt III: 40–41 and Exod. 32,
and thus possibly to Eglon.

2.3. Agag, King of Amalek

The Ehud story is thus in all probability a mythical tradition of the Gilgal
sanctuary: this seems particularly credible because that shrine itself with its
twelve maṣṣ^{e}bôth is based on traditions relating to the "birth" or creation of Israel and possibly to the battle of Yahweh against the (Reed) Sea.[49] Moreover,
that sanctuary is important in the narratives about the conquest and about the
origins of Israelite monarchy, and in particular the tradition of the capture and
killing of King Agag of Amalek (I Sam. 15) is a Gilgal tradition. So it would
seem that Gilgal is the scenery and possibly the cradle of both the biblical traditional narratives that recount of the violent elimination of an enemy king,
and, since one of those narratives may be seen as the biblical equivalent of a
cosmic battle myth between the forces of order and a monster of chaos, we
may assume that the quality of the other is not entirely different.

The story of Saul's war against King Agag is easy to summarize. Samuel,
who has anointed Saul king over Israel at Yahweh's command, communicates to him the "word of the Lord": "I have seen well what Amalek did to Israel in opposing them on the way [to the Holy Land], when they came out
of Egypt. Now go and smite Amalek, and utterly destroy him and all that he
has; do not spare but kill both man and woman, infant and suckling, ox and
sheep, camel and ass." Saul summons "the people" and leads them in war
against Agag, king of Amalek. "And he took Agag the king of Amalek alive,
and utterly destroyed all the people with the edge of the sword. But Saul and
the people spared Agag, and the best of the sheep and of the oxen—the
fatlings and the lambs—and all that was despised and worthless they utterly
destroyed." So the word of Yahweh comes to Samuel ("(10) I repent that I
have made Saul king . . .") and Samuel reaches Gilgal where Saul has arrived after leaving Carmel.

> (13) And Samuel came to Saul, and Saul said to him: "Blessed be you to
> Yahweh; I have performed Yahweh's commandment." And Samuel asked:
> "What then is this bleating of the sheep in my ears and the lowing of the
> oxen which I hear?" Saul said: "They have brought them from Amalek; for
> the people spared the best of the sheep and of the oxen, to sacrifice to Yah-
> weh your god; and the rest we have utterly destroyed." Then Samuel said to
> Saul: "Stop! I will tell you what Yahweh has said to me this night."

Saul is reminded that "to obey is better than to sacrifice" and be deprived of the kingdom. "(32) Then Samuel said: 'Bring here to me Agag the king of Amalek.' And Agag came to him with tottering step. Agag said: 'Bitter indeed is death.' (33) And Samuel said: 'As your sword has made women childless so shall your mother be childless among women.' And Samuel hewed Agag in pieces before Yahweh at Gilgal."

Who was this Agag, hewn in pieces in the Gigal sanctuary? Obviously, a foul enemy hated by Yahweh, if, for having spared him, Saul was deprived of his throne! In the Old Testament, we have two direct mentions and one indirect mention of Agag. One direct mention is the one I have just quoted. The other is more vague: in the second of Balaam's oracles (Num. 24:7) it is said that Israel's king shall be loftier than Agag, implying that Agag is a famous and powerful king. Since the text of Balaam's oracles is believed to be very archaic, if we consider King Agag of I Sam. 15 a historical figure, we must conclude that he and the King Agag mentioned in Num. 24 cannot be the same person; while if we believe the episode to be a Gilgal mythical tradition we can well identify the two Agags. Anyhow, the Agag of I Sam. 15 bears the name of a famous, or rather proverbial, king of the Israelite tradition, who was known to be a great monarch indeed and could be *in comparationem adductus* (Zorell)[50] in an archaic (and sacred) poetic text. As for the indirect mention quoted above, we are reminded of it by H. W. Hertzberg who in his commentary to the Books of Samuel writes that "the naming of the personification of anti-Semitism, Haman, in Esther 3.1 as Agagite shows clearly that Agag became almost the type of the enemy of Yahweh and his people."[51] If an arch-enemy of Yahweh and of Israel is termed an Agagite in the (late) book of Esther, we can well believe that at least by that time Agag was seen not as a mere historical kinglet of Amalek defeated by Saul but rather as a famous (mythical?) fiend, of whom it was recounted that he was justly hewn in pieces before Yahweh in his sanctuary at Gilgal, and possibly that the mention of Agag in Num. 24:7 is nothing but another though older proof of the importance and vitality of that same tradition. Turning now to the personality of this monarch, we shall note first of all that the name Agag may be connected to the Akkadian *agagu*, a term that means "fury, rage": *agagu* is used to indicate the terrible wrath of Irra in The Akkadian Epic of Irra[52] that M. K. Wakeman[53] classifies as a battle myth or monster myth, wherein that god nearly destroys the whole cosmos in a terrific fit of anger. This is a mere possibility; but other data indicate that Agag's is indeed a monstrous personality, strongly connected with death and the Netherworld.

We have seen that Agag, when his time comes, walks up to Samuel "with tottering step" and says: "Bitter indeed is death." Now, the verb I have interpreted as indicating a tottering or limping gait is usually translated "walked delicately," but T. H. Gaster has shown that "the Hebrew verb rendered 'delicately' really means 'with limping gait,' for the word is m'dnyt which KJV and RV (after Symmachus and the Aramaic Targum) vocalize ma'ʻʻdanît and derive from 'ʻ–d–n, 'be delicate.' But it should really be read mᵉʻôdanît, from *m-ʿ -d*, totter, stagger, as both the Greek Septuagint and the Latin Vulgate recognized."[54] The reference, Gaster adds, "is to a custom to be observed at Semitic funerals, whereby the mourners shuffle around the bier with a peculiar limping or hopping step"[55]: examples of such a ritual behavior are given by that author who quotes Roger's *La terre saincte* (1664), Lane's *Manners and Customs of the Modern Egyptians*, and a custom reported by Wetzstein, the German consul at Damascus, which was known in Syria by the same term (*maʿid*) as in our biblical text.[56] Moreover, "in Arabic and Syriac, 'to skip, hop' (*r-q-d*, *r-q-ṣ*) also denotes the performance at a funeral of a special kind of limping dance, and in an ancient Mesopotamian syllabary, the corresponding Akkadian word (*ruquddu*) is listed as the technical term for a professional mourner."[57] The term seems also to occur in the Ugaritic Poem of Aqhat "in connection with the mourning for him by his father Daniel."[58] If we note that Agag's "statement" that death is indeed bitter has a metrical structure and that "not impossibly, it was because they had to accompany this limping dance that Hebrew dirges were usually composed in a peculiar limping (scazontic) meter"[59] that corresponds to the form of the phrase uttered by Agag, we can well conclude that the king of Amalek approaches Samuel "in the manner of a mourner, intoning a typical dirge."[60] But there is no reason to observe with Gaster that Agag acts thus "like an arch-hypocrite."[61] The message conveyed by the mourning attitude of Agag as he goes to meet his own death is rather that the enemy king's very nature is that of a being connected with the sphere of death and somehow belonging to the Netherworld, so that Saul's abstention from killing him is not only sinful, but decidedly absurd.

2.4. *The Killing of Agag and the Destruction of the Golden Calf*

As for Samuel's action when he hews Agag asunder, we can only agree with T. H. Gaster, who writes that "Agag is not merely slain; he is slain 'before Jahweh at Gilgal,' and he is slain in a special way."[62] but, even though we may accept that there is some ritual aspect in the killing of that king, I do not think that it can be explained by comparing it to the Arab custom of selecting from the spoil a choice beast "which they sacrificed and upon the flesh of whom they feasted" as a way of "recementing commensality of kinship ties after the losses incurred in warfare or on forays,"[63] for Agag was emphatically *not sacrificed* (he could not be for he had to be destroyed according to the ban or *herem*), and was surely not eaten! What we should look to for comparison is rather the mythical breaking in pieces of the chaotic monster at the end of the cosmic battle that has been studied by M. K. Wakeman. In the ancient and widespread form of that myth the hero or god "vanquishes the 'serpent' whose body as a consequence is *broken in pieces*. The vital fluids are released *violently*,"[64] while it the Bible and in its Ugaritic background it is the parts of Mot, of the Calf, and of the Tannin that are scattered.[65] If we remember Agag's connections with death and the Netherworld and his sword that has rendered women childless, and if we bear in mind the proposed identification of Mot and the calf, and of Eglon as a chaotic monster, we can well venture to suggest that the story of Agag's destruction is similar in nature and meaning to the mythical destruction of monsters such as Mot or the (golden) calf.

In fact, it has already been noted by Hertzberg that

> Amalek was Israel's chief enemy during the time of the desert, as the saying in Ex. 17.16 shows: "the Lord will have war with Amalek from generation to generation." Amalek, then, is an adversary of the Lord. This people is regarded by the traditon as *the* opponent, which first and most obviously sought to deny Israel entry into the Promised Land. Therefore the victory over Amalek is expressly a victory of prayer (Ex. 17.8 ff.) and thus of the Lord; and the answer to anyone who puts himself in opposition to God "with a high hand" can only be the ban.[66]

It is thus clear that, even apart from the specific quality of Agag and of his execution in front of Yahweh, the Lord's victory in the war against his arch-enemy Amalek and its king has in itself a cosmic value, and can be compared to Yahweh's other victories over his chaotic opponents.

Moreover, the specific similarities in narrative structure between the golden calf episode in Exod. 32 and the story of the slaying of Agag in I Sam. 15 are indeed striking. In both stories a large army or mass of Israelites is intent upon an erroneous and sinful ritual action (in one case, the worship of a false deity; in the other, the offering of a sacrilegious sacrifice to the true god). In both stories, this happens under the guidance, and involving the responsibility, of a vicarious leader of the people (Aaron, Saul), who has previously been anointed by the people's original guide and Yahweh's "prophet" (Moses, Samuel). Again in both stories, the "prophet," who is absent, is warned by Yahweh that his people are committing sinful deeds, so he hurries to the place where this is happening and violently enters on the scene. In both cases, the "scene" is an important holy place (Sinai, Gilgal); Yahweh's "prophet" (Moses, Samuel) destroys the object of the sinful behavior (Mot, Agag), punishes the sinners ("the people," Saul) and thus restores the correct order. The similarity between the two narratives is so strong that they might well be considered as two different outcomes of one traditional tale, or at least as two very strongly connected Yahweh traditions. The common theme is obviously the reinstallment of Yahweh's order by his champion after a crisis, and through the destruction of a hated enemy, followed by the punishment of the Israelite sinners who have caused or permitted the critical situation.

Our assumption was that the Gilgal tradition about Agag, just like the Gilgal (?) tradition about Eglon, could be interpreted as the biblical ("actualized" and "yahwistic") equivalent of a cosmic battle myth involving the victory of a god of order against the monster of chaos. The evidence we have given to sustain our hypothesis is fourfold. First of all, the victory against Amalek, the arch-enemy of Israel, and of its god (Exod. 17:8), is a victory of Yahweh (Hertzberg)[67] and thus similar to the Lord's other victories against his chaotic opponents. Second, Agag's nature is that of a terrific champion of death and the Netherworld, who belongs there so justly that he comes dancing to his killer and is shown intoning "a typical dirge." Third, the dismembering of Agag "in front of Yahweh" is no mere execution but a ritual killing that corresponds well to the breaking in pieces of chaotic monsters such as the golden calf in Exod. 32:20 and Mot in UT 49:ii. Finally, the narrative structure of the Agag episode is so similar to that of the destruction of the golden calf in Exod. 32 that the two tales can be considered as one, and we have seen that there is a correspondence between the biblical story of the golden calf and the Ugaritic myth of ʿAnat and Mot. In the face of this evidence, we can reach the conclusion that our hypothesis is proved and that both the biblical accounts of the killing of enemy kings by Yahweh's champions are "microcosmic" tales about God's victory over the chaotic monster.

2.5. Kings and Monsters of the Bible

In the previous paragraphs I have shown that Amalek had to be utterly destroyed because it was an enemy of Israel and of its god Yahweh, and that its king Agag was finally hewn asunder, in a manner that reminds us of the treatment inflicted upon the golden calf in biblical tradition and upon the (serpent-) monster in many other cosmic battle myths. We have also seen that Israel's and Yahweh's hostility toward Amalek goes back to the time of the desert. But what is the cause of that hostility? Exod. 17:8–16 provides an answer to this question. Immediately after the solving of the two problems of hunger (Exod. 16) and thirst (Exod. 17:1–7), Israel is faced with an Amalekite attack: the enemy is defeated by the power of Moses' uplifted hands. Then follow the giving of the Law (Exod. 19–23), the organization of Israelite cultic life (Exod. 24–31), and finally the golden calf episode (Exod. 32). Since Israel is on the move toward Palestine, and since the Amalekite attack appears to be the last of the three main external menaces to such a movement, which is at the same time a movement toward the acquisition of the yahwistic religious and moral order (Exod. 19–31), it can well be stated that "this people is regarded by the tradition as *the* opponent, which first and most obviously *sought to deny Israel entry into the Promised Land*" (Hertzberg;[68] the last italics are mine). If we remember that in the cosmic battle myths studied by Wakeman "the repressive nature of the monster may be expressed . . . in terms of withholding water, and the sun . . ."[69] so that when the hero vanquishes the monster, "whose body as a consequence is broken in pieces," the vital fluids are released,[70] we shall not be able to avoid noticing that the function of such monsters (for instance, the Egyptian serpent-monster Apophis)[71] in the mythologies of the ancient East is not fundamentally different from that of Amalek in regard to Israel, as expressed by the equation:

(serpent-) monster: vital fluids:: Amalek: Israel.

Amalek, Yahweh's arch-enemy "from generation to generation" (Exod. 17:16), is thus in its function the equivalent of a "withholding" monster of mythology; and the "breaking in pieces" of its king Agag is perfectly consistent with such a function. As Seth in the Egyptian myth cuts Apophis, the withholding enemy, in pieces, so Samuel hews Agag, king of the "withholding" enemy Amalek, asunder before Yahweh. The correspondence is extremely precise.

We have no reason to suppose that Agag is in any way serpent-like. Yet we know that in Israel as well as in other cultures the serpent (*peten*)[72] is a monster, and sometimes a monster that withholds or bars the way. M. K. Wakeman writes that "the word *miptan*, 'threshold,' is derived from the same root as *peten*, 'serpent,' for which the meaning 'protect' is suggested" as shown by Ass. *patanu*, "protect," whence "'serpent' as protector, and 'threshold' as asylum."[73] "The evil serpent that guards the boundary is represented by Apophis, and Vritra 'the serpent lying on the mountain,' but the benevolent aspect of the serpentine guardians of the threshold is also familiar from Greek tradition."[74] To this last aspect of the serpent ideology we should connect Jacob's blessing of his son Dan in Gen. 49:17: "Dan shall be a serpent on the way, an adder in the path, that biteth the horses' heels, so that the rider shall fall backwards." In biblical tradition the basic concept of the serpent as a withholding monster that bars the way was liable to be developed in both a negative and a positive sense and to be "historicized" into the symbol of a border tribe. Likewise, the tradition of the hewing asunder of a (serpent-) monster that withheld the vital fluids inhibiting the construction of a correct world order developed into the account of the destruction of an enemy king, whose people were at war with Yahweh because they had tried to "withhold" Israel.

Now, the most typical example of a withholding serpent-monster is the snake Apophis of Egyptian mythology; and the victory over the serpent Apophis was repeated daily in the temple of Amon-Ra by its personnel, as shown by a hieratic papyrus of the fourth century B.C.E.[75]: by such an action the correct order was continually reestablished and upheld; the sun could rise every morning, the state and its king prospered. Like the monsters in the Bible, Apophis was bound and chained, trampled upon, pierced by a weapon. It is interesting to note, however, that in trampling the serpent that withholds the sun *the left foot was used*,[76] and that the monster was pierced with a knife or a short dagger,[77] and cut in pieces by Horus[78]: all these data remind us of the fate of the enemy kings Eglon and Agag.[79] It is clear that in the field of magical practice no less than in that of mythology, the form and function of the cosmic battle against the chaotic monster, and, in this specific case, against a serpent-monster, as it appears in a neighboring culture, corresponds precisely to the form and function of the victory over the two monstrous enemy kings in the Bible. The victory of order over chaos that the Egyptian culture expressed by the two means of mythical narrative and ritual (magic) practice, thus projecting it in the indefinite time of myth and at the same time repeating it every day throughout all time, was presented by the Bible as one or more punctual "historical" happening(s) apparently devoid of mythical or ritual aspects and firmly set in the continuous story of Israel and its god.

Yet, as I have shown so far, on the basis of some peculiar features of the biblical narratives a reconstruction of their cosmic and mythical import is possible, and the conclusion can be reached that the traditions in question, no less than the tales about battles between Yahweh and Leviathan, Mot or Tannin that Gunkel, Wakeman and others have reconstructed, are the equivalent of the cosmic battle myths of other ancient societies. Moreover, the possibility of connecting both narratives with one specific sanctuary, that of Gilgal, and thus of considering them as two distinct but similar narrative traditions of that shrine, allows us to envisage them as two different variations on a common theme, i.e., the mythical destruction of an oppressive and monstrous enemy monarch, seen as necessary in view of the construction of a correct religious and social order, or, in other terms, of the Israelite yahwistic society in Palestine. In the light of such a hypothetical interpretation of the two biblical episodes we can now synthesize their reciprocal similarities and discrepancies as follows:

Place	Gilgal (??)	Gilgal
Name of enemy	Eglon (Calf) king of Moab [cf. Golden Calf]	Agag (Fury??) king of Amalek [cf. Irra??]
Connotations of enemy	Fat; impure Lusts for tribute [cf. Yam]	Deadly "withholder" [cf. Apophis]
Hero	Ehud	Samuel
Disposal	Killed: stabbed with left hand [cf. Apophis]	Killed: hewn to pieces before Yahweh [cf. Apophis, Golden Calf]

3. The Serpent-King and a Tentative Conclusion

3.1. The Defeat of the Serpent-King and the Scattering of Ammon

In discussing the killing of Agag, king of Amalek, as it is presented in I Sam. 15, I have tried to show that Amalek was to be destroyed because it was Yahweh's arch-enemy, and that such an enmity arose out of the fact that Amalek had tried to interfere with Israel's march toward the Holy Land: like the Apophis of Egyptian mythology, it was a "withholding" monster. I have also proposed to see in the dismembering of king Agag the equivalent of the dismembering of the serpent-monster Apophis, and to interpret that monarch's fate as the most logical punishment of a mythical "withholding" monster. I was thus led to ask myself whether king Agag was in any way serpent-like, but I found no trace of this. In particular, while the king of Moab dispatched by Ehud bore a name that pointed to one specific Ugaritic chaotic monster and to the biblical golden calf, and an animal name at that, nothing of the kind was true of the enemy monarch hewn asunder by Samuel.

It is precisely in a biblical episode contained in the First Book of Samuel, centered on Saul and involving the sanctuary of Gilgal, that we find an enemy king bearing a name that means "serpent." We are told in I Sam. 11 that Nahash the Ammonite encamped against Jabesh Gilead; the men of Jabesh said to him: "Make a covenant with us, and we shall serve thee." But Nahash answered: "On this condition will I make a covenant with you, that I may thrust out all your right eyes." So the men of Jabesh asked for and obtained a seven days' respite, and sent messengers to the tribes of Israel. When news of this situation came to Saul, who was leading oxen out of the field, the spirit of Yahweh came upon him and his anger was kindled. So he took a yoke of oxen and hewed them in pieces, and sent them throughout Israel saying, Whoever does not come after Saul—and Samuel—so shall it be done to his oxen! The dread of Yahweh fell on the people and they came out as one man. Messengers were sent back to the people of Jabesh announcing that on the morrow they would have deliverance. And on the morrow Saul, having put the people in two companies, cut down the Ammonites and those who survived were scattered so that not two of them were left together. The people then asked Samuel for the head of the men who had opposed Saul when he had been chosen as a king, but Samuel answered that no man should be put to death that day: for on that day Yahweh had wrought deliverance in Israel. Then he said to the people: "Come, let us go to Gilgal and there renew the kingdom." So all the men of Israel went to Gilgal, and there they made Saul king before Yahweh in Gilgal. There they sacrificed peace offerings before Yahweh; and there Saul and all the men of Israel rejoiced greatly.

As Hertzberg observes,[80] we have here a new description of the Lord's nomination of Saul, who had already been anointed (I Sam. 9–10) and chosen (I Sam. 10:17–27), which resembles the way in which such acts of deliverance were introduced in the time of the Judges. Once again, "God has brought his help in a time of deep need, as he did before."[81] Yet, in the light of what has been argued so far in this chapter, there is more to say about this episode, which can well be compared to the two Gilgal (?) traditions we have just examined.

First of all, Nahash. Hertzberg reminds us that we find a hostile encounter with the Ammonites as early as the judgeship of Jephtah. Even then, as here, tradition holds that they were the ones who picked the quarrel. Hertzberg[82] again underlines that "Nahash, described as 'the Ammonite,' is, of course, the king," and warns us that his name means "snake." But *nāḥāš* is no mere name of a type of reptile, for in Job 26 we are told that Yahweh quelled the sea (or Yam), smote Rahab, bagged Yam, and pierced *nāḥāš bāriᵃḥ*, the slippery serpent. M. K. Wakeman[83] observes that, taking Isa. 51:9, Ps. 89:10–11, and Job 26:12–13, 9:13 together as references, *tannîn*, *ḥōlēl* and *nāḥāš bāriᵃḥ* are parallel to *rahab* and are all pierced (*ḥll*), so that "they might conceivably be designation of Rahab," the monster who (accompanied by helpers) was "hewn, crushed, smitten, stopped." Moreover, the $r^e h\bar{a}b\hat{i}m$ in Ps. 40:5 are foreign or false gods, and Rahab in Isa. 30:7 and in Ps. 87:4 is identified with Egypt; M. K. Wakeman holds that "it is precisely this close association with Egypt that makes the idea of permanent defeat possible, and allows the verb to carry the original connotation of oppression."[84] Of course, I do not think it in any way necessary to accept the identification $n\bar{a}\underline{h}a\check{s}$ $b\bar{a}ri^a\underline{h}$ = Rahab that not even Wakeman deems certain;[85] what I am interested in is the possibility of identifying associations, connections and profound symbolical values of the name Nahash; and the data quoted here surely provide good material for such an endeavor, testifying as they do that there is a strong connection between the name of the king of Ammon defeated by Saul and the biblical tradition about the destruction of a mythical, oppressive chaotic monster vanquished by Yahweh.

Second, Saul and Gilgal. It is evident at first glance that this Nahash episode is a kind of reversed copy of the Agag story we have examined in the previous sections of this chapter. In both stories, Saul must fight, vanquish and destroy an enemy people and its king (Amalek and Agag, Ammon and Nahash). In the earlier episode, the one we are now examining, the leader accomplishes his mission, and as a consequence of his successful initiative Yahweh, by means of his envoy Samuel, renews and confirms his kingly investiture. The ceremony takes place in the Gilgal sanctuary, before "the people," and in that same shrine sacrifice is correctly offered to the Lord. In the later Agag episode, the leader fails to accomplish his mission correctly, and as a punishment for this failure Yahweh, by the hand of Samuel, rejects Saul and deprives him of the kingdom. In this case too the rejection of the sinful leader takes place in the Gilgal shrine, where a paradoxically sacrilegious sacrifice has just been offered by the unfaithful Saul and by the people. Of course, this comparison, though it seems to me very fitting, does not explain *all* aspects of this complex and important traditional narrative. As Hertzberg[86] noted in the passage I have quoted, I Sam. 11 resembles the structure and style of many episodes of the book of Judges. For instance, it has been observed by that same author that "Saul's action under the influence of the spirit of God" (that is, the hewing in pieces of the two oxen) "is similar to the that of the Levite in Judg. 19. Strangely enough the [Levite's] concubine, too, is killed [and cut in pieces] in Gibeah. It is in the course of the same story that the connection of Benjamin with Jabesh Gilead [that is mentioned in Judg. 21 where it takes the form of a group marriage between the women of that town and the Benjaminites] is related."[87] Mizpah, the sanctuary where Saul was "chosen" by lot according I Sam. 10:17–27, plays an important role in this same episode, Judg. 19–21; and Mizpah is the shrine where a covenant is sworn between the elders of Gilead and Jephtah, whereby if Yahweh subdues the attacking Ammonites before Jephtah, that warrior will be the Gileadites' head: so in this other episode of the Book of Judges (Judg. 11) monarchic power is promised to the leader who shall vanquish the Ammonites, just as it is bestown officially on Saul after his victory over the same Ammonites. These specific connections with the Book of Judges show that the history of the tradition about Saul and the Ammonites is a long and very complex one; yet the perfect parallelism between I Sam. 11 (Saul vs. Nahash) and I Sam. 15 (Saul vs. Agag) that I have just illustrated cannot be denied or overlooked, and guarantees a very strong connection between the Nahash episode and the two Gilgal (?) monster-king traditions we have examined in the previous sections. To this we must add the observation that Gilgal plays an important role in I Sam. 15 as well as in the two episodes in question, so that we may well speak of a Gilgal triad involving the defeat and annihilation of the three (monster-) kings Eglon (Moab), Nahash (Ammon) and Agag (Amalek) by Yahweh and by means of an ambiguous Benjaminite warrior (Ehud or Saul). In the light of this, the fact that Eglon king of Moab "enlisted as allies the Ammonites and Amalekites" (Judg. 3:13) acquires new significance, for the structure of our hypothetical triad would then be: (1) Ehud vs. a, b, c; (2) Saul (and Samuel) vs. b; (3) Saul (and Samuel) vs. c.

Finally, the whole Nahash episode in I Sam. 11 is based on a continuous play with themes and concepts we have often met with in the course of the present essay, such as withholding, dismembering or scattering, unifying. At the beginning, the serpent-king of the Ammonites surrounds Jabesh Gilead and *withholds* its inhabitants. He does not accept their submission, and will enter with them under no disparity treaty: his sole condition for lifting the siege (and thus ceasing to "withold" them) is that he may thrust out all their right eyes, that is, that he may synthetically and symbolically *dismember* them. Messengers are then sent *in all parts* of Israel in quest of solidarity and unity. When he receives news of the Jabesites' plight, Saul kills and *dismembers* the oxen and then *scatters* the parts of the butchered animals in all the scattered parts of Israel. The explicit message to the tribesmen is: "Whosoever comes not forth after Saul and after Samuel, so shall it be done to his oxen," but the implicit message conveyed is that the tribes are all parts of one unity and that under such circumstances any division will lead to a bloody death, for a whole body (Israel) is a living one, while a body torn apart cannot live. The gruesome message is effective and the view of the fragments causes "the fear of Yahweh" to "fall on the people." So in Israel a unity so perfect is achieved that the people come out *as one man* (k'yš 'ḥd). From the morning to "the heat of the day" the Israelites slay the Ammonites, "and it came to pass, that they which remained *were scattered, so that two of them were not left together*" (wl' nš'rw–bm šnym yḥd; I Sam. 11:11). So Israel is united, the enemy is scattered, and the Israelites who were surrounded and withheld by the serpent-king are liberated by Yahweh. But at this point Israel's unity is endangered, for the people ask Samuel to "bring" the men that rejected Saul's kingship so that they may be put to death. Samuel refuses to do so, for this is a special day, on which Yahweh has wrought deliverance in Israel, and immediately leads the people to Gilgal where *all the men of Israel* make Saul king before Yahweh (the same expression is used as in the case of the dismemberment of Agag: *lpny-Yhwh*), sacrifice peace offerings before Yahweh and rejoice greatly. In this narrative both risks represented by the chaotic monsters studied by M. K. Wakeman, that of being "withheld" and that of being "scattered," are run by Israel, but once more the monstrous enemy king is vanquished and, though we hear no more of Nahash himself, we are told that his people are totally scattered. If this interpretation of the narrative is correct, the Nahash episode is related to the mythical complex of the cosmic battle not only because the enemy king of Amalek bears the name of a chaotic monster of tradition, and because the story of the defeat of Nahash is a reversed equivalent of the "mythical" narrative about the victory over Agag, but also, or rather especially, because its very content is the story of Yahweh's triumph over the dangers of dissipation and oppressive reclusion.[88] So Yahweh's "cosmic" victory, consistently with what we have seen to be the general trend of biblical "actualization," is inserted here in the continuous narrative that recounts the sacred story of Israel and of its deity, and thus firmly placed on the microcosmic level of that people's earthly adventure. On this level the mythological motifs and concepts of the traditional cultures of the ancient East are transposed and take over new values and meanings;[89] but the common ideological intent, i.e., the endeavor to found through narrative a correct order and to protect it from the continuous risk of a lapse into chaos, is still the fundamental scope, basis, and meaning of the narrative tradition.

3.2. Foreign King and Monster: A Biblical Equation

In the course of this chapter I have strived to show that biblical narrative traditions contain some specific episodes that are similar in nature and function to the well-known myths about a cosmic battle between a creator-god and one or more chaotic monsters that are so frequent and important in ancient mythologies. I have recognized and examined four such episodes: (1) the story of the destruction of the golden calf (Exod. 32) and the accounts of Yahweh's and Israel's victories over the enemy kings, (2) Eglon of Moab (Judg. 3), (3) Agag of Amalek (I Sam. 15) and (4) Nahash of Ammon (I Sam. 11). In all these narratives, Yahweh destroys a hated enemy by means of the action of his envoy and the leader of his people. As in the cosmic battle myths, the destruction of the monstrous oppressor, whose very existence is an obstacle to the forming of a correct cosmic order, is a necessary precondition to the building up of such an order; but in the biblical narratives in question that order is not the order of the macrocosm but the correct relationship between Israel and Yahweh and the religious, moral and social organization that stems from that relationship. So each of the narratives we have examined is in a way the equivalent of a creation myth, and not just of a cosmic battle myth.

One of the main aspects of the biblical narratives in question is a clear proof of their value as accounts of the creation of the microcosm Israel. All those narratives stress the importance of obedience to Yahweh and unity among Israelites as means to obtain liberation from the chaotic monster, but also as autonomous positive values. Episodes (1) and (3) show that any weakness or, worse, any betrayal in favor of Yahweh's enemies must be punished in order to reconstruct harmony, and that violence must be exerted against the enemy but also against the sinful Israelites who have permitted that enemy to prosper, or even to survive: the worshipers of the golden calf are killed, Saul is deprived of the kingdom. Episodes (2) and (4) insist on the opposite situation, i.e. unity in Israel and obedience to Yahweh's commands. In Judg. 3 Ehud's trumpet-blast unifies the Israelite (probably: Benjaminite) warriors, and in I Sam. 11 Saul's gruesome message succeeds in the same intent. As we have seen, in episode (4) a capital punishment of Israelite sinners, who, by opposing the king who has now won, have indirectly favored the enemy, is prospected, but on that day unity has already proved so strong and effectively successful that it need not be upheld by punishment, and the guilty men are spared.

So the defeat and destruction of the monstrous enemy monarch is in all cases accompanied and upheld, or followed, by a strong reassessment of the correct and compact structure of the Israelite-yahwistic cosmos: and this corresponds precisely to the creation that follows the battle in the battle myths examined by Wakeman. Here too "the direction of activity after victory is towards form,"[90] and Yahweh and his envoy are at the same time "separators" and "gatherers" (Wakeman) for Israel must be united under Yahweh, while the enemy must be scattered (the golden calf, Agag, the Ammonites). The creative aspect of the battle myth is prominent in the biblical narratives, and makes of them so many accounts of the construction of Israel.

The nature and significance of the biblical traditions we have examined in this chapter are thus clear. Two (possibly three) of them are connected with Gilgal, and with the Benjaminite heroes Ehud and Saul, so that we can well postulate for them a formation in the sanctuary of Gilgal or at least in the territory of the tribe of Benjamin, though of course, in the form that we now have, they are Israelite in the broadest sense. These "Gilgal" traditions are completely "actualized," referring as they do to (historical?) conflicts against historical neighbouring people, while the golden calf tradition is referred to a more paradigmatic and distant past, and more similar in language and structure to the corresponding Ugaritic material, and thus "logically," if not historically, more archaic. With these last observations I could well conclude my research.

Yet the main problem posed by the material I have examined has not even been mentioned. We have seen *what* biblical tradition substituted for the cosmic battle myth of many other ancient cultures, and we have seen *how* it transposed and transformed ancient concepts and narrative structures. But we have not seen *why* it did so. In other terms, we have not even asked ourselves what was the *Sitz im Leben*, or, rather, the economical, social, political and ideological basis and reason of such a striking evolution of ideas and narrative schemes. To this last question I cannot give an exhaustive answer here; yet I shall try to hint briefly at some possible lines of inquiry.

It is not necessary to insist on the well-known fact that the cosmic battle myths to which I have compared our biblical material are the expression of ancient societies centered upon agriculture, organized in urban communities headed by a monarch and worshiping the gods of polytheistic pantheons. The main concern of such societies is the maintaining of a stable though complex order of natural and social conditions and relationships, and the function of mythology and religious practice is precisely that of conferring value and supernatural protection to such a static order, given once and for all. Human events and historical happenings are disvalued, for the true positive value is that of continuity and stability, whose earthly warrant is the king, or rather the royal succession eternally repeated. So the mythical tradition of a battle between a God and a monster of chaos and disorder is one of the means whereby such societies reject outside "normal," actual time the menace of a subversion of the cosmic order that is for them so vital. As I have shown when quoting the Egyptian magic papyrus of the Amon-Ra sanctuary, the ritual, dehistoricizing, reenacting of the cosmic battle against the chaotic monster was meant to guarantee such an order, and connected strictly the daily sunrise, endangered by Apophis, to the prosperity of the state and of its monarch. Against the forces of dissipation, oppressive reclusion and anarchic disorder, the hierarchical, static and sacred structure of the state was defended by ideological means such as the cosmic battle myth and the magic ritual practices directed against the monster.

The meaning of the biblical narratives examined here is profoundly different, and results from what I would choose to call the biblical "actualization" of Near-Eastern mythical traditions. In his critical reconstruction of the origins of Israel, G. E. Mendenhall identified that process as a "symbolization of historical events" and explained that such a symbolization "was possible because each group which entered the covenant community could and did see the analogy between bondage and Exodus and their own experience (cf. Judg. 6:9)."[91] But through the examples quoted here I have shown that the process that led to the biblical narrative as we now have it was not a "mythization of historical *events*." Nor was it the opposite process, i.e., the "historization" of mythical traditions, for the ultimate result was *not* history in the common, modern, sense of the word, but rather a *sacred* narrative similar in function to mythology. It was, instead, a transposition of mythical language and tradition on an "actual" and a human, social level. Since the religious community of Israel believed itself to be built upon actual covenant and not upon a hierarchical order established from time immemorial, its main interest focused on warranting through history its own inner cohesion, which was seen as based not on the physical strength of a central authority but on the worship of the common supernatural Overlord; and such a task could be fulfilled only by insisting on the *actual*, not on the mythical, saving function of its fidelity to Yahweh and to the community. This of course meant that mythical tradition was bound to be transposed and altered into a continuous series of narratives about human ancestors of the actual Israelites, their traditional enemies and their god, and, what is more, that the value of such a continuous set of narratives was, as Mendenhall rightly puts it, "the mainstream of biblical religion."[92]

Of course, one of the main assets and advantages of the cohesion that was warranted by "national" narrative traditions in the history of Israel was the strength it gave poor peasants and herdsmen in their struggle against foreign kingly power and social and religious dissipation in Palestine. So it is not surprising that in the "actualized" narratives the tribute-thirsty monster is an oppressive monarch, and that the place of the warrior-god that destroys that monster in mythological tradition is often occupied by a tribesman who is a faithful executor of the royal commands of the covenant deity.[93]

NOTES

1. M. K. Wakeman, *God's Battle with the Monster: A Study in Biblical Imagery* (Leiden, 1973), henceforeward quoted as Wakeman, *Monster*. On the same subject A. Gunkel, *Schöpfung und Chaos in Urzeit und Endzeit* (Göttingen, 1895); U. Cassuto, *The Israelite Epic* (in Hebrew) "Kenesset" 8 (1943), Pt. 3, 121–142, now translated into English (1975). See also F. M. Cross, *Canaanite Myth and Hebrew Epic* (Cambridge, Mass., 1973).

2. Wakeman, *Monster*, vii.

3. Ibidem, *passim*, especially 118–138.

4. Ibidem, 111–112.

5. S. E. Löwenstamm, *The Making and Destruction of the Golden Calf*: "Biblica" 48 (1967). For criticism of Löwenstamm's article and a bibliography on the subject see L. G. Le Perdue, *The Making and Destruction of the Golden Calf—A Reply*: "Biblica" 54 (1973), 237–246. Some of Le Perdue's arguments seem convincing, but on the whole I accept Löwenstamm's interpretation of the Ugaritic and biblical texts.

6. Löwenstamm, *The Making and Destruction of the Golden Calf*, 458, quoted by Wakeman, *Monster*, 112, note 1.

7. See S. E. Löwenstamm, *The Ugaritic Fertility Myth—The Result of a Mistranslation*: "IEJ" 12 (1962), 80–88.

8. Wakeman, *Monster*, 1–51.

9. Ibidem, 112.

10. Ibidem, 71–72, note 1.

11. C. Virolleaud, *Le Palais d'Ugarit*, vol. 2 (Paris, 1957), 158.

12. Wakeman, *Monster*, 71, note 2.

13. T. H. Gaster, *Thespis: Ritual, Myth, and Drama in the Ancient Near East*, rev. ed. (New York, 1966), p. 134, note 49.

14. G. R. Driver, *Canaanite Myths and Legends* (Edinburgh, 1965), p. 102.

15. M. Held, *mḫṣ / *mḫš in Ugaritic and Other Semitic Languages (A Study in Corporative Lexicography)*: "JAOS" 74 (1959), 169–176. But see the criticism by S. E. Löwenstamm, *The Muzzling of the Tannin in Ugaritic Myth*: "Israel Exploration Journal" 9 (1959), 261.

16. Wakeman, *Monster*, 112 and note 3.

17. Ibidem.

18. *arš* in UT 'nt: III: 40–41 (now KTU 1.3 III: 40–41) is probably to be derived from the root *'rš*, "to love, to desire, to woo, to wed," attested both in West Phoenician (Pyrgi) and in biblical Hebrew: this seems probable also because *arš* is qualified as *mdd.ilm* ("beloved of the gods") in that same text.

19. H. Gunkel, *Schöpfung und Chaos in Urzeit und Endzeit, cit.*, 52–59.

20. Wakeman, *Monster*, 89–99. But for a more "normal" use of animal names of this type, see P. D. Miller, Jr., *Animal names as designations in Ugaritic and in Hebrew:* "Ugarit-Forschungen" 2 (1970), 177–186.

21. Ibidem, 106; 111–112.

22. Ibidem, 80: "the creation of Israel."

23. G. Dumézil, *L'heritage indo-européen à Rome* (Paris, 1949), 142.

24. Wakeman, *Monster*, 80.

25. M. Dahood, *Psalms*, 2 (Garden City, New York, 1973), 133–134.

26. Ibidem, 134.

27. On the divine nature of Pharaoh, see, e.g., H. Frankfort, *Kingship and the Gods* (Chicago, 1948), 15–212.

28. See esp. E. Lipiński, *La Royauté de Yahwé dans la poésie et le culte de l'Ancien Israel* (Brussels, 1965).

29. Wakeman, *Monster*, 136.

30. R. G. Boling, *Judges* (Garden City, New York, 1975), p. 85.

31. Ibidem, 87.

32. Ibidem, 86.

33. Quoted by W. Richter, *Traditionsgeschichtliche Untersuchungen zum Richterbuch* (Bonn, 1963), 19.

34. C. Grottanelli, *Un passo del Libro dei Giudici alla luce della comparazione storico-religiosa: Atti del I Congresso Italiano sul Vicino Oriente Antico* (Rome, 1978), 35–46.

35. Boling, *Judges*, 86.

36. See G. Dumézil, *"Le Borgne" and "Le Manchot": the State of the Problem* (G. J. Larson et al., *Myth in Indo-European Antiquity* [Berkeley, 1974]), 19.

37. Idem, *Mithra–Varuna* (Paris, 1940), 168–188; idem, *Mythe et Epopée* 1 (Paris, 1968); idem, *Mythe et Epopée* 2 (Paris, 1973), 267–281.

38. G. Dumézil, *Les dieux des Germains* (Paris, 1959), chapter 2.

39. A. Christensen, *Les types du premier homme et du premier roi dans l'histoire légendaire des Iraniens*, 1 (Paris, 1971), 184–189.

40. See Grottanelli, *Atti del Primo Convegno Italiano sul Vicino Oriente Antico*, 42.

41. So translated by Boling, *Judges*, 84.

42. Wakeman, *Monster*, 98.

43. Gunkel, *Schöpfung und Chaos in Urzeit und Endzeit*, 59.

44. So translated by Wakeman, *Monster*, 98–99. For *mōnē miṣrayim* = "Egyptian counters (of money or tribute)" see Dahood, *Psalms*, 2, 150.

45. Wakeman, *Monster*, 99.

46. So translated by Wakeman, *Monster*, 99.

47. A. H. Gardiner, *Late Egyptian Stories*, Bibliotheca Aegyptiaca 1 (Bruxelles, 1932), 76–81; G. Lefebvre, *Romans et contes égyptiens de l'époque pharaonique* (Paris, 1949), 106–113; G. Posener, *La légende égyptienne de la mer insatiable:* "Annuarie de L'Institut de Philologie et d'Histoire Orientales et Slaves" 13, 461–478.

48. H. J. Rose, *A Handbook of Greek Mythology*, 6th ed. (London, 1964), 182–185.

49. R. De Vaux, *Ancient Israel, Its Life and Institutions* (London, 1973), 302–303; R. Brinker, *The Influence of Sanctuaries in Early Israel* (Manchester, 1946), 143–148; H. J. Kraus, *Gilgal:* "VT" 1 (1951), 181–199. On the Gilgal connections of the Song of the Sea (Exod. 15), see F. M. Cross, *Canaanite Myth and Hebrew Epic, cit.*, 113–144.

50. F. Zorell, *Lexicon Hebraicum et Aramaicum Veteris Testamenti* (Rome, 1968), s.v.

51. H. W. Hertzberg, *Die Samuelbücher*, Das Alte Testament Deutsch 10, 2nd ed. (1960). I quote from H. W. Hertzberg, *I and II Samuel, A Commentary*, translated by J. S. Bowden (London, 1964), 125.

52. For a complete bibliography (up to 1969) on Irra, see L. Cagni, *L'Epopea di Erra* (Rome, 1969), passim; for the specific term agagu ('gg) in the Epic see the glossary, 263.

53. Wakeman, *Monster*, p. 47: insisting on the monster's fury.

54. T. H. Gaster, *Myth, Legend and Custom in the Old Testament, A Comparative Study with Chapters from Sir James Frazer's* Folklore in the Old Testament (New York and Evanston, 1969), 455–456, 543.

55. Ibidem, 455.

56. Ibidem, 456.

57. Ibidem.

58. Ibidem.

59. Ibidem.

60. Ibidem.

61. Ibidem.

62. Ibidem.

63. Ibidem, 456–457.

64. Wakeman, *Monster*, 136.

65. Ibidem, 22.

66. H. W. Hertzberg, *I and II Samuel, A Commentary*, cit., 124–125.

67. Ibidem, 124.

68. Ibidem, 124–125.

69. Wakeman, *Monster*, 16.

70. Ibidem, 12–14, esp. 14.

71. Ibidem, 15–16; R. T. Rundle Clark, *Myth and Symbol in Ancient Egypt* (London, 1959), 209.

72. Wakeman, *Monster*, 83.

73. Ibidem, 118–120.

74. Wakeman, *Monster*, 120.

75. F. Lexa, *La Magie dans l'Égypte Antique de l'Ancien Empire jusqu'à l'époque copte*, II (Paris, 1925), 83–98; the text in question (Bremmer-Rhind papyrus, British Museum n. 10. 188), published by M.E.-A.-W. Budge as *Facsimilies of Egyptian Hieratic Papyri in the British Museum* (London, 1910), is called Le Livre du Dragon Apop by F. Lexa.

76. F. Lexa, *La Magie dans l'Egypte Antique*, cit., 97–98.

77. Ibidem, 86–98.

78. Ibidem, 86–95.

79. Ibidem, 95: Apophis, having been vanquished, is "not furious any more": the monster's "fury" reminds us of Irra and, possibly, of Agag, if our etymology of the name is correct.

80. H. W. Hertzberg, *I and II Samuel, A Commentary*, cit., 98.

81. Ibidem.

82. Ibidem, 91.

83. Wakeman, *Monster*, 59–61.

84. Ibidem.

85. Ibidem, 61.

86. H. W. Hertzberg, *I and II Samuel, A Commentary*, cit., 90–93.

87. Ibidem, 93.

88. Wakeman, *Monster, passim*; esp. 1–51 and 118–138.

89. Ibidem, vii–viii.

90. Ibidem, 11–12.

91. G. E. Mendenhall, *The Hebrew Conquest of Palestine:* "Biblical Archaeologist" 27 (1964), 84.

92. Ibidem.

93. I have checked the philological aspect of this essay against later publications, the most important of which is the second edition of KTU (Münster, 1995). Though many details have changed, the generally accepted reading, translation, and interpretation of the Ugaritic and other texts discussed here is still consistent with the treatment presented.

4

THE STORY OF DEBORAH AND BARAK
A Comparative Approach

1. Myth

Against the complex reconstruction of many latter-day *khorizontes* (such as Richter, Schulte, Boling),[1] D. W. Gooding[2] has shown convincingly that the Book of Judges is a coherent text, perfectly structured, and possibly written, from beginning to end, as an autonomous unit by a single author (or possibly, I would add, by a single "school"). In spite of this, there is no way to deny that the book contains many distinct stories, and that the stories were surely not invented by the author (or "school"). They go back to traditions of various types and origins; and some of them are surely mythical.

Some years ago, I tried to discuss the mythical quality of the Ehud story (3:12–30), and some of my arguments have been accepted by J. A. Soggin in his recent commentary on the Book of Judges.[3] The Samson story (13:1–16: 31), though the old solar myth theories have justly been rejected long ago, is again being studied as a narrative (in some cases, almost as a mythical narrative)[4] rather than as a more or less reliable piece of historical evidence; and the same is true of the story of the Outrage in Gibeon (chapters 19–21).[5]

As for the story of Deborah and Barak (chapters 4 and 5), which is expressed first in a prose text, and then in the famous, and archaic, Song of Deborah, the very presence of the Song shows that the narrative is highly "traditional," even though I do not think one should consider the later prose text of chapter 4 as a mere rephrasing, with some free additions, of the Song: in this case, as often happens in many narrative traditions, the later text may contain aspects and episodes that are just as archaic, or even more so, than the ones contained in the earlier text. This "traditional" and archaic nature of the story, the quality of the Song, that has so many thematic, lexical, and stylistic elements in common with biblical poetry, notably with the Psalms,[6] and, through them, with Ugaritic epic (mythical) poetry, encourages scholars in viewing the narrative as essentially mythical. Weidner[7] has related the Song to a covenant celebration at an Israelite sanctuary; Gray[8] has followed him in connecting the Song to such a festive ritual, and proposes to identify the occasion in question with the autumn festival of Mowinckel's theory. Following suggestions by Mowinckel[9] and Kraus,[10] Gray suggests that the Song, in narrating the vindication by Yahweh of his power in the overthrow of the Canaanites and Sisera, is historicizing the cosmic conflict between Yahweh and the forces of chaos and death celebrated during the seasonal festival. Along very different lines, Garbini[11] has also recently proposed a mythical interpretation of the Song, and Soggin has dealt with this proposal in a long discussion of his Commentary.[12] Though they are profoundly different, all these interpretations of the Deborah-Barak story as myth agree in comparing the conflict described by the narrative tradition to a cosmic conflict opposing the deity of order and fertility to the enemies of the cosmos.

Moreover, all these studies share a *genetic* approach: they look for the (Canaanite, Aegean, or other) mythical prototype, then for the Israelite transformation of that prototype (the myth of Yahweh's conflict with the forces of chaos), and finally for the "historization" (the conflict against Sisera and "the kings"). In this chapter, I shall try to adopt a *typological* approach, by studying the story as a specific Israelite, biblical example of a type of myth that I shall, for the sake of brevity, term the "battle" myth.[13] This type of myth, which was most clearly identified by Wakeman,[14] is present in a vast number of ancient mythologies. In the Near East (and specifically in Egyptian, Babylonian, Ugaritic and biblical texts) a series of myths, all clearly cosmogonic, that tell of a conflict between some monstrous figure (who often usurps the cosmic kingship and lusts after tribute) and a warrior god that is often a storm god, belong to this type. But the type is present in many mythologies of peoples speaking Indo-European languages, as the fight of a warrior god or hero, connected in different ways with storm and lightning, against an enemy, often multiheaded or in other ways multiple, and often serpentine, who attacks and plunders, often raiding cattle and other goods. The Indo-European myths of this type have been recently studied by specialists, usually along genetic lines, and labelled "the Indo-European Cattle-Raiding Myth,"[15] or "le mythe du Dieu de l'Orage, poursuivant le Serpent."[16]

The typological approach I intend to adopt here enables me to profit from all the comparative analyses already produced by the scholars who have studied the story of Barak and Deborah as a (historicized) myth, and to project it against the far wider background of the mythical type I have described. At the same time, it allows me to study the story comparatively, without being hindered by the supposed necessity of constructing, through a series of genetic hypotheses, a historical justification of my comparative endeavor. For the "historical" (but really genetic) explanation of the similiarities between the biblical story and the type of myths it belongs to is neither possible (a reconstruction of the ways through which the mythical motifs in question have "entered" the culture of ancient Israel may only be hypothetical) nor important. Indeed, while it belongs to the "battle" myth typology, the story of Deborah and Barak is a biblical tale: it is in both positions at the same time, for, in telling of a conflict that has cosmic overtones, it opposes the people of Israel, protected by their god, and their human enemies: the "kings" and their army, led by Sisera. Moreover, a genetic hypothesis is necessarily faced with several possible lines of reasoning. For instance, in imitation of Dumézil's[17] interpretation of the mythical origin of some episodes of the most ancient history of Rome, one may suggest that, in order to become a coherent biblical story, a widespread mythical theme has been adapted to the new context: but then one would have to note that there is no such thing as a widespread mythical theme outside its single, different contexts, and that *each* of these is specific. On the other hand, following some recent suggestions by Sperber,[18] one may also imagine that an Israelite myth has here been shaped from common symbolic themes (e.g., the warrior as lightning and storm; the use of cunning and deceit against a prepossessing tyrant or enemy as the seductive behavior of a deceptive female) in ways that are culture-specific, and thus different from those used by neighbouring cultures in dealing with the same symbolic themes. This is not the right place to discuss these complex matters; but it should be clear that a historical explanation along genetic or diffusionist lines is neither the desired result nor the necessary justification for my typological and comparative suggestions.

The usefulness of the comparative and typological approach adopted here has to do less with reconstruction (of processes leading to the text as it is) than with interpretation (of the text). For it is true that the Deborah-Barak story can be explained only within its context, the Hebrew Bible, and that any interpretation must be culture-specific. But it is also true that our knowledge of the biblical context of the tale (the whole Bible and its cultural context and background) does not explain everything. The things it does not explain include precisely some of the aspects of the text that point to the approach I am suggesting. First, the name of the war leader: Barak, *brg*, i.e., "lightning," which is probably more than just the battle name of a warrior (cf. the Carthaginian general Hamilcar Barca), since the name of Deborah's husband (Lappidoth, i.e., "flashes") echoes it precisely. Second, the episode in which Barak's enemy is betrayed by a woman, Jael, who offers him hospitality and milk, then kills him—in his sleep, according to the prose text; Barak, who is pursuing him, arrives to his tent and is shown the dead man: even if one takes Jael's deceitful deed and her Qenite nationality as (traces of) historical facts, one then still has to explain why that female's duplicity is exalted and presented as heroic both in the prose text and in the Song, rather than played down or ignored; and our knowledge of the biblical context provides no solution to this problem, even though the stories of Judith and Delilah constitute possible parallels. Third, the peace relationship between Jael's Qenite group and Jabin, king of Hazor: why does the prose text insist on this relationship, which turns Jael's behavior into actual treason, an open violation not only of hospitality and the sacredness of a suppliant, but also of a holy, formally established bond between two communities? I think that at least these three aspects of the Deborah-Barak story, i.e., the "lightning" motif, the heroic duplicity of Jael, and the breaking of the peace relationship between Jabin and the Qenite splinter group by that heroine, may be explained only by considering the narrative comparatively and typologically, as a specific example of the "battle" type of myth presented above.

2. Lightning

It is clear from the Song that the victory over the kings is a victory of Yahweh, and that it is caused by a storm. In 5:4–5 Yahweh appears in what Boling,[19] citing J. Jeremias's[20] important study, considers to be a typical biblical theophany. That theophany involves rain and thunder (three times *ntpw*; plus *mym*, once). In 5:20 the stars fight, and stars in Ugaritic mythology, as well as in Greek conceptions, are the source of rain. Finally, in 5:21, surely because water (*mym*, 5:4) has fallen from the sky, and because the stars have fought (5:20), the Wady Qishon sweeps the kings of Canaan away.

The cosmic overtones of the battle are thus no mere epic embellishment of a victory, for, on the one hand, they indicate the intervention of Yahweh (see 4:14–15), and, on the other hand, they specifically involve rain, and the unexpected flowing of the *wady*, as the *cause* of the victory. The similarity between this victory and the Exodus victory at the Reed Sea noted by Freedman and Boling[21] also points in this mythical direction, for the connections between the Reed Sea episode and cosmic myths of the "battle" type are well established.[22] The same may be said of the last sentence of vs. 21, for the trampling of the defeated enemy, as shown by Wakeman,[23] is also a recurring theme in the Near Eastern myths of the same type.

In view of all this, I think the fact that the names of the only two Israelite males mentioned in Judg. 4–5 refer to lightning must be connected to the cosmic overtones of the battle, and I agree with Garbini,[24] who sees the victory by storm and the lightning aspect of these figures (especially, of course, of Barak) as two aspects of the same motif: the victory of storm-figures (Yahweh as a god manifest in the storm, Barak as a lightning-warrior) over an evil oppressor.

It must be noted, however, that, apart from his name, nothing in the narratives ties Barak directly to lightning or storm, which are presented as manifestations of Yahweh (and nothing may be said of Deborah's husband Lappidoth, who is, in fact, literally no more than a name). Nor does Yahweh seem to act like a thunder-god who hurls his lightning-bolt at an enemy: his hierophany *is* the storm; it is the stars that fight. And the champion whose name is lightning simply collects the victory the stars (Yahweh) have given him.

Since, in myths of the type considered here, the thunder-deity usually wields the lightning as a weapon (I think of Indra especially, but also of Thor, of Zeus, of Baal—Marduk used winds), the correspondence between our texts and those myths seems vague. But there is at least one important narrative of the type described above, in which the storm motif is treated as a favorable occasion for a victory against overwhelming forces.

Around 1930, a Northern Caucasic people of Iranian descent, the Ossetes, still possessed a rich epic tradition.[25] One of their main heroes was Batradz, a fierce and invulnerable warrior, and the champion of his people, the Nartian folk. Georges Dumézil has compared Batradz to the Indo-Iranian Indra,[26] and indeed Batradz is a killer of dragons, of multiheaded giants, and of other monsters. Though his sword is identifed with one type of lightning, Batradz does not wield the lightning, for he *is* the lightning. Since his birth, he is shown as a hero made of fiery steel (the substance of which lightning is made, according to Ossetian folk belief). Immediately after his birth, or, according to other versions, as soon as he reaches adulthood, he goes to live in the sky, whence he comes to the rescue of his people when his wet-nurse Satana invokes him with a prayer. When invoked, he plunges directly, all fiery and metallic, from the sky to the battlefields, and rescues the endangered heroes, defeating their enemies.[27]

The Abkhasian neighbours of the Ossetes also possessed a rich epic "Nartian" repertoire that is in many ways similar to that of the Ossetes,[28] and they celebrated a hero whose adventures are similar to those of the Ossetian Batradz: the hero's name is Patraz in some versions, Tsütsv in others. The Abkhasian hero, however, is never metallic, fiery, or in other ways identified with the lightning. Yet one episode, that Georges Dumézil has rightly identified as a recontextualized storm-myth, shows this hero winning a victory in conjunction, so to speak, with a sudden thunderstorm.

The Nartian warriors, we are told, were fighting against their oppressors, a race of giants, and they could not conquer their enemies' terrible stronghold. Tsütsv, whose valor was not commonly recognized, because he always acted *incognito,* had been left at home: but just when the situation was getting tragic and the army was beginning to draw back he appeared on the scene in his heroic aspect, riding his fiery horse, swift as a vulture, or as an arrow, and reprimanding the warriors with fierce words. The others followed him to a gate in the wall of the fortress; and Tsütsv ordered them to place their leader in front and to remain in battle formation before the gate. "A storm shall break out," he said, "the thunder shall growl, lightnings shall flash; but your hearts must not tremble! Great or small, your fears must vanish, for the gate shall open in front of you. At that point, you shall hit the giants with your swords, and only with your swords." As he has predicted, the storm breaks out, with thunder and lightnings, and the great gate opens up; Tsütsv leads the way, a naked sword in his hand, swift as a vulture, rapid as an arrow. What is one to do when, all of a sudden, a stone rolls on one's head? Where should one run, when one is enwrapped in flames? The giants do not understand what is happening to them; the heads of the most valiant fall, cut off by the Nartian swords, and the others drop their weapons and kneel down in submission. As a product of the sudden storm, wonderful trees suddenly spring out of the soil all around; the heroes take the fruits of those trees back to their homes. Today's fruit-trees and vines of Abkhasia derive directly from those mythical plants.[29]

The comparison with the Batradz mythology of the Ossetes shows that this Abkhasian epic narrative is a "reduced" version of the storm- and lightning-hero's victory over his people's monstrous oppressors. The last part of the story, centered upon fertility, shows that the double code of nature (storm and rain) and culture (battle and victory) still functions, and confirms the interpretation. The reduction that can be observed here must be compared to the reduction that may be present in the biblical story, where the storm is a theophany and the war-leader is connected to storm and lightning only by his name. The Caucasic material shows that a transformation similar to the one possibly attested by our biblical text has in fact taken place in the traditional cultures of archaic Near Eastern mountaineers of the modern era.[30] This transformation is, however, not identical to the transformation possibly attested by our biblical texts, for (1) in the Caucasic epic narrative the storm is only partially responsible for the victory, while in the biblical narrative the victory is totally due to the storm, seen as a yahwistic theophany, and then to Jael; (2) in the Caucasic epic tradition it is the correspondence between the Ossetian Batradz and the Abkhasian Patraz that connects the protagonist of the episode examined here to the lightning, while in the biblical text the protagonist's *name* reveals his quality.

3. Deceit

Yair Zakovitch[31] has recently studied the Jael-Sisera episode and rightly compared it to other biblical stories such as the Samson and Delilah episode (Judg. 16) and the story of Judith and Holophernes in the Book of Judith. What he has failed to point out clearly is, however, that all three biblical episodes correspond to a widespread motif of the same kind, which is frequent in Near Eastern mythologies. Such episodes occur often in myths of the battle of a god or gods against a (serpentine) monster: we can quote one of the two versions of the Hittite myth of the slaying of the serpent Illuyanka, the Hurrian myth of the dragon Hedammu, and possibly the Egyptian version of a myth about the Canaanite gods Astarte and Yam.[32] Such motifs are not present in the Indo-European myths of the "battle" type, apart from the Hittite evidence; but they are frequent enough to be considered specific aspects of the type in its Near Eastern versions. The presence of such an episode in the story of Deborah and Barak should thus be studied in the context of my general comparative and typological approach.

The correspondence between the episodes studied together by Zakovitch in their biblical contexts and the mythical theme in question is no recent discovery. To quote but one scholar who had dealt with this theme, Sir James G. Frazer[33] noticed the resemblance between the Samson-Delilah story and myths about the betraying of a monster or ogre by a female in favor of a heroic monster-slayer: the motif, he suggested, had been reversed in this case, or, so to say, seen from the other side. This reversal is not only found in the Samson story; it is attested in many other cases, and already in the Egyptian story of the two brothers, Bata and Anpu, that goes back to the thirteenth century B.C.E. (the "good" brother Bata is betrayed by his spouse, who had been made especially for him by the gods).[34]

In the texts in which the motif in question is an episode of the conflict between the gods (specifically the Storm-God) and a monstrous usurper, the female deceiver uses alcoholic beverages and/or sex to entice and then to stupefy the anticosmic enemy. In this case, Jael (= She-Goat) appears as a giver of milk, not of wine, and as a motherly wet-nurse who puts the confused war leader to sleep and then kills him, not as a seductive concubine. This particular transformation has no clear correspondence anywhere, as far as I know, and can only be explained by invoking complex association. I have tried to deal with this problem elsewhere, and I shall not repeat myself here.[35]

What becomes important in such stories is the fact that the enemy is defeated by a female, mortal or immortal. Of course, this is a good way to criticize, to ridicule, the monstrous, chaotic usuper: the motif of the proud, tyrannical champion defeated by a woman is used also in different contexts, as for instance in the stories of Abimelek (Judg. 9:50–54) and of the king of Epirus, Pyrrhus (Plut. *Pyrr.* 34).[36] But the motif also exalts female cunning and resourcefulness, the power of female seduction, over the warlike strength and efficiency of the male protagonist (who is often no less than the Storm-God, a warrior par excellence): the champion is not able to defeat the monster without help from a female. This is especially noticeable in the Hittite Illuyanka myth, where the importance of the female figure seems to have caused some problems.

> When the Storm-God and the serpent Illuyanka came to blows in the city of Kiškilluš̌a, we are told, the serpent Illuyanka defeated the Storm-God, and the Storm-God cried out to all the gods: "Come to my aid." Inara prepared a festival. She arranged it grandly: a vat of wine, a vat of *marnuwan*, a vat of *walhi*. She filled the vats full to overflowing. Now Inara went to the city Zigaratta and she encountered a man, Hupašiya. Inara said: "Look, Hupašiya, I say such and such—you must hold yourself apart for me." Then Hupašiya said to Inara: "Hail! I will sleep with you. I will come to you. I will do as you desire." And he slept with her. Inara led Hupašiya away and hid him. Inara adorned herself, and she beckoned the serpent Illuyanka out of his cave. "Look, I am celebrating a festival. Come for the food and drink." The serpent Illuyanka came up with its children, and they ate and drank. They drank all the vats and became drunk. Then they could no longer go down into the cave. Hupašiya came and he bound the serpent Illuyanka with a rope. The Storm-God came and killed the serpent Illuyanka there, and the gods were beside him.[37]

In this version of the myth about the Storm-God and the serpent, wine is used to trick the serpent, and sex is used to procure a mortal helper in order to tie the drunken monster down. But before calling the serpent out to feast, Inara adorns herself—just like Judith adorns herself before going to Holophernes' tent.[38] The enemy, however, is tricked by Inara, but bound by the man Hupašiya and killed by the Storm-God. So, on the one hand, the female does not kill the monster herself, and, on the other hand, the female's help against the monster is indeed indispensable.

The importance of the female figure in this myth, where she is more successful than the Storm-God, is reflected in her name: the name Inara is phonologically identical to that of the Vedic dragon-slaying, lightning-wielding god Indra (from a proto-Indo-European root *əner) and probably means "the manly." Moreover, the Hittite texts mention two forms of the deity Inara, giving the deity's name as KAL (= "the manly deity"): "Inara the effeminate" (KAL lu-li-mi-[e]š), and "Inara the manly" (KAL in-na-ra-u-wa-an-za). Typologically, this myth is intermediate between the "battle" myths of the type discussed above that are centered upon a male (Storm-God) figure, and the Near Eastern myths of the same type featuring a seductive female: the responsibility for the victory is divided between a male god, a man (to this we shall return) and a goddess; furthermore, the goddess is "manly" and bears a name that corresponds to that of the male monster-slayer and Storm-God of a linguistically connected culture.[39]

The central importance of the female figure, which seems to have been dealt with as a problem in the Hittite myth, is simply accepted, indeed even stressed, in the biblical texts: Jael does not only deceive Sisera, she kills him herself, so that, unlike the Hittite Storm-God, Barak finds his enemy already dead when he arrives upon the scene. In this, Jael resembles the female protagonist of Ugaritic mythic traditions, the goddess Anath, who kills Mot, the enemy of her brother, the Storm-God Baal, with her own hands, and destroys him completely.[40] Moreover, the victory of a female seems to be a true leitmotif in the biblical story of Deborah and Barak, as shown by Judg. 4:8, where the female prophet Deborah announces to the insecure Barak that Yahweh will sell Sisera by the hand of a woman: that woman, it would seem at this point, is Deborah herself—but the rest of the story makes it clear that the prophecy refers to Jael.[41] Indeed, the whole textual evidence, both in the prose narrative and in the Song, may be seen as a play on the rather ridiculous helplessness of *both* male protagonists, Barak and Sisera (the former will only go to war if Deborah accompanies him, and is deprived of the "diadem" of that day's glory by a woman; the latter loses his chariot, flees to a tent, is given milk and put to sleep by Jael, and immediately dies), and on the power of the female figures, who are the only really active figures in the whole narrative.

The "difficult" theme of the deceitful heroine is thus not reduced (as is the case with the lightning-and-storm motif) but underlined and expanded upon by the biblical text. Yet the reduction of the storm theme and the expansion of the theme of the deceitful female both result in the partial obliteration of the male protagonist: the enemies are defeated by Yahweh through storm and rain, or by Jael; Barak, in spite of his promising name, is only shown as he comes upon the scene to collect the results.

4. Guilt

The heroine Jael is thus a female deceiver similar to the goddesses of mythology who seduce and destroy, or help to destroy, the chaotic enemy (of the Storm-God). Her duplicity may well be exalted. But it is not only the duplicity of a seductive female; it is the treacherous behavior of a group that was offi-

cially allied to that of the betrayed leader.[42] *Because* there was a "peace relationship" between Jabin and the Qenite splinter-group, Sisera sought refuge in
Jael's tent; and *because* he trusted Jael in virtue of that official relationship, she
was able to betray him and to kill him. In the light of this, Jael's deed is not
only the behavior of a heroic female deceiver, but also the (doubly) guilty action of breaking a covenant relationship. This further aspect of the Qenite
woman's deed requires a further treatment.

Once more, if we envisage the story of Deborah and Barak as a specific
myth of the type presented above, this further aspect of the story may be explained, or at least dealt with, comparatively. For in the mythology of the warrior god Indra the killing of serpentine, three-headed and other beings by that
god is presented as a guilty act,[43] for reasons pertaining either to the sacredness
of the enemy (who may be a Brahman, as is the case with the tricephal
Viśvarupa) or to special kinship ties between Indra and his victim (who may be
the god's cousin), or to a "friendship" between the god and his antagonist (Namuci: Indra has established a tie of friendship with Namuci: *tenendrah
sakhyam akarot*) or his antagonist's father (Viśvarupa's father was a friend of Indra's). This situation is dealt with ingeniously in some myths: the killing of the
monster is attributed to a "human" hero, "pushed, encouraged by Indra" (*in-
dreṣitaḥ*): Tritá Āptya. And Tritá Āptya may be interpreted, as Maurice Bloomfield has shown,[44] as "the scapegoat of the gods," who, in various texts, pertaining not only to the mythical battle but also to sacrifice and to other rituals,
takes upon him the impurity of others, and, in addition to this, is presented as
a specialist of ritual purification.

In a famous study of these myths, Georges Dumézil[45] has compared them
to some episodes of the "early history" of Rome. He suggests that the battle,
dated by Latin and Greek historians to the time of Rome's third king, between
the Roman champion, the last surviving Horatius (a third brother like Tritá
Āptya), and the three Alban champions, the Curiatii (a "triple" foe, like the tricephal Viśvarupa) corresponds to Tritá's victory over the Tricephal, that Tullus
Hostilius' murder of the Alban king Mettius Fufetius corresponds to Indra's
victory over Namuci, and that all the narratives, Roman and Indic, derive from
the common mythology of the Indo-Europeans. Now, the Horatii and Curiatii
were cousins or future brothers-in-law, and the killing of the Curiatii was followed by a ritual treatment of the surviving Horatius, whose family, the *gens
Horatia*, was in historical times the "owner" of special rituals of purification.
The relationship of Mettius Fufetius with Tullus Hostilius was also a special
one: they were formal allies, *socii* (the term is phonologically identical to the
term *sakhā*, "friend," that is used in referring to Indra and Namuci); and it is
only through a special cunning device that Tullus could kill his *socius* (who
had, however, betrayed him).

Whatever we may think of the possible historical relationship between the
Indic and the Roman narratives, we are surely faced with two groups of myths
presenting the killing of a dangerous enemy as the betrayal of a sacred relationship (a kinship tie, a marriage bond, a sworn alliance, or "simply" friend-

ship), and dealing, in different ways, with the paradox. And one of the solutions adopted seems to be the shifting of the guilt (and also of the glory) onto a human, or nonroyal, scapegoat, who is then sometimes purified and/or presented as an expert purifier.

A similar strategy is probably at work in the Hittite Illuyanka myth. This is at least possible in the version I have quoted above: though the killing of the serpent is not presented as guilty per se, it is prepared by treachery and in part attributed to a mortal. The man Hupašiya goes on living with Inara after the deed, but he is homesick, and this displeases the goddess; so, though the end of the story is missing, we may well suspect that the human helper of the gods against the serpent comes to a bad end. The other version[46] features a half-human ally of the Storm-God. In the first round, the serpent Illuyanka defeated the Storm-God and stole his heart and eyes. To reconquer them, the Storm-God conceived a child from the daughter of a poor man, and, when the boy reached adulthood, he married him to the daughter of the serpent Illuyanka. "As soon as you enter your wife's dwelling, he then told his son, you must ask for my heart and eyes." The young male obeyed and the Storm-God got his heart and eyes back, and as soon as his body was whole again, he reached the sea, where the serpent came out to fight with him, and he defeated Illuyanka. But the Storm-God's son was then in his father-in-law's dwelling, and when the Storm-God came to kill Illuyanka, he cried out to his father: "Kill me too! Do not spare me!" So the Storm-God killed both the serpent and his own son. Obviously, the serpent Illuyanka was bound to both the Storm-God and his half-mortal son by marriage ties; the young man who took advantage of these ties in order to help the Storm-God to destroy the serpent, and then asked to be killed along with the father-in-law he had betrayed, seems to be taking the guilt upon himself, and paying for it, too. Like a good scapegoat.

Even if we leave aside the Roman traditions, which cause more problems than they solve, we are still confronted with several Indic, and at least one Hittite, mythical traditions about the killing of a monstrous or serpent-like enemy by a Storm-God, in which that deed is presented as the betrayal of an ally, friend, kin, or in-law, and in some cases attributed at least partly to a (half-)human figure, acting as a scapegoat of sorts. In the light of this evidence, we could suggest that the betrayal by Jael of the *šlm* relationship that enables her to kill Sisera may be seen as a further example of the same theme, and that, in the biblical narrative, Jael plays not only the part attributed, in the "first" version of the Illuyanka myth, to the goddess Inara, but also the part attributed in the "second" (and in the "first"?) version of that myth to the (half-)human, male helper of the Storm-God (and of Inara). Since in the preceding section (3.) I had suggested that Jael was given the function attributed by the Hittite myth to the Storm-God (i.e., that she herself killed the enemy she had deceived), I should observe here that, in the perspective I am adopting, the biblical narrative appears as a "simplified" example of the type of myth discussed: a version in which one figure (Jael) plays the roles that another (the "first" Hittite) version divides between no less than three distinct figures: the Storm-God, Inara, and Hupašiya.

If my suggestion is accepted, then the fact that Jael is both a heroine of Israelite epos and a Qenite also acquires a new meaning. For as a Qenite Jael is ready for her task as a traitor and killer: she is a descendant of Cain, the first murderer, the first brother and the first betrayer of a brother, a bloody, impure man, an accursed wanderer, protected from other men's wrath only by his immense capacity for taking revenge and by the mark Yahweh has placed upon him. If envisaged in the context I have tried to reconstruct, then, Jael is *the* perfect scapegoat, not only (among other things) *a* scapegoat held responsible, in the biblical narrative, for a deed that should not be attributed to a true Israelite.

5. Prophets

The typological and comparative approach adopted here has thus permitted us to understand three problems of the biblical story of Deborah and Barak that the traditional, culture-specific, internal approach could not explain. It should then, I submit, be considered as one possible, correct and useful, approach to the biblical texts (or at least to this biblical text).

I want to insist again, however, on the fact that the approach in question reveals differences as often as it permits us to point out similarities between the narratives compared and classified as belonging to the same type of myth. And I repeat that the narrative traditions compared are no less typical of each specific culture for the fact of being studied and classified together.

Thus, the Deborah and Barak story is the story of a (holy) war between (parts of) Israel and enemy kings, won by Yahweh by way of a storm and of a woman, Jael, and announced by another woman, Deborah. Monolatry, holy war, and the unexpected importance of female figures (see above, section 3) are its characteristic traits. All three traits are unified, so to say, in the figure of Deborah; and Deborah is a *prophet* figure. So one may well follow James S. Ackerman[47] in his brilliant study of the story of Deborah and Barak, and see the story as a perfect example of biblical prophecy-and-warfare: the people oppressed because they have been "sold" by Yahweh, the people's cry to Yahweh for help, the reassurance of the people, and the encouragement in view of war, by Yahweh through a prophetic figure, the divine choice of a leader, the victory oracle, and the victory.

That this structure is not merely biblical is shown by the Aramaic inscription of King Zakkur of Hamath (around 800 B.C.E.), which Zobel[48] has compared to biblical oracular forms: "All these kings laid siege to (my city) Hazrak.
. . . But I lifted up my hands unto Ba'alsha[may]n. And Ba'alshamay[n] answered me (*wy'nny*). And Ba'alshamayn [spoke] unto me by the hand of seers and diviners (*hzyn* and *'ddn*). And Ba'alshamayn [said to me]: 'Do not be afraid for I have made you king, and I will arise with you and I will deliver you

from all [these kings who] have set a siege against you.'"[49] As in the Barak and Deborah episode, we have the oppression, the cry to the deity, the deity's answer through inspired persons, the reassurance and encouragement, couched in typical prophetic speech ("Do not fear . . ."): the divine choice of the leader is implicit in the statement that (in a previous moment), Ba'alshamayn had made Zakkur king. Victory follows and is celebrated by the erection of the stele, just as it is presented as celebrated by the Song in the story of Barak and Deborah.[50]

As is always the case in the Hebrew Bible, in this specific instance too a cultural pattern that is widespread in the Near East is taken up and profoundly restructured: the *use* of inspired seers by a *leader* in moments of (military) crisis becomes the *expression* of the *deity's* will through prophets in the sacred war: the prophetic figure becomes central and the military leader is almost nonexistent. This specifically biblical version of the victory announced by the deity coincides with the specifically biblical version of the battle theme, in which the storm-aspect of the battle is presented as a Yahwistic theophany, while the deceitful behavior that completes the victory is attributed to a female figure. But the leader's name remains as a signal of the ancient and powerful symbolic potentiality of the battle theme, and the story of Barak's victory can be envisaged as the specific, "prophetic," biblical version of the type of myth I have called the "battle" type.[51]

NOTES

1. W. Richter, *Die Bearbeitung des "Retterbuches" in der deuteronomistischen Epoche*, Bonner Biblische Beiträge 210 (Bonn, 1964); H. Schulte, *Der Entstehung der Geschichtsschreibung im Alten Israel* (Berlin, 1972); R. G. Boling, *Judges: Introduction, Translation, Commentary*, The Anchor Bible (New York, 1975).

2. D. W. Gooding, *The Composition of the Book of Judges*: 'Ereṣ Iśra'el 16 (1982), 70–79.

3. C. Grottanelli, *Un passo del Libro dei Giudici alla luce della comparazione storico-religiosa: il Giudice Ehud e il valore della mano sinistra*: Atti del Primo Convegno Italiano sul Vicino Oriente Antico, Roma, 1978, 35–45; see J. A. Soggin, *Judges*, Old Testament Library (London, 1981), 48, 53. See also chapter 3 in this book.

4. J. L. Crenshaw, *The Samson Saga: Filial Devotion or Erotic Attachment?*: ZAW 86 (1974), 470–504. See also J. Blenkinsopp, *Structure and Style in Judges 13–16*: JBL 82 (1963), 65–76.

5. M. Liverani, *Messaggi, donne, ospitalità: Comunicazione intertribale in Giud. 19–21*: Studi Storico-Religiosi III (1979), 303–341.

6. For this aspect see F. M. Cross, Jr., and D. N. Freedman, *Studies in Ancient Yahwistic Poetry* (Baltimore, 1950; microfilm Xerox reprint, Ann Arbor, 1961); J. Blenkinsopp, *Ballad Style and Psalm Style in the Song of Deborah: A Discussion*: Biblica 42 (1961), 61–76; E. Lipiński, *Juges 5, 4–5 et Psaume 68, 8–11*: Biblica 48 (1967), 185–206; and the discussion of the implications of these parallels for the dating of the Song in Soggin, *Judges*, 93–94.

7. A. Weidner, ZAW 30 (1959), 67–97.

8. J. Gray, A Cantata of the Autumn Festival: Psalm LXVIII: JSS 22 (1977), 2–27.

9. S. Mowinckel, Die achtundsechstige Psalm: Avhandliger utgitt av det Norske Videnskaps-Akademi i Oslo II, Hist. Filo. Klasse, 1953, n. 1.

10. H. J. Kraus, Die Psalmen, Biblischer Kommentar, eds. S. Hermann and H. W. Wolff, XVI, II, 1978, 624–638.

11. G. Garbini, Il cantico di Deborah: La Parola del Passato 178 (1978), 5–31.

12. G. Soggin, Judges, Old Testament Library (London, 1981), 60–101.

13. See chapter 3.

14. M. K. Wakeman, God's Battle with the Monster: A Study on Biblical Imagery (Leiden, 1973).

15. B. Lincoln, The Indo-European Cattle-Raiding Myth, History of Religions 16 (1977), 42–65.

16. V. Ivanov and V. Toporov, Le mythe indoeuropéen du dieu de l'orage poursuivant le serpent: Reconstruction du schéma, in Echanges et Communications. Mélanges offerts à Claude Lévi-Strauss II (The Hague, 1968), 1180–1206.

17. G. Dumézil, Mythe et Epopée I. L'idéologie des trois fonctions dans les épopées des peuples indo-européens (Paris, 1968), 261–634.

18. D. Sperber, Du Symbolisme en général (Paris, 1974).

19. Boling, Judges (see above, note 1), p. 108; M. Weinfeld, They Fought from Heaven: 'Eres Isra'el 14 (1978), 23–30.

20. J. Jeremias, Theophanie: Die Geschichte eines alttestamentlichen Gattung (Neukirchen, 1965).

21. Freedman: oral communication to Boling, Judges (see above, note 1), 97.

22. Especially by F. M. Cross, Cannanite Myth and Hebrew Epic (Cambridge, Mass., 1973), 112–144.

23. Wakeman, God's Battle with the Monster (see above, note 13), 118–121, and chapter 3 in this book.

24. Garbini, La Parola del Passato 178 (1978), 5–31.

25. G. Dumézil, Legendes des Nartes (Paris, 1930); idem, Le Livre des Héros (Paris, 1965).

26. D. Dumézil, Romans de Scythie et d'alentour (Paris, 1978), chapters 1–6.

27. Dumézil, Romans de Scythie et d'alentour, chapter 1.

28. Ibidem, chapter 1.

29. Ibidem, chapter 1.

30. For a discussion of this transformation see Dumézil, Romans de Scythie et d'alentour, chapter 1.

31. Y. Zakovitch, Siseras Tod: ZAW 93 (1981), 364–375.

32. On the Hittite myth (KBo III 7; KUB XII, 66; XVII, 5 and 6), see H. Otten, Ein Text zum Neujahrfest aus Bogazköy: Orientalistisches Literaturzeitung 51 (1956), 101–105; on the Hurrian, J. Siegelová, Appu-Märchen und Hedammu-Mythos, StBoT 14 (Wiesbaden, 1971); on the Canaanite-Egyptian myth: A. H. Gardiner, Late Egyptian Stories. Bibliotheca Aegyptiaca I (Bruxelles, 1932); G. Lefebvre, Romans et contes égyptiens de l'époque pharaonique (Paris, 1949); G. Posener, La légende égyptienne de la mer insatiable: Annuaire de l'Institut de Philologie et d'Histoire Orientales et Slaves 13, 76–81, and chapter 3 in this book.

33. J. G. Frazer, Folklore and the Old Testament, vol. 2 (London, 1918), 480–502.

34. On this episode see S. Donadoni, *La seduzione della moglie di Bata:* Rivista degli Studi Orientali 28 (1953), 143–148.

35. C. Grottanelli, *L'Inno a Hermes e il Cantico di Deborah: due facce di un tema mitico:* RSO 56 (1982), 27–37.

36. In these texts the hero is killed by a stone object thrown by a woman from the walls of a besieged town: in both cases the type of a death is seen as ridiculous and causes loss of honor.

37. This is the text quoted above, note 32.

38. Judith 10:1–10.

39. KBo III 7. I follow the treatment of this myth by B. Lincoln, *Priests, Warriors and Cattle: A Study in the Ecology of Religions* (Berkeley, 1981), 117–121. The translation of the text given here is also indebted to Lincoln's translation in the same volume, 118–119, as well as to ANET and to other translations.

40. On Anath see A. S. Kapelrud, *The Violent Goddess: Anath in the Ras Shamra Texts* (Oslo, 1969), 67–79, who follows the traditional "agrarian" interpretation. Against that interpretation one should see S. E. Loewenstamm, *The Ugaritic Fertility Myth: The Result of a Mistranslation:* IEJ 12 (1962), 87–88; idem, *The Making and Destruction of the Golden Calf:* Biblica 48 (1967), 481–490. On Anath and Deborah: P. C. Craigie, *Deborah and Anat: A Study of Poetic Imagery:* ZAW 90 (1978), 374–381.

41. See Boling, *Judges* (quoted above, note 1), 96. On Anath and the monster, see chapter 3 in this book.

42. On the peace relationship between the Kenite group and Jabin, see Boling, *Judges,* 97, and the discussion by F. C. Fensham, *Did a Treaty Between the Israelites and the Kenites exist?:* BASOR 175 (October 1964), 51–54, and Soggin, *Judges,* 77.

43. G. Dumézil, *Heur et Malheur du Guerrier* (Paris, 1985, 2nd. ed.).

44. M. Bloomfield, *Trita, the Scapegoat of the Gods:* The American Journal of Philology 17 (1896), 430–437.

45. G. Dumézil, *Heur et Malheur du Guerrier,* 20–53.

46. The second version is contained in the same text that contains the first (KBo III 7): the text is a liturgy of the spring festival. See above, note 32.

47. J. S. Ackerman, *Prophecy and Warfare in Early Israel: A Study of the Deborah-Barak Story:* BASOR 220 (December 1975), 5–14.

48. H. J. Zobel, *Das Gebet um Abwendung der Not und seine Erhörung in den Klageliedern des Alten Testaments und in der Inschrift des Königs Zakir von Hamath:* VT 21 (1971), 91–99.

49. KAI I, Text 202: 9–15.

50. J. C. Greenfield, *The Zakir Inscription and the Danklied,* in Proceedings of the Fifth World Congress of Jewish Studies, I (Jerusalem, 1971), 174–191.

51. This chapter must be read as a continuation of my previous studies on biblical narrative, cosmogony, "battle" myths published in this periodical. SSR I (1977); SSR IV (1980). While I was reading the proofs, two important contributions to the study of Judg. 4 and 5 were published: B. B. Webb. *The Book of Judges. An Integrated Reading* (Sheffield, 1987) (a unified view of the Book of Judges, in the line of Gooding's article quoted above, note 2), and A. Caquot, *Les Tribus d'Israël dans le Cantique de Débora (Juges 5, 13–17):* Semitica 35 (1985), pp. 47–70 (where "l'anteriorité du Cantique de Juges 5 sur le récit en prose de Juges 4" is rightly questioned).

5

CHARISMATIC POSSESSION AND
MONARCHIC RATIONALIZATION
The Folly of Saul

For the author of an epic . . . the individuality
of the characters—that which is gleaned about
them by the reader—and all that is directly represented, constitute a system composed of concrete
representations whose role is to express the ideological substance of the work.

G. N. Pospelov

The student of mythology effects the translation of
mythological language into ideological language.
The direction is undeniable: to use Hjemslev's terminology, a "connotative semiotic" is transformed
into a "denotative" semiotic.

A. J. Greimas

1 . The Story of David and of Saul

1.1. From Saul to David: A Transition Told

Until now the biblical texts dealing with the birth of the monarchy[1] have been
studied as a series of "sites" in which to look for indices and traces of historical
facts if not the actual historical facts themselves. This attitude toward the texts
derives from a series of factors at the root of which may be a certain attitude
toward the Holy Book which has never been overcome (not even by the
staunchest nonbelievers).

In addition, the research into the sources of the Old Testament begun by
Wellhausen's school, in itself innovative and correct, has had the negative effect of encouraging a disinterest in the biblical text in its entirety, a text which
presents itself to us today as integral. Even though this unity is a constructed
and later development, it nonetheless responds to an intriguing design which,
with many subtleties, informs every book of the text and the text as a whole.
This tendency to avoid studying the books of the Old Testament as a unity that
transcends its diverse sources, coupled with the search for "true" historical

facts reconstructed on the basis of textual fragments, has generated the most childish of misunderstandings.

This being the case, it is not banal to state that the books of the Old Testament should be studied as any other text. It is right to apply to them, under the same constraints that apply to any other text, every new methodological approach that would clarify its entire semantic sense, its ideological intent, and its social and political value.[2] They comprise a message, as does any other text, replete with a sender and a receiver. The books of the Old Testament are not simply a cauldron in which older texts or oral traditions are badly fused.

A few steps in this direction have been taken. They have left intact, however, a pseudohistorical prejudice, due to a naive reading that is still in search of the "true anecdote." Such an approach fails to recognize that these texts comprise a semantic system in whose context the specific, individual propositions can be explained. At issue here is the opinion, which recurs even today among many scholars, that, at least for the second half of his life, King Saul was a poor unbalanced neurotic. In the final analysis it is to this historical fact (historical like Napoleon's ulcer!) that Saul's failure and David's success are attributed.[3]

The belief in such a historical "fact" arises from a rationalistic interpretation of those biblical passages where Saul acts in strange and absurd ways because he is possessed by an evil spirit. But this rationalism is not rational. It removes these specific biblical passages from the entirety of the biblical narrative concerning Saul and his successor David. This is precisely the context in which Saul's "strange behavior" should be set in order to uncover the meaning the text attributes to them, which is, in fact, the only "true" meaning that we moderns ought assign to them as well.

The stories of David and Saul coincide with the story of the origin of the monarchy in Israel, which is immediately preceded by the accounts of the last Judges (Gideon, Jephthah, Abimelech). The intended audience for that tale of origin consisted of the literate classes of Israel. The transmitters were scribes possibly tied to the monarchy, but wedded even more closely to the theocratic ideology of an evolved Yahwism and the complex social reality that both presupposes and guarantees it. The goal can only be to narrate the origin of the monarchy and the complex reality that underlies it, because these are linked to that ideology and guaranteed by the will of the god of Israel.[4] Insofar as they prove to be more conducive to the happy survival of the people of Yahweh, they can be set in opposition to the more archaic tribal regulations. These ancient customs held a certain fascination for those who connected them with the ancient glories of the patriarchs and the forms of "theocratic democracy" more consonant with their own religiosity than with the predatory (and in some ways foreign) regime of the monarchic state.[5] In short, it is a question of founding the monarchy and doing so precisely through the story of its origin.[6] The aim is to present the monarchy, which has an ambiguous value (and is "foreign" in that, according to the Old Testament itself, it is an imitation of foreign peoples), as something positive (and "national"). Of course, in the biblical context, to speak of "origins of the monarchy" is to speak of "origins of the state" with all its characteristics, from the functional division of labor and its social governance to the very existence of a capital and the tribute to an organized army.[7]

The need for the monarchy is clearly expressed in I Samuel, wherein the people request that the judge appoint a king. On that occasion Yahweh addresses Samuel: "It is not you [the people] reject, they are rejecting me as their king" (I Sam. 8:7). Still, continues Yahweh, Samuel must listen to the voice of the people, announcing in the meantime the rights of the king who will reign over them. Samuel tells the people that the king will take their sons and make them care for his chariots and his horses; he will make them military leaders, peasants on his lands, smiths for his weapons and wheelwrights for his chariots. He will make their daughters perfumers, cooks, bakers; he will appropriate the fields of the people, their richest vineyards and olive groves, their best servants, cattle and asses. He will tithe their seed grain and their grapes and give the earnings to his courtiers and ministers. He will also impose a tithe on their flocks and herds. "You yourselves will become his slaves," concludes Samuel; "When this takes place, you will complain against the king whom you have chosen, but on that day the Lord will not answer you" (I Sam. 8:17–18). In spite of this dark warning, the people insist on having a king to govern them and lead them in battle just as other peoples do (I Sam. 8:19–22).

Rather than simply look on this passage as an antiroyal polemic, perhaps inserted at this point, it seems we must seek in it a "dialectical" formulation of the characteristics of kingship.[8] The legitimation of this kingship is thus amply expressed and guaranteed by the will of the people (who, having been forewarned, thereafter forfeited the right to complain about the negative consequences of their own stubborn insistence). The kingship also is legitimized by acceptance on the part of Yahweh and Samuel. Further, its onerous burden for the people is closely linked to its state functions (its ministers, its army with its officers and its chariots, necessary for victory in war). From one point of view, one might speak of the people's nostalgia for a primitive anarchy. This primitive anarchy is, in its turn, opened up to criticism in ways that legitimate the monarchy, as, for instance, when the book of Judges (Judg. 17–18) comments on the conditions in which an antimosaic cult could be autonomously established by a man of Ephraim in a domestic shrine containing a statue recast from stolen silver: "In those days there was no king in Israel; everyone did what he thought best" (Judg. 21:25).

As in the Mesopotamian world, also in Israel kingship has a divine sanction. In the Mesopotamian world, however, kingship descends from heaven in a mythical time,[9] whereas, in the case of Israel, the kingship is requested by human beings in "historical time." Before the kingship, there is no primordial chaos but a different, and *relatively* chaotic, social organization.

After all, it is almost necessary that Samuel condemn the onerous burdens of kingship, since the dialectical opposition between judge and king includes, among other things, a confrontation between the "free" juridical-military services provided by the judge and the social costs of the royal court. In stepping down from the judgeship, Samuel dwells on this contrast by asking: "Whose ox have I taken? Whose ass have I taken? . . . From whom have I accepted a bribe in order that I close my eyes?" (I Sam. 12:3). In this context, then, a judge can accumulate wealth only if he is corrupt. This is reminiscent of Hesiod's motif of the *dorophagoi basileis*, but with the effect of negating it,[10] for there is no *institutional mechanism* that would allow a judge to live off the people. After his prophetic call, the eyes of Samuel, which no one had closed with bribes, are opened wide to the supernatural. In the simple premonarchic world, Samuel's character as a seer inspired directly by Yahweh can make him, at one and the same time, a folk diviner who, *for a fee*, helps peasants recover their livestock (as still happens today on the margins of our industrial and state societies) and the supreme leader of the people, who does not live off his fellow Israelites.

The behavior of Samuel's sons, judges like himself, makes clear that this formula fails. They accept bribes and allow themselves to become corrupted, justifying by their behavior the discontent of the people: "Now that you are old, and your sons do not follow your example, appoint a king over us . . ." (I Sam. 8:5). Paradoxically, that the king is maintained at the expense of the entire community is precisely the guarantee of his justice and *incorruptibility*.

1.2. Narrative Modules

An indirect confirmation of my proposal for a global reading of the origins of state order in Israel comes from comparative studies. These reveal noteworthy structural assonances between the biblical events, which have been the objects of this study, and Livy's history of the origins of the republican state order in Rome around the time of the Gallic invasion (late fifth to early fourth century B.C.E.).[11]

Here follows an account of the events common to both stories under examination. As we will see, they form a complete and coherent series of events, which could be entitled "the new birth of Rome (or of Israel) as a harmonious state, through the efforts of a pious military leader."

In both cases, one encounters a community in which the old orders of governance are in grave crisis. Conflicts are numerous, whether internal, among social groups, or external, against foreigners. One foreign group in particular (the Gauls for Rome, the Philistines for Israel) emerges as archenemy and oppressor. Tradition has a major impact on the category of external conflicts, using them to express even the situation of internal conflict, as has been shown by D. Sabbatucci's critical studies of Roman traditions,[12] in contrast for those of A. Alt in the case of Israel.[13]

Whoever possesses charismatic power (King Saul, on the one hand, or the ruling class of senators on the other) confronts a crisis. Meeting opposition from within the society, they can neither auspicate in the traditional manner (I Sam. 28:6; Livy IV, 1–9) nor stave off external enemies. Thus they show themselves to be completely ineffective either on the religious or the military plane. A great military leader who has often been victorious (David, Camillus) is closely tied to the center of charismatic power. When he comes into conflict with it, however, he is forced into exile and must withdraw from national territory (I Sam. 18–31; Livy V, 32). While the community is thus sundered, the group that holds charismatic power is practically destroyed by external enemies (Gauls; Philistines) (I Sam. 18–II Sam. 1; Livy V, 41–42). Only when the exiled leader returns at the head of a group of expatriates can victory over the enemy and the restoration of the social order be obtained (II Sam. 1–8; Livy V, 42–55). The community, which had, so to speak, lost its center, finds it once again with the definitive choice of a capital city, ruled by the "savior" with divine consent (II Sam. 5–6; Livy V, 55).

Even so, the crisis is not completely resolved. Through bloodshed (the killing of the Gibeonites; the killing of Marcus Manlius), the prior holders of charismatic power had provoked a plague, followed by famine and military defeats (Rome), or by a famine (Israel). Once again the new leader intervenes to reorder things, putting an end to the new crisis and providing a harmonious and ordered rule for the society (II Sam. 21; Livy VI, 18–22). With this reordering, the series of victorious battles continues, and at his death the old leader, the true "new founder," leaves behind a peaceful and powerful society (II Sam. 23:1–7; I Kings 2:1–12; Livy VI, 22–31).

The essence of these two juxtaposed narratives lies in the circumstance that, while Saul and the power of the *patres* (and the reality that they represent) "do not work" or work "in reverse," David and Camillus (and the reality they establish) work well. The two terms of comparison contrasted in the biblical text are completely different from those that Livy presents. Nonetheless, the narrative modules that express these two vastly different social transmutations are analogous both in function (showing the functional superiority of one social reality over an older one) and with respect to the social settings that created them (dominant classes which authored a "national [sacred] history").

2. The Confrontation between Saul and David

2.1. Saul and David

Given what we have observed thus far it seems superfluous to insist that the biblical tale establishes an opposition between David and Saul. This opposition consists fundamentally in the fact that David functions well as protector and guarantor of the interests of Israel, whereas Saul functions poorly. For two figures to be truly comparable, however, they must have something in common. The common element is: they are both kings of Israel.[14] As those charged with the functions of guiding and guarding the people, they are judged on their performance of these duties. As kings, therefore, they are contrasted with their predecessors, the tribal or intertribal leaders whose functional inadequacy made Israel ask (the biblical text claims) for a king. These leaders are called Judges, and the last of these in chronological order is Samuel.

Throughout the entire biblical narrative, Saul's failure and David's success as kings are closely tied to the *behavior* of these two narrative characters, who are described as determining, directly or indirectly (by evoking reactions from Yahweh) the fate of their people. It follows, of course, that the failure of Saul is the failure of the Saul model, that is, of a certain model of sovereignty. The success of David, on the other hand, coincides with the success of the ethic, the religiosity and, in general, the cultural and pragmatic profile of a hero from whom the reigning dynasty will be born. The people of Israel will look to David, throughout the entire course of its history, as to a figure that is, in a certain sense, messianic. The return of his descendant is awaited with hope.

In order to clarify the real meaning of this biblical account we must carry out a systematic comparison of the principal characteristics of the two figures in question. This will clarify the real terms of the opposition previously mentioned. The analysis is divided into several headings, taken in order. Emphasis falls on religious aspects of the comparison, which appear to be central from the point of view of the redactor of the books of Samuel.

2.2. *The Spirits*

Saul. Right after being anointed by Samuel, Saul follows the instructions of the old Judge. The last of these instructions is the order to go to the hill of Elohim where, according to the predictions of Samuel himself, the new king comes across a group of prophets. They are playing musical instruments and have entered a state of trance. At this point "the Spirit of Yahweh" (*rwḥ Yhwh*) takes possession of Saul, who becomes " a different man," and he prophesies in their midst (I Sam. 10:9–13), although the verb "to prophesy" does not mean precisely to "make prophecies" but rather "to behave like a prophet," that is, like an ecstatic, or, better yet, like "one possessed," with connotations of madness. There is very precise evidence in the Old Testament regarding the relationship between "the Spirit of Yahweh" and the prophets: the phenomenon is one of possession.[15]

The "popular" reaction to this event is not the reaction that one would have expected, one marked by religious respect. The proverbial comment "is Saul also among the prophets? . . . and who is their father?" (I Sam. 10:11–12) has been interpreted in various ways.[16] The most likely interpretation is confirmed by a passage which will be dealt with shortly. This interpretation takes note of an expression of amazement in seeing a high-profile personality such as Saul mixing and associating, through his violent behavior, with those "nobody's children" ("Who is their father?"). These are, in fact, the prophets, described in social terms. On the one hand, Saul has a long genealogy ("Son of Kish, son of Abiel, son of Zeror, son of Becorath, son of Aphiah, a Benjaminite"; I Sam. 9:1). This indicates a certain nobility, even independent of his recent royal unction, which was relatively secret and unknown to most. On the other hand, the prophets may be sacred persons, but their sacrality appears to be ambiguous. No one knows who their father is, and their possessed behavior clashes with a rising "aristocratic" ethic. After all, certain aspects of that behavior are explicitly condemned in the books of the Pentateuch.[17]

The "Spirit of Yahweh" in this episode hastens to restore Saul to normalcy, but it reappears in the episode concerning the reconquest of Jabesh-Gilead (I Sam. 11:1–11). Hearing of the humiliation to which Jabesh was subjected, Saul becomes inflamed with rage because "the Spirit of Yahweh rushed upon him" (I Sam. 11:6). With his bare hands he tears to pieces the two oxen that he was leading back from the field after plowing. He sends the fragments to the tribes as a warning about their own fate should they not run to help Jabesh. Leading the arriving contingents, he avenges the city by defeating the Ammonites. It is noteworthy that, by means of the terrorist ruse of the dismembered ox, Saul succeeds in mediating between the tribal militia, based on voluntary service, and an army of conscripts as a regularized function of the state.

On the heels of Saul's errors, Samuel anoints David king (I Sam. 16:1–13). At this point we are told that the Spirit of Yahweh departed from Saul and "an evil spirit sent by Yahweh" filled him with terror (I Sam. 16:14). This evil spirit, it should be noted, is sent by Yahweh and appears precisely at the moment when the Spirit of Yahweh departs from Saul. The evil spirit provoked in Saul excesses of melancholy, alternating with bursts of fury and murderous revolt against David, who (as we shall see) had been entrusted with the task of placating him with music. The errors of Saul thus compounded themselves, with disastrous consequences for Israel.

None of this should lead one to think that this situation represented a radical or irreversible change in the person and function of Saul. On the contrary:

a) Saul remains always and everywhere a sacred person, the anointed of Israel, even in the eyes of the hated David. He must not be physically hurt. One must prostrate oneself before him, an act which, in the biblical text, is expressed by the same verb that designates the adoration of Yahweh (I Sam. 24:9).[18]

b) The departure of the spirit of Yahweh from Saul is anything but irreversible. In a passage that follows those just cited, the Spirit of Yahweh takes possession of the king once again, and in ways similar to those of the first possession near the "hill of Elohim": that is, through an encounter with a group of possessed prophets, this time with Samuel in their midst (I Sam. 19:18–24). The fact that the very same proverb is cited, by way of an etiology, is confirmation of the fact that we are dealing with a *duplicatio*. It is significant that this episode is endowed with a series of details (for example, Saul's nudity) that differentiate it neatly from the other episode. In addition, it is placed by the redactor *after* the incident of the evil spirit and in a phase of total misfortune for Saul.

The diachronic sequence of Saul's possessions is, therefore, as follows:

Spirit of Yahweh	I Sam. 10:10–13
Spirit of Yahweh	I Sam. 11:6–7
Evil spirit	I Sam. 16:14–23
Evil spirit	I Sam. 19:9–11
Spirit of Yahweh	I Sam. 19:18–24

In light of these facts it is reasonable to interpret Saul's possession by the Spirit of Yahweh and by the evil spirit "sent by Yahweh" as a single phenomenon, and in particular to interpret the arrival of the evil spirit as an inconvenient side effect of possession. An indirect confirmation of this interpretation comes from a comparison with documents from classical antiquity. E. R. Dodds has collected evidence showing that the place a divinity occupies in one possessed may be usurped by deceitful inferior demons. Among other such cases, the British scholar refers to one that involves a Delphic Pythia, a priestess of Apollo. Possessed by a demon who had substituted himself for Apollo, she spoke in a hoarse voice, fled from the sanctuary, and died a few days later.[19] In other cases, however, the intrusion was only temporary.[20] In the biblical text, one may note, the specific theology of Yahwism requires that it be Yahweh who sends the evil spirit.[21]

The possession of Saul is, therefore, doubly ambiguous. It is strongly positive in that it makes the king of Israel the receptacle for the divine spirit. But the possession runs counter to a (new) aristocratic ethic insofar as it imposes attitudes that are less than dignified and association with ignoble and disorderly people. Moreover, possession is dangerous because it disrupts one's personal equilibrium. In and of itself, such possession is portrayed as ambivalent, for it opens an entryway even for evil spirits.

David is anointed king by Samuel in his natal Bethlehem and immediately the Spirit of Yahweh descends upon him "from that day forward" (I Sam. 16:13), but one hears no more about this in the rest of the narration. Neither does it occur for any other ruler, so much so that to see the Spirit come down upon the head of a descendent of David one must wait for the "baptism" of Jesus Christ. No other king will have, as did Samuel, a direct contact with the divinity, who thenceforth expresses himself only through prophetic intermediaries or by other canonical means. As for David himself, the biblical text does nothing but provide proof of the degree to which he is master of himself: not least among these proofs is the *simulated* madness that is shown to us at Gath while he is "drooling onto his beard" (I Sam. 21:14) to confuse the Philistines. (According to authors like Lucan such drooling happened spontaneously to a Pythia.) It is difficult to imagine a more striking contrast with the possessed king, Saul.

For the Judges (Samson, Gideon) the possession by the Spirit of Yahweh does not occur in connection with anointing (as it did for the kings), but rather in moments when it was least expected. This possession provoked in them a bellicose fury (perhaps comparable to the *berserk* state of the Germanic warriors). For the possessed, this fury foretold their command in the battles into which they led certain tribes of Israel, and, for the people, it foretold victory over their enemies and oppressors.[22] In Saul's time the descent of the Spirit of Yahweh was the prerogative of the prophets, and was very closely connected with divination, but also, as we have seen, with an extraordinary fury and strength not unlike that of some of the Judges. In the successive books of the Old Testament such phenomena are the prerogative of the (most ancient) prophets, and are linked above all with divination.[23]

2.3. Music and Dance

Saul. As I have indicated, in one case out of three the possession of Saul by the Spirit of Yahweh has a musical origin, in that it is born of an encounter with prophets "preceded by harps, tambourines, flutes anhd lyres," who were "prophesying." This is a feature which falls within the normal typology of ecstatic phenomena and of possession, which are closely associated with music and whirling dance in numerous cultures, from ancient Greece to modern Africa and even, for example, in Sardinia.[24] In particular, as regards the Syro-Palestinian area, the figurative art of the ninth to the eighth centuries B.C.E. already provides evidence of dancers who play instruments similar to those mentioned.[25] Classical literary sources bear witness to ecstatic followers of the Syrian goddess who wandered through the streets of the Roman Empire playing cymbals and flutes, whipping themselves and prophesying.[26]

One component of "prophetic" behavior seems to be nudity: at the sheds near Ramah, Saul "stripped himself of his garments and he, too, remained in the prophetic state in the presence of Samuel; all that day and night he lay naked" (I Sam. 19:24).

David is closely tied with the world of music, not only because he plays the harp, but because, according to the biblical tradition, he is the author of numerous liturgical psalms which were sung in the cultus of Israel.[27] In the narrative under study, David's musical ability is explained precisely in connection with Saul's possession by the evil spirit sent by Yahweh. David's music had the goal, more often than not achieved, of calming the possessed Saul (I Sam. 16:14–23). To a Saul who suffers the music and its charm one can contrast a David who makes the music; to a music which is, so to speak, *intoxicating*, one can contrast a music that *soothes*. The temptation is strong to recall the very Greek contrast between Apollonian and Dionysiac music (and, more technically, between two extremes such as the "Lydian mode" and the "Phrygian mode"). The musical instruments are distributed in the same way (wind and percussion, in addition to stringed instruments, in the case of the prophets; and unaccompanied harp, in the case of David). It is reminiscent of the contrast, for example, between the Dionysiac Marsyas, who plays the double flute, and Apollo with his harp.[28]

The fact that David plays soothing music does not stop him from dancing. On the occasion of the entrance of the ark of Yahweh into Jerusalem we see him dancing nearby to the sounds of instruments of every kind which accompanied it, dressed in a linen *ephod* (II Sam. 6:12–15). The reaction of his wife

Michal, Saul's daughter, is no different from what has been reconstructed as the "popular" reaction toward the "prophesying" of Saul himself. She chastises David: "How the king of Israel has honored himself today, exposing himself to the view of the slave girls of his followers, as a commoner might do!" (II Sam. 6:20). The expression "exposing himself" probably refers to the use of the *ephod*, which in this particular case must have been a very skimpy garment, appropriate for the dance.

The "prophesying" of Saul, who was taken by the Spirit of Yahweh, and this dance have in common a certain disturbing quality, insofar as they are at the same time both "common" and "abnormal" behaviors. But there are some differences between them. David is not presented as one possessed, as is Saul when he is "prophesying"; he is not in the midst of a group of "nobody's children" but he dances, to all appearances, alone; in dancing before the ark of the Lord he performs a quintessentially cultic act; and finally, even if he is accused of exposing himself, he is not naked, as is Saul when he "prophesied," but dressed in an *ephod*, a sacred canonical vestment. In addition, he is not "taken" by this dance, but chooses it. The rest of the story demonstrates that this choice was an entirely positive one, both in his eyes and in those of Yahweh. David, in fact, answers his wife Michal by praising his own actions, and immediately Yahweh acts upon Michal so that she remains childless to the day of her death (II Sam. 6:21–23).

2.4. Sacrifice and Priests

Saul's two gravest errors are cultic ones, or, more precisely speaking, errors pertaining to sacrifice. In one case (I Sam. 13:7–15), the error, which was committed in a moment of grave crisis, consisted in his failure to wait for Samuel, as called for by the prescriptions, and in offering sacrifices to Yahweh before Samuel's arrival. This error cost Saul the eternal preservation of his reign over Israel. In another case (I Sam. 15:7–35), Saul offers in sacrifice part of the booty plundered from the Amalekites, against whom he should have put into effect a ban (*herem*) which implied the destruction of every member of their people and all their goods. This grave sacrilege inspires the wrath of Yahweh and of Samuel, who declares: "The Lord rejects you as king of Israel" (I Sam. 15:26). Both of these errors, and in particular the second, which consists precisely in offering a *sacrifice* that is actually a *sacrilege*, reveal in Saul a ritual clumsiness that borders on the pathetic. He does the right thing in the wrong moment and with the wrong material. He produces effects that are the opposite of what he intends. As opposed to a priest who is schooled in sacred things, he reveals himself to be absurdly ignorant. On the other hand, we see David offering sacrifice only two times. This he does correctly and in exceptional circumstances, as in the transporting of the ark to Jerusalem (II Sam. 6:17–19), and in the raising of a new altar (II Sam. 24:25). Here is a good place to note that the succeeding kings will offer few sacrifices, if any (Solomon in I Kings 8:62–66; I Kings 3:3; 3:15), giving over the task to the priests and/or Levites. It is said of King Uzziyah that, having usurped the sacrificial functions of the chief priest Azariah, by offering incense to Yahweh on the altar of incense, he was afflicted with leprosy and died in isolation (II Chronicles 26:16–23).

On the contrary, Samuel is presented throughout this entire account as a correct sacrificer. As for the Judges, one of them has priestly functions but with some negative overtones. Gideon went so far as to forge an *ephod* and put it in a sanctuary where he served as priest. He claimed that position even for his descendants, although he refused the title of king (Judges 8:22–27).

As for their attitudes toward priests, it is enough to recall the warm welcome and help offered to David by the priests of Yahweh in Nob (where he receives Goliath's sword) (I Sam. 21:2–10). Recall also the impious behavior of Saul, who punished the priests with death, entrusting an Edomite with the task of killing them, when his own Israelite followers refused (I Sam. 22:6–23). A crime similar to this is perhaps the cause of a famine that struck Israel and of which I spoke in section 1.2 above. The need to remove this impurity, which weights on Israel, will transform David into an avenger of the Gibeonites, whose city was the site of a great sanctuary (II Sam. 21:1–14). Solomon will later mention this event when he receives a response about it in a dream (I Kings 3:4–15). All this demonstrates a privileged relationship between the sanctuary and the household of David, on the one hand, and a hostile relationship between it and Saul, on the other.

2.5. Divination and Prophets

Saul, as an upstanding Yahwist and as a king who now has power over his country, expels "mediums and fortune tellers" (I Sam. 28:3), and tries to know the future and the divine will through canonical means; that is, "in dreams or by the *urim* or through prophets" (I Sam. 28:6). This formulation is still extremely vague and things can easily turn topsy-turvy. In fact, Yahweh does not answer him through any of these means. The need to have a response concerning the war with the Philistines, who have already assembled in Shunem on the plain of Jezreel, forces the king to consult the witch of Endor. She, with her magical art, conjures up Samuel, and thus obtains for the king a totally negative response (I Sam. 28:7–25).

The complete lack of communication between Yahweh and Israel by means of the king, caused by the malfunction of the correct means of divination, is one of the most serious outcomes that Saul's misconduct brings upon his people. From it derives the ultimate contradiction (and guilt) of Saul, who is constrained to violate his own laws (and to do it secretly: but even in this he fails!) (I Sam. 28:20–25). He is forced to turn to the abhorrent practices of necromancy, disturbing the eternal rest of Samuel, and to depend on the lower world rather than on the divine for an answer.

Here, paradoxically, he who obtains no response through the prophets is himself a "prophet," and he who has no communication with Yahweh is the very charismatic leader who is so often filled with the Spirit of Yahweh himself. The possession of the king in the story of Saul does not bring anything that is decisively good, and, above all, it does not bring any divine inspiration. At best, it brings the superhuman strength seen above in the episode of the dismembered oxen.[29]

It is also significant that it is Samuel who is evoked in this incident of I Sam. 28. Even in death he remains the necessary intermediary between Saul and the divinity. The king is not able to establish, autonomously and by means of the correct use of the required techniques, a relationship with Yahweh that makes him the right intermediary between Israel and its god.

David. Throughout much of his career, David is followed, not by generic "prophets" or "priests," but by the prophet Nathan and the priest Abiathar, who consults *urim* and *tummim* for him on all important occasions, especially in war. The figure of Nathan is particularly significant for David and for Israel, because it is through him that Yahweh communicates the oracle that promises an eternal reign to the Davidic dynasty (II Sam. 7:1–19). These two characters will reappear, but on different sides of the dynastic dilemma, when King Solomon is anointed and the proper succession of the kingdom is ratified (Abiathar: I Kings 1:19; Nathan: I Kings 1:38).

Samuel, the last of the Judges, was himself a seer, and he is presented as such from the beginning, in a passage that explains the identity of the figures of "seer" and "prophet" stating that the term "seer" is the ancient name of that which is "nowadays" called "prophet" (I Sam. 9:9). His contact with the divine sphere was *direct*, without any intervening technology except (perhaps) for the music used to achieve a state of possession. We have explicit reference to the use of music only for the "prophets" (I Sam. 10:5), who are linked only obscurely to Samuel in the biblical text.[30]

2.6. War, Fasting, Death

The very serious reversals suffered by Saul in war are almost always the effects of the religious mistakes examined above. In addition, Saul is frequently at fault even in the *specific field* of warfare, where he often appears indecisive or even afraid.

Other mistakes are even more specific. Take, for example, the problem of *fasting*. In a great battle in the hill country of Ephraim against the Philistines, Saul "swore a very rash oath that day, putting the people under this ban: 'Cursed be the man who takes food before evening, before I am able to avenge myself on my enemies'" (I Sam. 14:24). His son Jonathan transgresses the oath, gathers some honey, eats it, and to those who chastise him he answers that, if the people had eaten some, the victory over the Philistines would have been greater. Discovered in this transgression, he is condemned to death by his father, but is saved by the people in gratitude for his prowess of the preceding day, when he won a victory for Israel (I Sam. 14:24–30). Saul's oath, then, remains hollow, and is transgressed precisely by the brave warrior who determines the good outcome of the battle. Comparisons with the Iliad[31] clarify that the choice of imposing a fast on the troops or of feeding them is resolved, in the traditional Greek epic, in favor of the second possibility. This highlights a conflict between a solution that we would call religious and a solution that we would call "technical" to a military problem. In this case, Saul is, once again, disproportionately religious.

The refusal of food is a recurrent characteristic of Saul's behavior (see I Sam. 28:20). Focusing on the "possessed" character of Saul and on his trances of musical origin, a historico-religious comparison would call into play phenomena such as ascetic and shamanic fasting, and would lead us to reject psychological interpretations (which would view Saul, for example, as a "mental anorexic"). At this point one must keep in mind that Saul is not a shaman and not even a pure and simple "prophet," but a *king*. As such, he has the obligation toward his people of caring for his own well-being, even his physical condition, since the good fortune and the very life of Israel are tied to it (and not only in a "political" and "natural" sense). In this context, therefore, Saul's fasting can only be seen as negative and is the culminating error in a consistent pattern of errors that weigh on Saul.

Finally, regarding Saul and war, one should recall that he finds there not only numerous defeats, but even his death—an ignominious death, which definitively confirms his failure as a military leader. Mortally wounded during a complete rout, he attempts to flee from the end which he fully understands to be shameful by having himself killed by one of his soldiers. Even this last scene presents a truly chaotic reversal, showing a warrior who uses his weapons against his own king rather than against the enemy (I Sam. 31:1–7). But even this is not enough: the king's corpse is beheaded, the head being taken as a trophy, and his weapons hung in the temple of a foreign god (I Sam. 31:8–10). Finally, even the recovery of Saul's corpse by his friends results in a funerary rite, which, although not given an explicitly negative cast in the biblical passage (I Sam. 31:11–13), passes beyond the strange to something negative in the context of the religious tradition of Israel. This is especially true if the treatment of Saul's body can be likened to death by burning, which was reserved, in the Old Testament, for perpetrators of incest and for those who looted lands that were under a ban. This last sin coincides, perhaps by chance, with the gravest of Saul's sacrificial errors.

David, who dies of old age (I Kings 2:1–10) and always wins in war, is a brave warrior from the time of his duel with Goliath. Above all, he is an excellent military organizer, who, as we have seen, knows how to appoint able leaders.

It is, perhaps, superfluous to recall here that Samuel and the other Judges are the fortunate *military leaders* of spontaneous tribal formations. Their main function is precisely to guide Israelite contingents into war, thus periodically freeing them from the foreign oppression authorized by Yahweh, from time to time, to punish his guilty people.

3. Conclusions

3.1. The State and the Separation of Functions

A common element, indeed, the lowest common denominator, of the oppositions revealed thus far is the contrast between the strongly negative character of Saul and the "correctness" of the Judges (even if it has limits which explain the need for a king) and David. If we consider that Saul is, for the most part, endowed with characteristics that intermediate between those of the Judges and those of David, we may conclude that the king performs so badly precisely because he is neither fish nor fowl. As an unbalanced and transitional figure, Saul can only engender crises that constitute the "crisis of growth" of Israel from the time of the Judges to that of the kings.[32]

What does Saul, who, as we have seen, is clearly a king just like David, have in common with the "tribal" leaders that preceded him? One can answer this question in a summary way: that which makes Saul like the Judges is the multiplicity (and, in this context, the contrariety) of his functions. At one and the same time, he is "prophet," military leader, and sacrificer. These three aspects coexist in the context of his broadest mission as king of Israel, but, as we have seen, they impede that mission in the end. In fact, each of these dimensions becomes its very opposite. On the one hand, the possession that draws him near to the prophets is looked upon poorly by the people, insofar as it runs contrary to "noble" behavior, which should be serious and dignified; and, on the other hand, possession can at times transform itself into an evil intrusion. To his military function one must contrast both his tendency, clearly excessive in some cases, to find "sacred" solutions, and his unstable "character" (both problems traceable to a negative tendency to impose a grid of religious functions). Finally, his role as sacrificer is carried off incorrectly and in a disordered way.

These are no longer times in which a tribal structure (classless, we would say) allowed "Judges" to assume command (for limited periods), Judges who were simultaneously possessed seers, administrators of the law, ritual experts, and leaders in war. Such an aggregate of functions, as the book of Judges shows, gave rise to errors and abuses in its day, but, in that different context, was considered altogether normal. Now this aggregate of functions was no longer adapted to the needs of a people who were calling loudly for a king.

Given the above premise, it is not surprising to observe that, while Saul *is* prophet, sacrificer, and military leader at the same time, David, on the other hand, in preserving the supreme power of Israel, *has* a prophet (Nathan), a priest (Abiathar), and a leader of his army (Joab). This diversification of specialized functions well suits this king. In contrast to David, Saul is never presented as an organizer (but rather, as unruly and "disorganized"). But David gives himself over entirely (except for war) to the political organization of Israel in a new form, that of a state. Note that this activity is attributed to David by Saul (with a clearly negative cast) even during the period of exile. Saul ad-

dresses the men of Benjamin asking if David, whom they are accused of protecting, has promised them fields and vineyards, or positions of prestige in the
military hierarchy (I Sam. 22:7), since fields and vineyards, Samuel had asserted (I Sam. 8:14), are taken by a king from his people and given to his ministers. A *failure* of David demonstrates how such an undertaking might be reli-
giously revolutionary: he is forced to interrupt the attempted census in order to
confront and stave off the pestilence brought on by such a clearly blasphe-
mous measure (II Sam. 24). The process of organizing a society into a state
has, therefore, in the biblical text we have examined, a lower limit, expressed
in the figure of Saul, but also an upper limit that cannot be surpassed, indicated by the census attempted by David and by its disastrous consequences.

David's "moderation," that is, his knowing when to stop, is even attested to
by his behavior before the ark of Yahweh. We have seen above the points of
similarity and contrast between David's attitude and the "prophetic" attitude of
Saul. Here the mediation is not directly between "tribal" religiosity and the
exigencies of the new state organization of Israel, but rather between the ritual
behavior imposed by an ancient tradition (now "popular" to the point of being
vulgar?) and the norms of a new ethic, which highly values controlled and dignified behavior. David is distant from these "prophetic" attitudes of Saul,
whose negative aspects, as we have seen, he is even able to cure. He is equally
resolute in confronting extreme rationalization which, in the second book of
Samuel, is expressed through the reaction of Michal to the dancing king. The
punishment of Michal, stricken by Yahweh with barrenness, can be compared
to the fate of Saul, who left not one surviving descendent in Israel, with the exception of the lame Meribbaal.

The character of organizer of the state microcosm, which David assumes in
this view, is made extremely clear by the internal organization of the final part
of the text under examination. In fact, chapters seven and eight of the second
book of Samuel contain: (1) The prophecy of Nathan concerning the eternal
reign of the household of David (the "prophetic" functions are performed,
regularly, and with positive outcomes, by the prophet *of* David who has heard
the word of Yahweh directly) and the prayer of David; (2) the victorious wars of
David against the Philistines, the Moabites, and the Arameans of various
cities, followed by a list of the peoples subjugated, with mention of the prefects
set over them; (3) the formula that so clearly defines the royal functions of
David: "David reigned over all Israel, judging and administering justice to all
his people" (II Sam. 8:15). It is immediately followed by (4) an explicit statement of the separation and the coordination of the various politico-religious
functions: "Joab, son of Zeruiah, was in command of the army. Jehoshaphat,
son of Ahilud, was chancellor. Zadok, son of Ahitub, and Ahimelech, son of
Abiathar, were priests. Shawsha was scribe. Benaiah, son of Jehoiada, was in
command of the Cherethites and Pelethites. And David's sons were priests"[33]
(II Sam. 8:16–18).

Here the royal function is identified with the administration of justice and
with the conduct of war (by means of a commander of the army). The priestly

and "prophetic" functions are given over to the respective specialized personnel linked to the king. The step from here to the great reign of Solomon,
which was heavily bureaucratized, is not so large. In the *beginning* of his reign,
in fact, Solomon is consecrated in the presence of a significant group of "faithful," including the *prophet* Nathan, the *priest* Zadok, the warrior Benaiah, a
member of the "thirty warriors" of David, and a group of foreign mercenaries.
Nevertheless what a distance there is between the divine "wisdom" of that
powerful solver of riddles and the nakedness of the prophesying Saul, filled
with the spirit of Yahweh!

3.2. The Integration of Manía in Plato

The division of functions and their organization under the direction of a centralized power; the complex articulation of society into classes and functional
sectors; the creation of a team of specialists centered on the palace, the seat of
royal power: this is the new *state* framework that issues, as a superior synthesis,
from the struggle between the "old" and the "new" models of kingship,
between David and Saul. Within this framework, as we have seen, the
"prophetic" function, based on divine possession, can no longer maintain its
ancient centrality, which made of it, in "tribal" society, the mark and guarantee of power. Now it must serve the rational organization of the state and, in
this instance, the monarchy (that is, the power concentrated in the palace and
the classes that hold that power). Regarding the normalization of prophetic
possession in Israel, as treated in the biblical narrative concerning the struggle
between Saul and David, it will help to examine an analogous rationalization
from another ancient culture. This rationalization of an ideal state was proposed in the thought of Plato where he treated the relationship between "mantic" function (and "madness") and state power.

In his 1974 study, L. Brisson[34] examines Plato's theory of the irrational activity of the human soul, demonstrating how Plato distinguishes four types of
"madness" (*manía*) whose value is not always totally negative, but may result
in (limited) beneficial effects. These four sorts of madness are mantic, teles-
thetic, poetic, and erotic. To the mantic type of madness belongs that "unruli-
ness" that is characteristic of fortune-tellers and diviners; and, according to the
early Plato, it is to this category of psychic activity that political "wisdom" is as-
signed. In fact, politicians owe their competence not to reason, of which, apparently, they make no use, but to divine intervention. Politicians, who are in
the throes of possession and enthusiasm, make decisions under the influence
of inspiration and divine intervention. They then impose these decisions without being able to give any reasonable account for them.[35]

In a thinker like Plato such a series of considerations amounts to a criticism
of a thoroughly negative situation. In fact, in the more mature and construc-
tive part of his works, and, in particular, in texts such as the Republic, the
Laws, and especially the Phaedrus,[36] the philosopher postulates an optimal
state, ruled by a philosopher king, which is capable of integrating in itself

the various forms of psychic (and "technical") activity, even activity identifi-able as *manía*. In a similar context, divination, with its aspects of *manía*, be-comes, in Brisson's words, "un art adjuvant de la royauté," and the *Laws* place the mantic function within the complex organization of the state, assigning to it specialized personnel. And so, even on the political level, Platonic ration-ality recuperates "l'irrationnel d'origine divine"[37] (but views it as an imperfect and auxiliary function).

From the verification of a point of fact (political leaders are not "rational" but "possessed"), Plato passes to an optative formulation (the state leaders should be philosophers, that is, "rational" and employ mantic *manía* as a form of "auxiliary knowledge," enfolding its functions within the framework of state order). The two formulations that are so opposed are, nevertheless, quite simi-lar to those we have seen *succeeding one another* in chronological order, and presented as equally "real" in the books of Samuel. This comparison should inspire caution in discussing the "historicity" of the biblical events. It is not ab-surd to think that the redactors of the passages under study intend to commu-nicate, in narrative form, something analogous to what Plato communicates in discursive and dialectical form. Let us not forget that the narrative form is the "most ancient form" of ideological expression, as is attested by primitive mythologies. Plato himself does not disdain this form of expression (recall the myths of Er and of the cave), but uses it alongside the discursive-dialogical form. An observation of this kind would not in the least deny every form of his-toricity (in the narrow and banal sense of the term) to the biblical narrative, but would only deny *that type* of historicity that attempts to attribute Saul's failure to his mental disequilibrium, thus losing sight of the true value, indeed "historical," of the biblical text as the conveyor of an ideology.

3.3. The "Prophetic" Function

Moreover, it is a historical given that the "prophetic" function is "un art adju-vant de la royauté." We are assured of this for the ancient Near East, by the texts of Mari (eighteenth century B.C.E.)[38] and the account of Wen Amun, which depicts the king of Byblos availing himself of the suggestions of one of his subjects, suddenly fallen into a state of possession (eleventh century?);[39] and, for the classical world, the cases of Megistias in the retinue of King Leonidas,[40] Abas in the retinue of Lysander,[41] and Marius, assisted in war by the Syrian "prophetess" Mara.[42]

In the culture of Israel the value of such a phenomenon lies in the fact, seen above, that *prophetic behavior* (both in connection with possession and with the supernatural capacities related to it) *was* (in a "tribal" phase still very much alive in national "memory") the *guarantee of power and of command* in and of itself. The new systematizing of "prophetic" possession as an auxiliary function is, therefore, also its *degradation*, and was probably accomplished by dint of force. In this way, a religious formation, at one time hegemonic but later "reconfigured" from on high, acquires an ideological value that grounds the transformation of that type of religiosity into a "popularized" and, in a certain sense, alternative, reality. In addition, the attitude of the spectators before the "prophesying" Saul (and of Michal before the dancing David) can be explained only as a reaction to an implicit social decree which, ex post facto, represented such behaviors as chaotic, undignified and more appropriate to a "no account" whose father is unknown. This decree, in its turn, presupposes the division of Israelite society into social classes.

It is not surprising to observe that, throughout the history of Israel, it is precisely the prophets, unfettered more and more from relations of dependence on the royal court, who play a "dialectical" role, rather than an "integrated" one, such as that performed by Nathan (who however, it should be remembered, judged the sins of David!). They defended the rights of the poor and the tradition of Yahwism, both of which were often betrayed in the corrupt atmosphere of the rapacious court, which inclined to the cultic practices of "foreign peoples" (practices which were more in keeping with a state order of society than with an archaic monolatry). This dialectical role will enable them, under direct orders from Yahweh, actually to "make" new kings by opposing them to their predecessors, just as Samuel opposed David to Saul.[43]

The Pentateuch does not name the prophets as such, except in Deuteronomy (which is also the only book of the Pentateuch to mention the king of Israel). Chapter 18 of Deuteronomy, which teaches how to distinguish true from false prophets, attributes the following words to Moses: "A prophet *like me* will Yahweh, your God, raise up for you from among your kinsmen" (Deuteronomy 18:15). The prophets come, therefore, from "the people" (is this the "other side of the coin" in the criticism of Saul, who was both "noble" and "prophet"?) and not, for example, "from Levi," like the priests, or "from David," like the kings. The prophets are, therefore, "like Moses," that is, like the charismatic leader of old, who enjoyed a *direct* relationship with the deity. This same Moses we find in the New Testament, as a mark of continuity, alongside Elijah and Jesus. As a healer and a seer from the countryside of Galilee, Jesus reminds the powerful of Jerusalem of their wickedness toward the prophets, and he acts through the power of the Spirit, which descended on him as it did on Saul. The continuity of the "prophetic function," that true guarantor of Yahwism, did not pass away.[44]

NOTES

1. Concerning this period, see J. A. Soggin, *Das Königtum in Israel: Ursprung, Spannungen, Entwicklung* (Berlin, 1967); G. Buccellati, *Cities and Nations of Ancient Syria* (Rome, 1967); O. Eissfeldt, *The Hebrew Kingdom*, CAH II, 34 (Cambridge, 1965), pp. 537–587, in addition to the fundamental contribution of A. Alt, *Die Staatenbildung der Israeliten in Palästina* (Leipzig, 1930), republished in A. Alt, *Kleine Schriften für die Geschichte des Volkes Israels* II (Munich, 1953), pp. 1–65.

2. Concerning this approach to the text of the ancient Near East see the stimu-

lating contribution of M. Liverani, *Memorandum on the Approach to Historio-graphic Texts* 1: Orientalia 42 (1973) (Gelb Volume), pp. 178–194.

3. I will mention here only two examples among many, referring to the works by two excellent scholars of the Old Testament: J. Bright, *A History of Israel* (London, 1972), pp. 186–187 ("Saul was always of volatile temperament capable of frenzies of excitement [chs. 10:9–13; 11:6 f.]; it appears that as the pressure was put on him he became increasingly disturbed in mind, swinging like a pendulum between moments of lucidity and black moods in which, incapable of intelligent action, he indulged in behavior calculated to alienate even the closest to him. Before the end Saul was probably no longer quite sane"); and J. A. Soggin, *Introduzione all'Antico Testamento* (Brescia, 1974), p. 268 ("Da questa sordità spirituale [di Saul] sorge un conflitto interiore che porta il protagonista a forme patologiche di diffidenza, ipocondria e mania di persecuzione, che avrebbero condotto chi era stato [e restò sino alla fine] un cavaliere senza macchia e senza paura all'autodistruzione se la morte gloriosa sul campo di battaglia non l'avesse, pietosamente si potrebbe quasi dire, liberato").

4. Concerning the problem of the relationship between Yahwism and the monarchy in Israel see the exhaustive treatment of G. Fohrer, *Geschichte der Israelitische Religion* (Berlin, 1968), pp. 122–222 (with bibliography). On the peculiar character of the royalty in Israel see the interesting "epilogue" of H. Frankfort, *Kingship and the Gods* (Chicago, 1948), pp. 337–344. The only real king in Israel is Yahweh: E. Lipiński, *La Royauté de Yahwé dans la poésie et le culte de l'ancien Israel* (Brussels, 1965). The earthly monarchy is nonetheless a sacred institution, comparable to that in Mesopotamia: J. De Fraine, *L'Aspect religieux de la Royauté Israélite, L'Institution Monarchique dans l'Ancien Testament et dans les Textes Mésopotamiens* (Rome, 1954), because the king is chosen by the divinity: ibid., pp. 168–213, and R. De Vaux, *Le Roi d'Israel, vassal de Yahwé: Mélanges E. Tisserant*, I (1964), pp. 119–131. On the other hand, A. Lods accentuates the "foreign" character of certain aspects of the monarchy in Israel in his "La divinisation du roi dans l'Orient méditerranéen et ses repercussions dans l'ancien Israel," *Revue d'Histoire et de Philosophie Religieuses* 10 (1930), pp. 209–221. J. A. Soggin insists on the religious "syncretism" of the courts of Israel in "Der offiziel geförderte Synkretismus in Israel während des 10. Jahrhunderts," *Zeitschrift für die Alttestamentliche Wissenschaft*, 78 (1966), pp. 179–204.

5. See the dated work of J. W. Flight, "The Nomadic *Idea and Ideal* in the Old Testament," *Journal of Biblical Literature* 42 (1923), pp. 158–226. For a critical recontextualization of the "nomadic ideal" through a revision of an important passage see F. S. Frick, "The Rechabites Reconsidered," *Journal of Biblical Literature* 90 (1971), pp. 279–287. On "tribal" society in Israel and on its vestiges in the monarchic period, H. Schaeffer, *Hebrew Tribal Economy and the Jubilee, as Illustrated in Semitic and Indo-European Village Communities* (Leipzig, 1922), is still of great interest.

6. For criticism concerning the biblical narrative about the origins of the monarchy see in particular F. Langlamet, "Les récits de l'institution de la royauté (I Sam. VII–XII)," *Revue Biblique* 77 (1970), pp. 162–200; R. E. Clements, "The Deuteronomistic Interpretation of the Founding of the Monarchy in I Sam. VIII," *Vetus Testamentum* 24 (1974), pp. 398–410, N. H. Nübel, *Davids Aufstieg in der frühe israelitischen Geschichtsschreibung* (Bonn, 1959).

7. Concerning such phenomena see, for example, E. Neufeldt, "The Emer-

gence of Royal-Urban Society in Ancient Israel," *Hebrew Union College Annual* 31 (1960), pp. 31–53, and the earlier article by A. Causse, "La crise de la solidarité de la famille et du clan dans l'ancien Israel," *Revue d'Histoire et de Philosophie Religieuses* 10 (1930), pp. 24–60.

8. Opposed to an antimonarchic reading of the passage was J. De Fraine, *L'aspect religieux de la Royauté Israélite*, pp. 108–112, and more recently B. C. Birch, "The Choosing of Saul at Mizpah," *Catholic Biblical Quarterly* 37 (1975), pp. 447–457, with the bibliography there cited. In support of the "dialectical," as opposed to the antimonarchic, character of the episode recall the identical situation of the frogs in the fable of Aesop and Phaedrus: the little creatures insist that Zeus provide them a king, not a do-nothing king (as was the stick thrown initially from the sky into the swamp), but an *active* king. When at last the serpent who had been sent to rule over them by Zeus takes to devouring them, they complain to the king of the gods, but in vain. According to Phaedrus, the fable was narrated by Aesop, in a polemical fashion, to those who were late in joining the opposition to the tyrant Peisistratus: "hoc sustinete," proclaims the conclusive injunction, "maius ne veniat, malum." In fact: "quia noluistis vestrum ferre bonum malum perferte." Which is equivalent to saying: you have brought all this on your own heads and therefore cannot complain. Finally, concerning this passage, see I. Mendelssohn, "Samuel's Denunciation of Kingship in the Light of Accadian Documents from Ugarit," *Bulletin of the American Schools of Oriental Research* 143 (1956), pp. 17–22.

9. Reference is made here to the myths of Etana: Langdon, *Babyloniaca*, 12 (1931), pls. 1–14; see also ANET, p. 114.

10. Hesiod, *Erga* vv. 38–39. The *basileis* in this context are "judges," not "kings."

11. D. Sabbatucci, "Demitizzazione nell'antica Roma," *Studi e Materiali di Storia delle Religioni* 41 (n.s. 1) (1972), pp. 539–589.

12. Ibid., pp. 549–559.

13. A. Alt, *Die Staatenbildung der Israeliten in Palästina* (Leipzig, 1930), reprinted in A. Alt, *Kleine Schriften für die Geschichte des Volkes Israels* (Munich, 1953), pp. 1–65, and in particular pp. 3, 10, 24.

14. After the studies of G. Buccellati, it is doubtful whether, in the biblical text, Saul is the right and proper king of an embryonic state. See G. Buccellati, "Da Saul a David, Le origini della monarchia israelitica alla luce della storiografia contemporanea," *Bibbia e Oriente* I (1959), pp. 99–128.

15. See II Kings 9:11; Hosea 9:7; Jeremiah 29:26, and the illuminating pages in Y. Kaufmann, *The Religion of Israel from Its Beginning to the Babylonian Exile* (Chicago, 1960, pp. 275–277). Fundamentally important to this day is H. Gunkel, *Die Propheten* (Göttingen, 1917), chapter 2.

16. V. H. W. Hertzberg, *Die Samuelbücher* (*Das Alte Testament Deutsch* 10) (Göttingen, 1960), pp. 53–57. For a different reading see J. G. Williams, "The Prophetic 'Father': A Brief Explanation of the Term 'Sons of the Prophets,'" *Journal of Biblical Literature* 85 (1966), pp. 344–349.

17. Dance and nudity (around the golden calf): Exodus 32:19–25. Perhaps even the prohibition against sweating, imposed on the Levites, should be understood in this sense (Ezekiel 44:17–19): see E. A. S. Butterworth, *The Tree at the Navel of the Earth* (Berlin, 1970), pp. 76–77.

18. On the presumed "divinity" of the king see J. De Fraine, *L'Aspect Religieux*

de la Royauté Israélite (Rome, 1954), pp. 276–284. On the inviolability of Saul and, in general, of the king, see ibid., pp. 196–197.

19. E. R. Dodds, "Supernormal Phenomena in Classical Antiquity," *Proceedings of the Society for Psychical Research* 55 (1971), now reprinted in Dodds, *The Ancient Concept of Progress and Other Essays on Greek Literature and Belief*, pp. 201–202. For the episode of the Pythia see p. 197.

20. Ibid., p. 203, where Dodds cites Synesius, *de insomn* 142 A (PG LXVI 1300) and Iamblichus, *de mysteriis* 3.31.

21. Thus, it is Yahweh who sends the deceitful and the "false" spirit. Concerning this problem see J. Hempel, *Vom irrenden Glauben* (1930) = *Apoxysmata* (Berlin, 1961), pp. 174–197; G. Quell, *Wahre und falsche Propheten*, Gütersloh (1952); E. Jacob, "Quelques remarques sur les faux Prophètes," *Theologische Zeitschrift* 13 (1957), pp. 479–486.

22. Othniel (Judg. 3:9); Gideon (Judg. 6:34); Samson (Judg. 13:26; 14:6; 14:19; 15:14).

23. On the spontaneous possession of the prophet, the following are particularly illuminating: Numbers 11:16–25; Amos 3:8.

24. An important contribution to the study of possession in the Mediterranean, both ancient and modern, is E. de Martino, *La Terra del Rimorso, Contributo a una storia religiosa del Sud* (Milan, 1961) (expecially chapters 1–7 of Part 2, which are given over to historico-religious comparisons). Concerning Afro-American culture see A. Métraux, *Le Vaudou Haïtien* (Paris, 1958). Concerning modern Sardinia see C. Gallini, *I Rituali dell'Argia* (Bari, 1967). Fundamental to the study of Dionysiac possession in Greek culture is still H. Jeanmaire, *Dionysos, Histoire du culte de Bacchus* (Paris, 1951).

25. See H. Frankfort, *The Art and Architecture of the Ancient Orient* (Harmondsworth, 1963), table 167 B and pp. 191–195.

26. Particularly significant sources are (pseudo) Lucian, *De Dea Syra*, and Apuleius, *Metamorph.* VIII, 27–28.

27. Concerning David and music see R. North, "The Cain Music," *Journal of Biblical Literature* 83 (1964), pp. 373–389.

28. See E. A. Pillmon, *Musical Thought in Ancient Greece* (New York, 1964), passim, and A. Sendrey, *Music in the Social and Religious Life of Antiquity* (Rutherford, 1974), pp. 282–290, 300–302.

29. Dionysiac possession in Greece is "nondivinatory" par excellence. H. Jeanmaire, *Dionysos*, pp. 193–195, contrasts it with the divinatory *manìa* of Apollinism. In the context of Greek polytheism, Dionysian religiosity has an autonomous and highly significant field of action that is missing completely from the nondivinatory *manìa* in the religion of Israel.

30. R. Press, "Der Prophet Samuel," *Zeitschrift für die Alttestamentliche Wissenschaft* 56 (1938), pp. 177–225; W. F. Albright, *Samuel and the Beginnings of the Prophetic Movements in Israel*, The Goldenson Lecture for 1961, Hebrew Union College Press, Cincinnati; M. Newman, *The Prophetic Call of Samuel: Israel's Prophetic Heritage, Essays in Honor of James Muilenburg* (New York, 1962), pp. 86–97. Samuel as the last of the Judges: J. Bright, *A History of Israel* (London, 1972), pp. 181–182. Again concerning the figure of Samuel: A. Weiser, *Samuel* (Göttingen, 1962); H. Wildberger, "Samuel und die Entstehung des israelitischen Kònigtums," *Theologische Zeitschrift* 13 (1957), pp. 442–462; J. L. McKenzie, "The Four Samuels," *Biblical Research* 7 (1962), pp. 3–13. These three works just men-

tioned attempt, in different ways, a "global" interpretation of the figure of Samuel. Still interesting but superseded in part is W. A. Irwin, "Samuel and the Rise of the Monarchy," *American Journal of Semitic Languages* 58 (1941), pp. 113–128.

31. P. Roussel, "Le jeûne funéraire dans l'Iliade," *Revue de l'Histoire des Religions* 66 (1912), pp. 171–182.

32. The "intermediary" character of Saul, placed, historically and "typologically" halfway between "judgeship" and kingship, has already been amply brought to light but, as far as I know, not so much from the point of view of functional polyvalence but as regards the "charismatic" or "institutional" character of his office. See J. A. Soggin, "Charisma und Institution in Königtum Saul," *Zeitschrift für die Alttestamentliche Wissenschaft* 75 (1963), pp. 54–65; for a different position on this problem, W. Beyerlin, "Das Königscharisma bei Saul," *Zeitschrift für die Alttestamentliche Wissenschaft* 73 (1961), pp. 186–201. But the entire problem of the contrast between "charisma" and institution, which results from a misapplication of Weberian formulations concerning "charismatic" power, is a misunderstanding: in fact it should be clear from the studies cited in note 2 that in Israel kingship is no less "charismatic" than "judgeship." If anything, the *forms* in which charismatic investiture are verified and manifested differ: direct possession or direct "calling" for the Judges, consecration (anointing) by a prophet or priest for the Kings. On the "intermediary" character of Saul see also F. Langlamet, "Les Récits de l'Institution de la Royauté (I Sam. 7–12)," *Revue Biblique* 77 (1970), pp. 161–200.

33. See, however, G. J. Wenham, "Were David's Sons Priests?" *Zeitschrift für die Alttestamentliche Wissenschaft* 87 (1975), pp. 79–82, who proposes the leading *sknjm* (meaning functionaries, administrators of kingly power) rather than *khnjm*.

34. L. Brisson, "Du bon usage du dérèglement," in Jean-Pierre Vernant et al., *Divination et rationalité* (Paris, 1974), pp. 220–248.

35. Ibid., pp. 228–229, where he cites various passages from the *Meno*.

36. Ibid., pp. 228–234: an evolution of platonic thought has been identified which, especially in the Phaedrus, places the diviner (even the diviner who is driven by mantic madness) in the third social class, well below the superior class represented by the philosopher and the king.

37. Ibid., pp. 246–247.

38. F. Ellermeier, *Prophetie in Mari und Israel* (Herzberg, 1968); H. B. Huffmon, "Prophecy in the Mari Letters," *Biblical Archaeologist* 31 (1968), pp. 102–124; W. L. Moran, "New Evidence from Mari on the History of Prophecy," *Biblica* 50 (1969), pp. 15–56.

39. H. Gardiner, *Late Egyptian Stories* (= *Biblioteca Aegyptiaca I*) (Bruxelles, 1932), pp. 61–76; E. Bresciani, *Letteratura e poesia dell'Antico Egitto* (Turin, 1969), pp. 508–515; especially p. 510.

40. Herodot. VII 219, 221, 228.

41. Paus. X 9, 7.

42. See C. Gallini, *Protesta e integrazione nella Roma antica*, Bari (1970), p. 126 (Plut. C. Mar. XVII 1).

43. Recall the case of Elijah and Elisha. On the social function of the prophet: H. Donner, "Die soziale Botschaft der Propheten in Lichte der gesellschaftlichen Ordnung in Israel," *Oriens Antiquus* 2 (1963), pp. 1–30; K. Koch, "Die Entstehung der Sozialen Kritik bei den Propheten," *Festschrift G. von Rad* (Munich, 1971), pp. 236–257; G. Wanke, "Zur Grundlage und Absicht prophetischer Sozialkritik,"

Kerygma und Dogma 18 (1972), pp. 2–17; and regarding the critique of the monarchy, H. W. Schmidt, "Kritik am Königtum," in H. W. Wolff, ed., *Probleme biblischen Theologie, Festschrift G. von Rad* (Munich, 1971), pp. 410–441.

44. See N. W. Porteous, "The Prophets and the Problem of Continuity," *Israel's Prophetic Heritage: Essays in Honor of J. Muilenburg* (New York, 1962), pp. 11–26.

6

SPECIALISTS OF THE SUPERNATURAL
IN THE HEBREW BIBLE

1. The Three Models

In the portion of the Hebrew Bible describing the pre-exilic period the text presents three distinct social models. To each model there corresponds a precise typology of relations between power and techniques of the supernatural. These models are not perfectly consistent, either internally or in their application in various passages of the biblical text. These inconsistencies can be attributed to discrepancies among the sources and to the re-editing that occurred throughout the centuries of the formation of the texts. To complicate matters further, various redactional hands emphasized one or another point from time to time.

Nevertheless, the models are not merely the fruit of a modern reading. In fact, throughout the history of the redaction of these biblical texts, there perdures a fundamentally unitary and coherent attitude among the tradents and redactors precisely in the identification and description of the three models, each of which shapes a part of the narrative of the Hebrew Bible. In order to describe these models, as I will attempt to do, one cannot simply extract some coherent system from the texts, as seen from a modern point of view, however useful such an enterprise might be. The description must also identify with precision that which is formulated explicitly and coherently in the text, even if not in a fully systematic way.

I will call the first model "patriarchal." It is contained in the second part of the book of Genesis, and is the easiest model to describe, for it presents a somewhat simplified picture. It aims to gather and present in a coherent way the exploits of the mythic progenitors Abraham, Isaac, and Jacob, in order to establish the distinctive characteristics of Israel, the nation descended from Jacob, the last in this series, who also bore the name Israel. Given that the characteristics of the nation include its relations with neighboring peoples, these also appear in the exploits and are represented by eponymous ancestors or prototypical characters. The mothers of all these characters are important because they differentiate the heads of distinct lineages, above all in the case of the sons of Jacob. Though sons of the same father, they must be distinguished because from them spring different tribes.

This is the patriarchal framework: few personalities, family-based organization, and many relocations. The family-based organization is the only one that interests the narrators of the mythic genealogies and the only one possible, given that the tribes do not yet exist—these will consist of the families of the sons of Jacob. The many relocations were less the product of nomadic or semi-nomadic life (as many think), than of the need to connect a small set of ancestors with many places.[1]

I will call the second model the tribal model. It is contained in the books of Exodus, Joshua, and Judges. It concerns the internal differentiations of the people of Israel, that is, the tribes. Taken together, the tribes are the people of Israel, and this is presented as a given, in order to found Israel. The origin of this situation is recounted in a tale that includes the arrival of the tribes (reflecting the common assumption in antiquity that various ethnic groups came from abroad), and their formal unification through solemn treaties (which modern historians have interpreted uncritically as the foundation of the so-called league of twelve tribes). In addition, the reciprocal relations among the tribes are described in the smallest detail, from the exchange of brides to open hostility. Finally, it is told how the tribes, both separately or together, fought against the non-Israelites. The workings of tribal or intertribal institutions are demonstrated in these narratives.[2]

The third model is that of the state monarchy. The origins of the monarchic state are narrated, also with foundational intent, in the books of Samuel. And this gives shape to the only texts describing events that we would call historical, in the final parts of the books of Kings and of the books of Chronicles. This model consists in the more or less successful superimposition of a palace and its administration on a tribal model. The tribal model seems to be overshadowed especially in the books of Kings and in the Chronicles, due to the character of the texts, but it never ceases to have an underlying influence. The palace and king have a particular relationship with the underlying national-tribal structure. The monarchy of Israel is of the type described by Giorgio Buccellati[3] in a famous book, as a "National Monarchy," and opposed by that author to monarchies based on purely dynastic criteria or on the raw power of the palace.

The biblical text presents the three models as occurring diachronically. As a result, nearly all modern scholars have mistaken the three models for three phases of evolution through which the ancient Israelites supposedly passed. Therefore, they speak of a period, a society, and a religiosity which are either patriarchal, tribal, or monarchic. This view runs up immediately against the fact that the historical and archaeological documentation of the ancient Near East and of Palestine in particular in no way corresponds to such an interpretation. In reality, societies of the pure patriarchal type (first model) or purely tribal societies (second model) had ceased to exist in Palestine in particular and in the ancient Near East in general, by at least the third millennium B.C.E. The state and the monarchy were everywhere. In the lower ranks of society, the producers (agriculturalists and so called seminomadic pastoralists—that is, herdsmen given to transhumance) were variously organized in families, in villages, and possibly in tribes. The three models of the biblical text were three real models that coexisted in the Palestine of the Iron Age. In mythic form, the Bible offers grounds for these models, narrating respectively the genealogies of the ancestors of the people (that is, events featuring the families), the adventures of the tribal heroes, and the origins of the national monarchy.

In this sense, the Patriarchal Age, the Conquest, and the Period of the Judges never existed as such. Rather, patriarchal families, tribes, and the monarchic state all coexisted in the first half of the first millennium.[4] This must be kept in mind in order to examine the ways in which each of the models articulates relationships between power and techniques (and specialists) of the supernatural.

2. The Patriarchal Model

From the point of view of the techniques of the supernatural, the patriarchal model possesses a structure that is disconcerting in its simplicity. This model allows for no religious specialists, with the exception, perhaps, of Joseph. Even in this exceptional case, one must take note of a significant fact: Joseph exercises his function as a specialist and his gift as interpreter of dreams in a royal palace (a foreign palace, naturally, because the Hebrews "still" had neither tribes nor king, only ancestors). Within his own patriarchal family, Joseph remains only a "dreamer." Relations with the supernatural are the responsibility of adult males, who make autonomous and sovereign decisions regarding the livestock, the family tomb, the children, and the idols called *teraphim*. (Perhaps one can find a trace of a "feminine" sacred sphere in the mandrakes of Leah and Rachel [Genesis 30].) Then again, the auxiliary function of the young men (*ne' arim*) in the practice of bloody sacrifice has initiatory value, as does their auxiliary function in war within the other two models.[5]

Sacrifice is the essential sacred function exercised by the patriarchs. This is animal sacrifice, which, as in Greek myth, can take the form of hospitality offered to a deity or deities. In the case of Abraham and Isaac, it is human sacrifice—the sacrifice of the only son, with the later substitution of a ram for the human victim initially required by the deity. Power, sacred and otherwise, devolves on adult males. However, three vehicles of sacred power belong only to certain adult males and not to others, and, thereby, guarantee and sanction (or, better, formalize) the greater power of certain adult males compared to others. These three vehicles are: (1) the blessing (*berakah*) given by the senior adult male; (2) the privileged relationship with the god of the fathers; (3) the possession of the family figurines called *teraphim*. The only information we have regarding the *teraphim* concerns those associated with Laban, Jacob's maternal uncle and father-in-law, which were stolen by his daughter, Rachel, unbeknownst to Jacob. We do know, however, that the blessing and the privileged relationship with the god of the fathers were closely linked, and that the *berakah* went normally to the first-born son. As often happens in the narrative traditions, however, the exception becomes the rule throughout the accounts of Genesis: the blessing and the privileged relationship with the deity falls to the last-born son.

The attainment of these three vehicles of special sacred power is of great importance in the accounts of Genesis. It is not to be separated from the attainment of what, in modern terms, we might call material goods. For example, the story tells how Jacob-Israel came to acquire much livestock, gold and silver, more wives and concubines, many children, the birthright, the paternal blessing, the privileged relationship with the god of Beth-El (identified with the god of the fathers), the blessing of an anonymous supernatural being at the ford of the Yabbok, a new name, the *teraphim* of his maternal uncle, and, finally, the land of Canaan rather than that of Edom. Jacob is identified with Israel, just as the god of his fathers is identified with Yahweh-Elohim.

The tale of the attainment of such powers on the part of the Abraham-Isaac-Jacob lineage is thus the mythic form of the story of the origins of Israel and of its relationship with the national god.[6] The model at work here implies a relationship between the patriarch and the god of the fathers, whereas the function of the model is to found the relationship between Israel and Yahweh. The discrepancy between the model and the function should not be explained by the greater antiquity of the patriarchal model (and the accounts that describe it). Rather, it can be explained simply as the result of a logical but synchronic disjunction. The values and the sacred practices of the ancient Israelite family group (that is, of the model) did not completely tally with the values and practices that were a function of the foundation stories. That is, they did not tally completely with the reality of the people and their god Yahweh. Some of these discrepancies and contradictions may be credited to the need to overcome the disjunction. On the other hand, the very reappearance of elements from the "patriarchal" model within the other models confirms that the "patriarchal" model was reflecting a reality consonant with those reflected by the other two models. Consider, as examples, the *teraphim* of David in I Samuel 19:11–17, the similarities between the Jacob-Laban relationship and the David-Saul relationship, the sacrifice of children repeatedly presented even outside of Genesis.

3. The Tribal Model

The tribal model presents differentiation and specialization. First of all, there is territorial specialization. Within the nebulous unity of Canaan, certain sacred places emerged through the work of the patriarchs whereas other sacred places were founded in the narrative of the Conquest. In addition, there are specializations within the national body, where certain groups of cult adepts appear, which were apparently understood as tribal-clan groups or ethnic groups. These groups can be classified in what Weber[7] called the category of *Gastvölker*. The Hebrew Bible employs the term *gerim* for the same category. These are groups without their own territories, "guests" of the various territorial tribes, and tied to the exercise of the cult in stationary sanctuaries (as in the book of Judges) or mobile sanctuaries (as in the books of Exodus, Joshua, and so on).

a) In the first place are the Levites. Scholars argue in vain about the existence of an original nonpriestly Levitic tribe.[8] What is clear, however, is that the Levites were a caste of priests, spread throughout the national territory. They carried out sacred functions for cities, sanctuaries, and tribes.[9] The Levites can be considered a "tribe" if by tribe we mean a social group that is considered unitary, bound by kinship ties, and descending from a single ancestor. The Levites cannot be considered a tribe, however, if by this term we mean a social group with its own well-defined territory. On the one hand, the Levites are privileged, because they maintain an institutional relationship with the sacred; on the other hand, they are marginalized, because they have no territory. They are tied to sacred places, and, in the end, not even to these, but rather to the cult in and for itself.

This is demonstrated by the figure of the Levite who, in Judges 17, is first enlisted to officiate in the sanctuary that the Ephraimite Micah had built for himself, placing there some *teraphim*, and an *ephod*. As the Danites passed by in their northerly migration, they stole the Levite away together with the objects of the sanctuary. The Danites said to him: "Be still: put your hand over your mouth, come with us and be our father and priest. Is it better for you to be priest for the house of one man or to be priest for a tribe and a clan in Israel? The priest, agreeing, took the *ephod*, the *teraphim*, and the statue[?] and went off in the midst of the band" (Judg. 18:19–20). The Levite became the founding head of the lineage of priests in the sanctuary of Dan.

Having no territory of their own, the Levites gained their livelihood from their priesthood, which consisted mainly in sacrificial and mantic functions, the latter through the medium of the *urim* and *tummim*. Either they received a portion of the sacrifice or a stipend from the "owners" of the sanctuaries (as we know from the Levite of Micah in Judg. 17:10: "I will give you ten silver shekels a year, a set of garments and your food" in addition to housing: Judg. 18:4). Recompense could include both forms of payment. The payment through a portion of sacrifice lent itself to certain abuses, and became the subject of critical traditions, as in the description of the sons of Eli (I Sam. 2:12–17):

> The sons of Eli [priest of Yahweh Sabaoth in Shiloh] were wicked; they had respect neither for Yahweh nor for the priests' duties toward the people. When someone offered a sacrifice, the priest's servant would come with a three-pronged fork, while the meat was still boiling, and would thrust it into the basin, kettle, cauldron, or pot. Whatever the fork brought up, the priest would keep. That is how all the Israelites were treated who came to the sanctuary at Shiloh. In fact, even before the fat was burned, the priest's servant would come and say to the man offering the sacrifice, "Give me some meat to roast for the priest. He will not accept boiled meat from you, only raw meat," and if the man protested to him, "Let the fat be burned first as is the custom, then take whatever you wish," he would reply, "No, give it to

me now, or else I will take it by force." Thus the young men sinned griev-
ously in the presence of Yahweh; they treated the offerings to Yahweh with
disdain.

This twofold sin, of quantity with respect to the boiled meat, and of inap-
propriate timing with respect to the roasted meat, is summed up well in the final phrase: "I will take [the meats] by force." For those acquainted with things
Greek, this calls to mind the *machaira*, the sacrificial knife of Delphi, which,
in turn, corresponds to the large fork of Siloh.[10] In the Homeric hymn Apollo
guarantees that the Delphic priests will be able to live off of the sacrifices.
These priests were proverbially gluttonous, and a popular saying warned: "If
you sacrifice at Delphi, you must buy yourself some extra meat as a side dish."
It is said that "if someone enters the sacred precinct to offer a victim to the
god, the Delphic priests surround the altar, each one armed with a knife.
When the sacrificer has slit the victim's throat, skinned it and gutted it, each of
those present take a piece of meat, however much they can grab, and run
away. So it happens that the one offering the sacrifice is left with nothing." According to the myth, in one of these frantic rushes, Neoptolemos-Pyrrhos, son
of Achilles, was killed by a Delphic knife and was buried in the sanctuary.

The gluttonous and bloody violence of the Delphic priests is perfectly mir-
rored in the myth of origin of the Levites. According to Genesis (49:5–7), the
eponymous ancestor Levi was cursed by his dying father Jacob because, together with Simeon, "in their fury they slew men, in their willfullness they
maimed oxen." For this reason his tribe received no land. Jacob is referring to
the massacre of Shechem (Genesis 34) undertaken to avenge the defilement
of his daughter Dinah, by the son of the city's prince—a massacre begun
through the trickery of Simeon and Levi. Levi is, therefore, a social group both
sacred and cursed, descended from an ancestor who had tainted himself with
blood. It is a tribe of priests without a territory, and in this respect, not unlike
the group of Kenites, the ironworking descendants of Cain.[11]

More humble service awaited the so-called Gibeonites. According to the
book of Joshua (chapter 9), they had the task of procuring water and wood for
the sacrificial fire of the tribes at Gilgal. These Gibeonites can probably be
identified with the *gerim* in Deuteronomy. Following Blenkinsopp,[12] we can
identify them with the *netinim* or attendants in the Temple of Solomon. It is
said of the Gibeonites, identified as Canaanites, that they too were a group
founded in an original sin, which was the cause of the humbled position they
were destined to occupy. This original sin consisted in their having tricked the
Israelites. They posed, not as Canaanites from the city of Gibeon, but as a
group of refugees from a distant land, acceptable within the alliance of Israel.
This permitted them to survive the massacres of the Conquest imposed by the
rules of *ḥerem*. Once the ruse was discovered, however, they suffered the curse
of Joshua, the status of *gerim*, and the obligation to provide water and wood at
the altar.

In II Samuel 21 the Gibeonites reappear. Saul, "on account of his zeal for

Yahweh," massacres them and a famine follows. Saul's successor David turns to them and asks how reparation could be made so that they might "bless the inheritance of Israel." They respond not by seeking recourse to existing law, but by asking that seven descendants of Saul be turned over to them, so that they might hang them in the sanctuary at Gibeon. The text explains that "the Gibeonites were not Israelites, but survivors of the Amorites; and the Israelites had given them their oath" (II Sam. 21:2). These guests were, therefore, both sacred and cursed; tied to Israel by a pact, but cursed by Joshua; without inheritance in Israel, but capable of blessing the inheritance of Israel. They did not invoke the customary laws against the family of the offender but invoked the handing over of seven of his descendants. They were tied to the altar by the exercise of a servile task and were possibly authorized, in their capacity as *gerim*, to consume impure foods (Deut. 14:21). In places they may be compared to the strange figure of the *xyleus*, the provider of white poplar wood for the sacrificial fire of Olympia, who served both the altar of Zeus and the cult in the circle of stones of the hero Pelops. The *xyleus* ritually tasted some of the black ram sacrificed to Pelops, thus becoming contaminated and excluded from the precinct of Zeus, to whom he was still bound to procure the firewood.[13]

In sum, mantic and cultic practices did not devolve exclusively on the specialized personnel, but only preferentially. This is attested to by the contents of the book of Judges regarding the sanctuaries respectively founded and officiated at by Gideon of Manasseh and his descendants (Judg. 8:22–35), and by the above-mentioned anonymous Ephraimite and his son, later replaced by the Levite from Judah (Judg. 17).

b) If the cultic practices in the sanctuaries are, at least in principle, a function incumbent upon the Levites and *gerim*, the tribal model also presents specific sacred statuses that appertain to members of the territorial tribes. These individuals are often tied to the practice of sacred warfare and strongly qualify as Yahwists. Furthermore, they are bound together, not by birth into a social group endowed with specific sacred functions, but by a common choice, calling, and investiture that transform these individuals from simple producers into possessors of a specific quality and power. Thus, for example, the Nazirite is a man dedicated for a determined period (or, according to a variant testimony of the life of Samson in Judges 13–16, dedicated for his entire life from before birth) to Yahweh and subjected to particular ritual restrictions and obligations. The one who is possessed by the spirit of Yahweh is suddenly invested with that spirit and thus acquires a certain status, with functions that are more warlike than mantic.[14]

There are cases in which the Nazirite's consecration of himself and the sudden investiture of a possessed person do not coincide ipso facto with a definable vocation. In such cases, the producer and the warrior do not carry out separate fixed functions, but, at most, lend power to their warlike achievements. However, there do exist members of territorial tribes who, called directly by Yahweh (I Sam. 3; 4:1), exercise mantic functions and eventually (Judg. 4:5) even judicial ones in a precise location. This is the case for the seer (*ro'eh:* I Sam. 9:9, in the land of Zuph) and the prophetess (*n^ebi'ah:* Judg. 4:4–7, near the Palm of Deborah, between Ramah and Bethel). In the well-known case of Samuel in I Samuel 9:7–8, the "seer's" mantic functions are exercised for a fee: in order to find out where his father's asses had gone, Saul wanted to offer Samuel a quarter of a silver shekel. On another occasion, however, it appears that Saul, upset by the response of the necromancer of Endor, did not pay her, but instead was offered refreshment by her.

Whether they imply only a temporary modification or transform the producer into a specialist of the supernatural, these qualities acquired by members of territorial tribes are forerunners of power. The power that they carry is exemplified by the power that the legendary saviors and liberators in the book of Judges exercised often on some, sometimes on many, practically never on all the tribes. As I have shown for Ehud[15] and could demonstrate for the other Judges, these figures are none other than the heroes of tribal sagas, whose historicity is dubious at best.

Here is where the model becomes a matter of interest. Within the tribal model, it becomes clear that the legendary figures of the savior-leaders are modeled on real figures of particular individuals, members of territorial tribes, invested from time to time with sacred powers and values:[16] Samson is both possessed and a Nazirite; Othniel and Gideon were called, devoted to Yahwism, and also possessed (Judg. 3:10; 6:34); Jephthah was possessed (Judg. 11:29); Deborah was a prophetess; Samuel was a seer inspired by Yahweh.

The tribal model can, therefore, be read in the key of this dichotomy: on the one hand were institutional specialists, understood to be tribal groups or "remnants" of national groups different from the territorial tribes (and their guests); on the other hand were members of the territorial tribes who were eventually raised to a sacred status. The first group lives at the expense of the territorial tribes, and possessed what Victor Turner[17] called "the powers of the weak." The second group is composed of either producers and warriors (Nazirites, possessed), or those who exercise specialized sacred functions for compensation (seers). These specialists thus sprout among the producers, acquiring authority and power, especially in judiciary and military fields. The only exceptions to this dichotomy are the great cultural heroes and religious founders Moses and Samuel, who seem to accumulate in their persons aspects of both these categories.[18] It is noteworthy that, although Moses was a Levite, he did not have pronounced priestly characteristics, but conferred these priestly functions on Aaron. Deuteronomy classifies Moses as a prophet. A. Cody[19] has also noted that although Samuel was a disciple of Eli and presided at sacrifices he never became a priest in the true and proper sense of the word.

4. The Monarchic Model

In the monarchic state model the dichotomy that I have just pointed to is both confirmed and complicated.

a) Here, objective affinities between the priesthood and the monarchy, two institutions that, by their very nature, fall outside the organization of the territorial tribes, are revealed. In the tribal model, the priests are "different" and "guests" (for example, "Canaanite," as in the case of the Gibeonites) among the territorial tribes, while the monarchy is a "foreign" institution. Conversely, in the monarchic model, the kings have complicated relations with the large sanctuaries, making some their own and giving them power. Meanwhile, the priests who are in charge of the large sanctuaries bear "royal" names, and certainly not by chance.

The name of Ahimelech, priest of Nob, is one case that can be typologically compared to that of the kings, Melchizedek of Salem (Gen. 14) and Abimelech of Shechem. Abimelech's father, Gideon, after having refused the royalty offered him by the Ephraimites, had a sanctuary built for himself and became its "owner" (Judg. 8–9). These two figures with "kingly" names do not appear to be true king-priests. Even if the king has not taken on genuinely priestly traits, however, the texts indicate that the rationalizing control of the palace over the priesthood was a strong element in the state model. This model provides for the regulation of official positions as well as the regulation of fixed incomes of Levitical personnel.[20] It also regulated the priestly hierarchy, both within the tribe of Levi (with the establishment of a class of super-levites, the Aaronites), as well as outside (with the superimposition of non-levitical Zadokites, who became the hegemonic priestly caste of Jerusalem). Further, the state model tends toward centralization. This tendency, however, was always frustrated because the large tribal sanctuaries never ceased to function. Even the smallest sanctuaries of the countryside were empowered by some kings and destroyed by others, but more often empowered than destroyed. The division of the kingdom put an end once and for all to the dream of unifying the cult, especially as the north had more than one royal sanctuary. As for the "deuteronomic" reform of Josiah (ca. 620 B.C.E.), which theoretically applied only to the kingdom of Judah, it seems to me to be nothing other than the rationalization of a negative status quo (widespread nonsacrificial butchery). Moreover, this reform was never put into practice; it was launched in a time of crisis and disorder, and was followed, only decades later, by the final disappearance of the kingdom. This period can be seen as a lost opportunity for Yahwistic rationalization, an opportunity to be recalled one hundred years later, at the return from Babylonian exile.

In a climate of dynastic stability, the power of the priestly hierarchies seemed one with the monarchic power, as we will see, at least in those cases in which the priests were seen as functionaries of the royal sanctuaries. In a climate of dynastic crisis, however, the priests had a certain role to play, since they were in a way strangers to the tribal conflicts and they controlled places of sacred refuge. The accounts of the priests of Nob, narrated in the books of Samuel and of Kings, strike me as significant in this regard: Ahimelech and the other priests of Nob receive David, banished by King Saul, in their sanctuary, and consult the oracle for him (I Sam. 22). They offer consecrated bread for him and for his men, and give him the sword of Goliath, preserved in the sanctuary. The priests of Nob are exterminated in a reprisal carried out by Saul, but Abiathar, son of Ahimelech, survives (I Sam. 22:6–23), to become a priest of David. He disappears only after siding with the son of David, Adonijah, against the other son of David, Solomon, in the struggle for succession. Abiathar is banished by Solomon, who wins the succession, and is replaced by Zadok as chief priest of Jerusalem (I Kings 1:5–31; 2:26–27).

b) The differences between the monarchic model and the tribal model are especially apparent in the sacred figures that arose among the producers. The reason is obvious: the type of preeminence and power conferred on such figures by their sacred status within the framework of the tribal model is not easily sustainable within a monarchic state. Furthermore, it should not be forgotten that, for the most part, the Judges fought against (foreign) monarchic states. In the state monarchic model there are no figures presented as members of territorial tribes whose special connections with the deity (established by means of a calling, a consecration, or possession) confer on them precise powers in the juridic or military spheres. In the state model, such spheres are controlled by the palace. There is evidence that other sorts of members of territorial tribes, however, were recruited to positions of sacrality. These are the prophets, the direct spokespeople of the deity: figures called and possessed, active within the inspired mantic sphere.

Within the category of prophets (sacred "inspired" specialists of the monarchic state model), one should distinguish between "dependent" and "autonomous" prophets. The "dependent" prophets seem to maintain a more or less direct economic relationship with the court (such as Nathan, prophet of David) or with a (possibly royal) sanctuary, which they furnish with their inspired mantic speech. "Autonomous" prophets, in contrast, exercise mantic techniques and other magico-ritual techniques in their own right, commanding their own symbolic languages.[21] They offer their services to the king if he requests this, also to other Israelites and (as illustrated in the accounts of Elijah and Elisha) to foreigners. In return, they are compensated with hospitality and with gifts, or only with gifts. The economic autonomy of these specialists and their large numbers served to establish a sort of competitive regime, attested to by the story of the prophets called by Kings Ahab of Israel and Jehoshaphat of Judah.

The first book of Kings (22:1–26) recounts that 400 prophets went voluntarily to the two kings, and predicted for them both, in a collective performance, a favorable outcome for the military campaign about to begin. But one lone prophet, who kept himself apart from the others, was called forward. He denounced the other prophets as liars—possessed, by order of Yahweh, by a deceitful spirit. Finally, he announced the defeat and the death of Ahab, events that happened shortly thereafter.

Micaiah, the protagonist in this episode, was exhorted by the royal messenger, who was sent to call him, to predict the success of the venture along with the others. But Micaiah answered: "As Yahweh lives, I shall say whatever Yahweh tells me" (I Kings 22:14). The autonomy of the prophets is connected with their professional need to prophesy correctly, and it is this that runs the risk of offending the powerful. Nevertheless, the function of messenger of truth goes beyond the professional ethic of inspired diviners. The prophet, in fact, is also the bearer of unsolicited messages that transcend the mantic logic. Some prophets are actually critical of the king and refuse to accept royal gifts. In the name of the god that inspires them, some prophets fight in the name of an intransigent Yahwism against the kings, in defense of tribal norms (above all, the norms regarding the possession of land and the carrying out of warfare). As the stories of Elijah and Elisha demonstrate in more than one place (for example, II Kings 4:8–36; 8:1–6) the possibility of gaining their own livelihood from sources other than the palace and the sanctuaries confers upon the prophets a certain freedom of movement, based on the authority that their acquired sacred status confers upon them in the eyes of the people.

I shall choose one episode among the many that the text provides. This episode shows the direct confrontation between the king and a "man of Elohim." It illustrates a conflict between the autonomous prophet and a prophet who is dependent on the royal sanctuary of Bethel, who deceives the prophet antagonistic to the king, and causes him to be lost.

The event unfolds as follows: The man of Elohim presents himself at the sanctuary of Bethel while King Jeroboam is standing at the altar to offer perfumes. The man of Elohim curses the altar in the name of Yahweh, describing the sign that will announce the fulfillment of the curse. When the king raises his hand against him, ordering his people to seize him, the hand of the king withers and the promised sign appears. The king then beseeches the man to ask Yahweh to heal his hand. The man of Elohim does so and the hand is healed. The king invites the man of Elohim to his house where, he says, he will be refreshed and will receive a gift. The man of Elohim refuses, explaining that Yahweh has commanded him to bring the message and to return without eating or drinking. At this point the king yields. However, an old prophet *nabi'*) who is "father" (that is, teacher) of a group of young prophets living in Bethel, overtakes the man of Elohim and introduces himself. "I too am a prophet like you," he says. He describes a vision in which an angel told him, by order of Yahweh, that the man of Elohim should stop to eat at his house. "He was lying to him," the text specifies, but the man of Elohim, taken in by the deception, accepts, eats with him, and departs only to be mangled by a lion along his way (I Kings 13).

Here a prophet constantly termed *nabi'* and followed by disciples called his "sons" is contrasted with a prophet called man of Elohim (like Elijah and Elisha, who also refused royal gifts and opposed certain kings). It is important to notice that a passage nearly identical to this narrative can be found in the book of Amos (7:10–17). In it, the priest Amaziah of Bethel is set against the prophet Amos, who announces the ruin of Jeroboam.

To Amos, Amaziah said: "Off with you, visionary, flee to the land of Judah! There earn your bread by prophesying, but never again prophesy in Bethel;

for it is the king's sanctuary and a royal temple." Amos answered Amaziah, "I was no prophet [*nabi'*], nor the son of a prophet [that is, a disciple of a *nabi'*]; I was a shepherd and a dresser of sycamores. The Lord [Yahweh] took me from following the flock, and said to me, Go, prophesy to my people Israel."

In this passage the condition of being a producer called by the divinity while at work seems to be put forward as a reason for not abiding by the orders of the priest attached to the royal sanctuary. This sanctuary priest has a function quite similar to that of the prophet and "father" of other prophets, who resides in Bethel. In the above cited passage, we have seen the prophet of Bethel deceive the man of Elohim. Amaziah, the priest of Bethel, and the *nabi'* of the sanctuary of Bethel, with his prophetic school, are on the side of the king. Against the king, on the other hand, stand the anonymous man of Elohim from the first narrative and Amos, from the second narrative. Amos denies being part of a group of *n^{e}bi'im* and recounts the calling that transformed him from a producer into a prophet. Cases of nonspecialists who are suddenly possessed and caused to prophesy are familiar in the ancient Near East.[22] Familiar also are oracles that contain a reproof to the king, but in no other instance are the sides so clearly drawn.

5. Synchrony, Diachrony, Prospectives

If we examine the three outlined models synchronically, we see that they can be combined more or less adequately to form a single socioreligious reality, articulated on three distinct levels. At the level of the family, the configuration includes *berakah*; the god of the father; *teraphim*; the sacrifice offered by the head of the household; the inheritance of powers and functions by primogeniture. At the level of the tribe, the configuration would include local sanctuaries, both tribal and intertribal; priests and other adepts of the cult as *Gastarbeiter* or *gerim*; productive members of the territorial tribes transformed, by means of consecration, possession, or calling, into persons endowed with particular sacred status and repositories of mantic, judicial, and military functions and powers. At the level of the monarchic state, the configuration would include a hierarchic priesthood that tends to be centralized; royal sanctuaries (tending towards a single royal sanctuary); consultation with specialists of mantic inspiration.

It is immediately evident that no level meshes perfectly with another. Discrepancies and contradictions arise, especially between the tribal model and the monarchic one. These discrepancies and contradictions are windows into social conflicts. It is also evident that, with respect to these contradictions, the biblical text is not impartial, but skewed.

The Hebrew Bible is the sacred book of fully developed Yahwism. The social context of Yahwism is not the ancient Hebrew society in general. Neither the monarchic state level (with its "official syncretism," to use Soggin's phrase) nor the family level (with its so-called religion of the patriarchs) provides the social context for Yahwism. Neither is the social context provided by the community of producers as such, for whom the religion of Baal is rather more functional. The social context of Yahwism is to be found at the level of the *nation* divided into tribes, especially in that moment when the tribal model is structured in a perfect way: the moment of (holy) warfare, for the purpose of which the *maḥanah* is organized: that is, the military camp of the tribes, which plays a leading role in the Exodus.[23]

The heroes of the Hebrew Bible are, therefore, the heroes of Yahwism. They are members of territorial tribes sacralized by a special personal and direct relationship with Yahweh. This is true whether one speaks of Joshua and the Judges, endowed with judicial and military functions and power, or whether one speaks of "autonomous" prophets, who transcend their mantic functions to take on the more complicated characteristics of spokespersons sent by Yahweh. The former belong to the tribal model: within that model, the king is a foreigner, and the leadership of the group rests with the member of the territorial tribe who is "called" by Yahweh. The latter belong to the state monarchic model, which shows, so to speak, the other side of the coin: the king is an Israelite, and the leadership of the group devolves upon him. More precisely (as told in the books of Samuel, which mediate the two models), the monarchy is, certainly, a foreign institution, but Israel has requested it and Yahweh has conceded to that request. Moreover, the correspondence among the figures is very clear. It is subsequently illustrated in accounts wherein the Judges, the charismatic tribal leaders, and the prophets are recruited by Yahweh while they are carrying out their work as producers (with regard to Gideon: Judg. 6:11–32; with regard to Saul: I Sam. 11:4–8; with regard to Elisha: I Kings 19:19–21; with regard to Amos: Amos 7:10–17). The presence of Saul in this list confirms the reading proposed here, as I have tried to demonstrate elsewhere, for Saul "mediates" between judge and king. In the new model in which he belongs, that is, in the fledgling, monarchic state model, Saul is classified (I Sam. 10:9–13) as a prophet.[24]

The juxtaposition of these levels may be understood in synchronic fashion, for families, tribes, and kings were always present in pre-exilic Israel. Conversely, the juxtaposition may be understood as partially diachronic (earlier, the kings were not Israelites, later they were; earlier the possessed were Judges, later they were prophets; earlier one could prophesy with the *urim* and *tummim*, later only with the prophets). From the meeting between Abraham and Pharaoh and from the conflict between Pharaoh and Moses, there perdures a conflict between the member of the tribe "called" by Yahweh and the king (one thinks of Ehud opposing the king of Moab, and of the *'iš Elohim* against Jeroboam). The superiority of one who has had direct contact with Yahweh over one who holds institutional power also perdures (one thinks of Moses anointing Aaron, Samuel anointing first Saul and then David, and Elisha anointing Jehu). Yahweh, who stands above the kings, is in direct contact with a member of his people.

In this fashion, the relationship between supernatural practices and power in the Hebrew Bible can be configured in a wholly new way with respect to its ancient Near Eastern context. We cannot rule out the possibility that members of other ancient Near Eastern societies had a conception analogous to this biblical one. But we can be sure that the only place where we see traces of this conception is in the biblical text, where it is not only present, but dominant. This unprecedented situation can be explained with a general premise and with two specific causes. Here diachrony makes a reappearance, to the satisfaction of those readers who have become nostalgic for it. The general premise and specific causes unfold in chronological order. The premise is the "national" character of the monarchy of Israel,[25] that is, the way in which Israel effected an accommodation between the tribal model and the monarchic model—an accommodation that made room for a religion of the god of an armed nation. The causes are: the existence of Yahwist kings such as Jehu and Josiah; and the existence of an exilic and postexilic Israel, which, as a people still devoted to their national god, managed to outlive their own monarchy.

NOTES

1. C. Grottanelli, review of De Pury, *Promesse divine et légende cultuelle dans le Cycle de Jacob* (Lausanne, 1975): "Oriens Antiquus" 18 (1979), pp. 357–362; more in general, see Mario Liverani, *Le 'origini' di Israele. Progetto storico irrealizzabile di ricerca etnogenetica:* "Rivista Biblica" 28 (1980), pp. 9–31.

2. See Mario Liverani, *Messaggi, donne, ospitalità. Comunicazione intertribale in Giudici 19–21:* "Studi Storico-Religiosi" 3 (1979), pp. 303–343.

3. Giorgio Buccellati, *Cities and Nations of Ancient Syria* (Rome, 1967).

4. See Liverani's article quoted above, in notes 1 and 2.

5. H. C. White, *The Initiation Legend of Isaac:* "Zeitschrift fur Alttestamentlische Wissenschaft" 91 (1979), pp. 1–30.

6. Concerning the god of the fathers, Albrecht Alt, *Der Gott der Väter*, BWANT III, 12 (Stuttgart, 1929), is still important. For further bibliography, see Alfred de Pury's work in two volumes, *Promesse divine et légende cultuelle dans le Cycle de Jacob* (Lausanne, 1975).

7. Max Weber, *Gesammelte Aufsätze zur Religionssoziologie*, III. *Das Antike Judentum* (Tübingen, 1921).

8. Alfred Cody, *A History of Old Testament Priesthood*, Analecta Biblica 35 (Rome, 1969).

9. B. Mazar, *The Cities of the Priests and the Levites*, in Supplements to Vetus Testamentum 7 (Congress Volume, Oxford, 1959) (Leiden, 1960), pp. 193–205.

10. See Walter Burkert, *Structure and History in Greek Mythology and Ritual* (Berkeley, 1979).

11. Robert North, *The Cain Music:* "Journal of Biblical Literature" 83 (1964), pp. 373–389.

12. Joseph Blenkinsopp, *Are There Traces of the Gibeonite Covenant in Dt?:* "Catholic Biblical Quarterly" 28 (1966), pp. 207–219.

13. See W. Burkert, *Structure and History in Greek Mythology and Ritual* (quoted above, note 10), pp. 82–86.

14. Regarding this possession and its implications, see this book's chapter 5.

15. On Ehud and his deed, see this book's chapter 3.

16. In this respect, Weber's work quoted above, note 7, is still the best guide to the main problems.

17. Victor Turner, *The Ritual Process. Structure and Antistructure* (Harmondsworth, 1974).

18. Walter Eichrodt, *Theologie des Alten Testament*, 2d ed. (Göttingen, 1939).

19. A. Cody, *A History of Old Testament Priesthood* (quoted above, note 8), pp. 39–50.

20. See Roland De Vaux, *Les Institutions de l'Ancien Testament* (Paris, 1960), 2, chapter 4.5.

21. On the symbolic language of prophets see chapter 9 in this book.

22. See H. H. Huffmon, *The Origin of Prophecy*, in Frank Moore Cross, Werner E. Lemke, and Patrick D. Miller (eds.), *Magnalia Dei: the Mighty Acts of God: Essays on the Bible and Archaeology in Memory of G. Ernest Wright* (Garden City, New York, 1976), pp. 171–186.

23. See Gerhardt von Rad, *Die Heilige Krieg im Alten Testament* (Zürich, 1951); R. Bach, *Die Aufförderung zur Flucht und zum Kampf im Alttestamentliche Prophetenspruch* (Neukirchen, 1962).

24. On Saul and the prophets, see chapter 5 in this book.

25. See G. Buccellati, *Cities and Nations of Ancient Syria*, quoted above, note 3.

HEALERS AND SAVIORS OF
THE EASTERN MEDITERRANEAN
IN PRECLASSICAL TIMES

I

"Salvation" in the sense it acquired in some of the "Oriental" religions of the Roman Empire was not a concern of the cultures of the Eastern Mediterranean, at least before Greek mysticism (Sabbatucci[1]) or "mysteriosophy" (Bianchi[2]) was "invented." Whether such a "salvation" *ever* became a popular concern is a problem that has often (Teixidor[3]) been discussed, and possibly still should be; but I for one lack the competence to do so.

In the ancient Mediterranean and Near Eastern societies of the period indicated, "salvation" meant safety from the three main calamities, i.e. from famine, epidemics, and (defeat in) war, and of course from the other calamity that often ensued as a consequence of the main three, i.e. becoming a slave. After death, there was no "salvation" but, for the common people, at best a vague but not too unhappy survival as a shade; for the king, various types of afterlife that in some cases and in different ways were considered (especially, of course, in Egypt) to be somehow divine.

Now, while the gods, if well treated, provided safety in life, and the pious continuity in ritual practice on the part of the descendants provided a not too unhappy though of course not exciting afterlife in the realm of the shades, the king was at least in principle the only detainer of expectations of a distinguished afterlife, as well as a mediator between gods and men and thus in various ways responsible for the welfare of the whole society. He was thus, both during his life and after his death, *a "healer" and a "savior,"* in the sense, of course, of "una 'salvezza' che investe i valori terreni più rilevanti, come appunto la salute e l'integrità fisica" (Xella); and it is not surprising to note that many have found the roots of what is usually known as "messianism" in Near Eastern kingship ideology.

However, the "sacred," and the "saving," quality of Near Eastern kingship even within its own ideology is more and more a matter of debate. Liverani[4] has suggested that the "saving" quality of kingship in Mesopotamia and Syria was firmly linked with the concept of royal justice, which was deified in both areas, and that the main aspect of such royal justice was the systematic remission of debts, and freeing of debtors, through royal decrees often in connection with new accessions. In the Late Bronze Age there were no more such decrees; social differences and conflicts increased, while consensus to kingship and social cohesion diminished.

The beginning of the Iron Age meant no less than the total collapse of the whole social and political system of the Eastern Mediterranean, from Mycenae to Egypt. This was an *internal* social phenomenon, and even the "invasions" that we usually connect with the beginning of the Iron Age are in reality increasingly interpreted as social upheavals. In F. M. Heichelheim's[5] words:

> The storms of the beginning of the Iron Age not only undermined the money system, the system of trade, the strategy, and the political organization of the Ancient Orient. They had an even more lasting effect because *Ancient Oriental kingship itself was no longer the strongest guarantee for the* survival of civilization and *lasting political power* [my italics]. Soon, and especially after the development of the Hellenic states to *polis* civilizations, it even had no longer any cultural advantage. The foundations of the spiritual and material organization of the Ancient Orient had been rendered unsafe to the last degree by . . . structural changes. All the attempts at a comeback made by the Egyptian, Assyrian, Neobabylonian and Persian kingdoms had to remain ineffectual in the end.

The transition between the Late Bronze and the Iron Age was thus a period of collapse, in some areas, and of profound crisis, in others, for the complex mode of production that Heichelheim calls the Ancient Oriental Pattern.

The collapse took place in a more violent way in Palestine and in Greece:

In Palestine where after the fall (or rather: during the fall) of the Bronze Age kingdoms a new society (Israel) emerged, only to be rapidly reorganized in the shape of a "national" monarchy that was different from the old Bronze Age pattern, as Buccellati[6] has shown; and in Greece where the Mycenaean palaces and their culture were destroyed, and after a "dark period" we know little about, society reshaped itself as a series of free townships, not ruled by monarchs.

In both areas, crisis was endemic for all the first half of the first millennium; and though Greece and Israel were extremely different from each other, yet they produced the first cultures (and the only ones in the Mediterranean before Rome) expressed by texts not thought and written by palace bureaucracies.

In those texts of a new type, the king is present, but not central; and new charismatic figures are present, not royal, often in conflict with monarchs, and always endowed with special powers that enable them to be more successful than the king in protecting, in "saving" individuals and societies from the calamities that endanger their lives.

2

When Israelite society developed into a peculiar type of monarchic state (whose "first king" was presented by biblical narrative as a possessed "prophet"!), the religious "prophetic" movement that is sometimes described as *nabism* was "rationalized" in various ways that I have tried to illustrate elsewhere.[7] Neverthe-less, "prophecy" remained an autonomous phenomenon in Israel, and both the behavior and the beliefs of the "inspired persons" (Pedersen[8]) were those of "men of god" often antithetical to kingly power, always faithful to ideals of social justice and apparently endowed with spiritual, even with supernatural, powers of their own.

The most famous of the early prophets were Elijah and his disciple Elisha, usually dated to the ninth century B.C.E. The traditions about them, reflected by the biblical passages relating to them (I Kings 17–19, 21; II Kings 1–2, 4–10) are usually considered archaic and often dated to the ninth through seventh century B.C.E.

Elijah and Elisha are presented as extraordinary men, first of all, from the point of view of their *way of life*. Though Elisha is probably shown to be at-tached to the sanctuary of Gilgal (Fohrer[9]), both prophets are presented as be-ing *without any fixed abode*.

They wander in the territory of the two kingdoms of Judah and Israel, often moving from one place to another at great speed, and occasionally dwelling in, or visiting, foreign countries like the Aramean lands or Phoenicia. When a drought breaks out, Yahweh forewarns Elijah, ordering him to go and dwell in the open country, by a brook, where crows miraculously bring to him bread and meat twice a day. When the brook dries up, Elijah is ordered by Yahweh to move to Phoenicia, where he is the guest of a widow of the town of Sarepta (I Kings 17).

The *dress* of the two men is also of a special type: they wear a hairy mantle of goatskin, that can be rolled up and used as a ("magic") wand (II Kings 2:8, 14). Their relationship with *animals* is also interesting: We have seen Elijah fed by crows; as for Elisha, we are told (II Kings 2:24) that once when, shortly after Elijah's ascension, he was being teased by some children, he caused two she-bears to attack them and to devour them.

Though Elijah's only disciple seems to be Elisha, the latter "gathered a guild of prophets about him," though I would not follow Fohrer in stating that he usually lived with them "in a fixed location."

Secondly, Elijah and Elisha were notable for their supernatural qualities. Divination was the main activity in which they employed those powers; but they also worked many miracles. I quote from Fohrer's[10] list of wonders worked by prophets, a list wholly drawn from the stories of Elijah and Elisha:

A prophet could make use of visible means to perform a miracle: he could use salt to make the water of a spring wholesome (II Kings 2:19–22), meal to coun-teract poisoned food (II Kings 4:38–41), a cut piece of wood to retrieve the iron head of an axe from a river as though with a magnet (II Kings 6:1–7), or his staff, laid upon the face of a dead man, to restore him to life . . . (II Kings 4:29). If this did not succeed, he would stretch himself upon the dead man so as to transmit his own vital force (I Kings 17:21; II Kings 4:34–35). Even a prophet's bones could still miraculously restore life (II Kings 13:20–21). He was likewise able to feed a multitude with scant provisions (II

Kings 4:42–44), cause the oil of a single jar to fill many jugs (II Kings 4:1–17), and prevent meal and oil from running out (I Kings 17:14–16)."

To these miracles that gave life (whether in the form of nourishment, of healing or of "breath," i.e., resurrection) one must add the great contest between Elijah and the prophets of Baal on Mount Carmel. This episode (II Kings 18) in its biblical *context* is a clash between the "foreign" deity Baal and the god Yahweh; but its *form* is the rain-making contest between a group of prophets and the solitary yet more powerful Elijah, and its *conclusion* is rain, salvation from famine for the people, and death for Elijah's unsuccessful rivals.

But the yahwistic healers are not only more powerful than the prophets of Baal; they also detain more charismatic power than the king of Israel. We are told (II Kings 5) that Na'aman, captain of the army of the king of Syria, was a leper, and was sent by his master the king to the king of Israel with a letter asking that monarch to cure him of his leprosy. "When the king of Israel had read the letter, he rent his clothes, and said: 'Am I God, to kill and to make alive [*h'lhym 'ny lhmyt wlhḥywt*], that this man sends to me to recover a man of his leprosy? Surely he seeks a quarrel with me'" (II Kings 5:7). So the leper is sent to Elisha, who cures him, accepts no reward, proclaims that Yahweh is the only God, obtains Na'aman's (partial) "conversion," and transfers leprosy on his servant who had run after Na'aman and extorted from him the gift Elisha had refused.

Of course, Elisha succeeds where the king has failed because he is the prophet of Yahweh, and it is the god who operates through him, as is clear from his words to Na'aman. However, it is significant that we have here an explicit statement of the fact that *the king cannot heal* because he is not the god (*ha'elohim*), that the statement is proffered by the king, and that the prophet Elisha heals the man the king was unable to heal. Elsewhere (II Kings 1) the king of Israel is sick, seeks "salvation" in a "foreign" cult, and is predicted to die by Elijah, who thus appears as an antihealer.

The motif of the sick king is already present, as Xella has shown, in Ugaritic mythology: but here it acquires a new meaning, in contrast with the motif of the healing prophet. Another "new" motif, that we find in the Bible (King Uzziyah, II Chron. 26:16–23) and possibly, according to J. Morgenstern,[11] also in Josephus (Ant. XIX.viii.2) is that of the king who becomes sick (a leper in the case of Uzziyah) because he usurps sacral functions that are not his.

The episodes I have just quoted show some aspects of the complex relationship between the king and the prophet in the stories of Elijah and Elisha.

Both Elijah and Elisha opposed kings like Ahab, who had a wicked Phoenician wife, Jezebel, followed gods other than Yahweh, and did not respect the tribal rights of the people of Israel, or Ahaziah, the sick king we have quoted. They were persecuted by them, and gleefully foresaw their terrible doom. But, if Yahweh gave the order, they could *make kings*, as happened with Haza'el of Damascus and with Jehu of Israel (I Kings 19:15–18; II Kings 8:1–18; 9:1–10), who "destroyed Baal out of Israel" (II Kings 10:28).

This great power that was even power over kings is probably to be connected with some traits of Elijah and Elisha that are without doubt "kingly"
traits, like the fact that when Elijah is ordered to *anoint* as kings Haza'el and
Jehu, he is also ordered to *anoint* Elisha to succeed him as a prophet (I Kings
19:16), or the symbolic value of Elijah's mantle (II Kings 2:13–14) that can be
compared to the mantle of King Saul (I Sam. 15:27–28). But the most extraordinary trait of all, which has no exact parallel in previous tradition, is the account of the ascent of Elijah.

We are told (II Kings 2) that Elijah and his disciple Elisha traveled together
for a long way, while intimations came by way of "the sons of the prophets"
that Elijah would be taken away from him on that day. While fifty "sons of the
prophets" stopped in sight not far from the river Jordan, Elijah rolled up his
mantle, split the waters of the river with it, and crossed over, followed by Elisha; then asked his disciple whether he could do something for him before
being taken away. Elisha asked for "a double portion of the spirit" of Elijah,
and was promised it if he could see Elijah while the prophet was taken from
him. As they spoke, a chariot and horses of fire divided them and "Elijah went
up by a whirlwind into heaven." Elisha saw this, cried out, rent his clothes,
took up Elijah's mantle that had been left behind, parted the waters with it,
and went back across the Jordan to the "sons of the prophets." They persuaded
him to have Elijah searched for in the surrounding mountains; but all search-
ing was vain.

It is useless to say that such great powers which involved even a victory over
death that few (if any!) kings could boast of, involved no institutional "political" power: not even an "economical" advantage, for we have seen that gifts
were turned down.

3

In the biblical Elijah-Elisha stories the point is reached where not only the
prophet and his disciple have more *charisma* than the kings, but one king is sick
and in vain asks to be healed, while another king declares he is unable to heal,
and Yahweh's envoy, the prophet, heals in his stead. If we turn to the Greek
world, we can easily find another healer who cures a sick king: as in some of the
biblical stories I have quoted the person healed is a foreigner, is very grateful,
and offers to compensate the healer. Herodotus (III 129–138) writes that the Persian king Darius once twisted his foot so violently that the ball of the ankle joint
was dislocated from its socket. The "first physicians of Egypt" [Αἰγυπτίων τοὺς
δοκέοντας εἶναι πρώτους τὴν ἰητρικήν] whom he had till then kept near his
person, were called by Darius, but for seven days and nights only made things
worse. On the eighth day the king was in a frightful state; but someone who had
heard at Sardis of the skill of Democedes of Croton, one of the men captured by
the Persian Oroetes after murdering the tyrant Polycrates of Samos, told Darius
about him; and Darius bade Democedes be brought to him without delay. The

physician was found somewhere all unregarded and forgotten, and brought forth, dragging his chains and clad in rags. At first he tried to deny having knowledge of his art, for he feared that by revealing the truth about himself he would be cut off from Hellas. But to avoid torture he confessed that he had some poor acquaintance with the physician's art, so that the matter was entrusted to him, he made the king able to sleep and in a little while cured him of his hurt. After this, Darius rewarded him with the [significant!] gift of two pairs of golden fetters, but his witty refusal led the king to send him to the royal wives who, learning that he was the man who saved the king's life, rewarded him generously, so that his servant collected a very great sum of gold for him. Democedes, who now had a very great house and ate at the king's table, pleaded for the lives of the Egyptian physicians who had till then attended the king, and were condemned to be impaled for being less skillful than a Greek, and saved them [ἐρρύσατο], saved [ἐρρύσατο] an Elean diviner who had been of Polycrates' retinue, made whole by treating her [ἰώμενος ὑγιέα ἀπέδεξε] Atossa, Cyrus' daughter and Darius' wife, who had "a swelling growing on her breast, that broke and spread further." Through her he devised a scheme to escape back to Hellas; but this is another story (Herodot. III 134–149).

Democedes, we are told (Herodot. III 131), had reached Samos from Croton, where he was troubled by a harsh-tempered father he was unable to bear, by way of Aegina and Athens: the Aeginetans had paid him a talent to be their public physician; in the next year Athenians had hired him for a hundred minae, and Polycrates the next again for two talents. "The fame of the Crotonian physicians [ἰητροί]," says Herodotus, "was chiefly owing to him; for at this time the best physicians in Greek countries were those of Cyrene. About the same time the Argives had the name of being the best musicians."

Of course, Democedes was not a charismatic healer, he was a professional physician; yet this story attests the existence of a tradition about a Greek healer and "savior" who worked wonders at the Persian court, healing the king and the king's wife who was also the daughter of the previous monarch. We are also told that he saved a Greek *diviner*, who was in a sense a colleague; and his art is significantly quoted in connection with *music*. Like Elijah, he contended alone against a whole group of (foreign) rivals, and won, but unlike the yahwist champion he saved his unsuccessful mates. Now, the story of Democedes is highly topical, and it should be compared, for instance, to the mythical traditions about the hero Melampus who, according to Herodotus (II 42, 47, 49, 123, 145), introduced the cult of Dionysos to Greece.

Melampus, the son of Amythaon and eponymous ancestor of the Melampodidai, a clan of diviners, was the hero of the town of Aigosthena where a small shrine and an annual feast (Melampodeion) were dedicated to him. He was exposed as an infant, and understood the language of animals. Two distinct tales were told about him. Of the first there is an echo in Homer (*Odyss.* XI 284–297): his brother Bias wanted to marry the daughter of King Neleus of Pylos, who would give her only to the man who could offer him the oxen of Iphikles; so Melampus set out to steal them for his brother, but was captured (the *Odyssey* speaks of "chains"). In prison he overheard two insects commenting on the fact that the wooden structure of his jail had been totally consumed by them and would soon collapse: he asked to be transferred and explained why, but was not believed until the building fell, killing of course not him but another person. He was then recognized as a successful diviner and ordered to cure the king's son, who was impotent: this he did by overhearing two vultures who discussed a frightful episode they had witnessed, during which the boy had received a terrible shock. The healer's "psychological" approach agrees with the quality of the second tale about Melampus: the daughters of King Proitus of Argos went crazy and ran away in the woods, and Melampus offered to heal them at the price of a third of Proitus' realm. The king refused, and all the Argive women became mentally disturbed and went about killing sheep and oxen and devouring them raw. So Proitus asked Melampus to help him, and Melampus accepted but added a further third of the kingdom to the previous price, intending to give it to his brother Bias. The women were cured, either with certain ritual dances or with herbs, and Melampus and Bias received their due, plus Proitus' two daughters in marriage.

I have suggested elsewhere[12] that the mythology of Melampus is strikingly similar to the biblical story of Joseph, the eponymous ancestor and (mythical) diviner who was sold by his brothers and ended up as a slave in Egypt.

Like Melampus, Joseph, a lonely foreigner, was in prison when recognized by an important fellow-prisoner as a successful diviner, and was summoned by the Egyptian king who asked him to interpret his dreams. This he did correctly, succeeding where all the Egyptian diviners and wise men had failed. But he did more, for the dreams turned out to be the announcement of seven years of plenty followed by seven years of famine, and Joseph was freed and promoted by the king and saved not only the kingdom, but the whole world, from a sterile and deadly future.

These traditions, Greek and biblical, about healers and diviners saving kings, royal families and kingdoms, are surely to be considered together, for coincidence in details (e.g. the fact that both Democedes' and Joseph's rivals were Egyptian specialists) and what seems to be a reversal of common motifs (e.g. the fact that, in tone with the "Egyptian" origin of Dionysism according to Herodotus, Melampus bears a name that identifies him as an Egyptian) show that they were probably formed in a common Mediterranean "international" milieu. Peculiar combinations occur, and the whole group of stories is nothing but a series of variations on the theme of the humble man, often a foreigner, a slave or a prisoner, or all these things together, who has more charisma than the king and his men.

The relationship between the king and the charismatic person is often one of mere hostility: The founder of Yahwism, Moses, was a foundling like Melampus, and later a murderer and a fugitive, and the leader of a rabble of slaves, persecuted by the king; but he worked wonders more wonderful than those worked by the "magicians" of Egypt summoned by Pharaoh. In the end, Moses triumphed, and the king and his men were miraculously drowned.

King Pentheus of Thebes was hostile to Dionysism and thrust a mysterious stranger, who was in reality (a priest of) Dionysos, into the dungeon of his palace, but soon the stranger was miraculously delivered and the king died torn to pieces by Dionysos' votaries, led by his own mother, who, not unlike Jezebel, had been the greatest opponent of the "new" religion.

In other cases, the healer's or diviner's conflict with the king (which seems to be a common trait) does not keep him from saving the king himself and the kingdom. Such are, of course, the cases we have examined at the beginning of this section; but we could add, among others, some traditions about David, who was introduced to the court of Saul because he was "a cunning player on an harp" and cured the king by playing this instrument when Saul was troubled by an evil spirit sent by Yahweh, just as Melampus is said to have cured the raging women of Argos. It is interesting to note that such a task was a dangerous one, for Saul hated his healer David who, like Melampus in Argos, had won the king's daughter, and one day as the evil spirit was upon Saul who "sat in his house with a javelin in his hand, and David played with his hand," the king tried to kill the young musician, but David "slipped away out of Saul's presence, and he smote the javelin into the wall" (I Sam. 19:9–10).

Herodotus (III. 36) tells the same story about Croesus, the vanquished Lydian ruler who had become Cyrus' friend and counsellor, and crazy King Cambyses, who ordered his attendants to kill him, but soon wished the wise man back. This last is the well-known motif of the wise counselor, diviner, or healer, injustly imprisoned or persecuted by the king, but sought when the moment comes for him to save the kingdom.

I have found other instances of this motif in the widespread Near Eastern traditions about the courtier Ahiqar, which are already present in an Aramaic papyrus of the 5th century B.C.E found in Egypt, as well as in the Greek *Life of Aesop*, the poet, *mythopoios*, and diviner, who according to Greek tradition solved difficult riddles for King Lykeros of Babylon, and spoke with animals.[13]

All the stories of this type stress the point that the king is unable to save his kingdom, and needs the man he hates, so that he is forced to free him and to use him. The evil that is to be averted is always one of the three calamities I have mentioned at the beginning of this chapter; special attention is given to the "epidemics" or "illness" theme, often involving psychological or psychosomatic ailments, while war is often replaced by other, ritualized conflicts between kings like the riddle contests in the stories of Ahiqar and Aesop.

4

In most of the traditions we have examined in the course of section 3, the savior or healer possessed a power that was clearly supernatural, even though he often used specific technical skills — in the fields of music, of divination, and of "medicine." Now, in the stories of Elijah and Elisha (section 2), such a supernatural power was firmly connected with a specific "faith," in the sense that it stemmed directly from that "faith" and from the divine power of the god Yahweh. The charismatic healers had something to teach and to preach, and their conflict with the king was due to the fact that the monarch was influenced by his evil Phoenician wife and did not believe (only) in Yahweh.

This would seem obvious in a biblical context, for the Bible is the holy book of Yahwism; so we are not surprised to note that, among the "healers and saviors" I have quoted in section 3, Moses is another case of such a miracle-making preacher; and I must at least mention another such figure, i.e. Samuel, the "prophet and judge" who is directly ordered by Yahweh to make and to dismiss Israel's kings, just as happens with Elisha. Yet, even in the Bible, not all healers and saviors are preaching prophets, for both Joseph and David cure kings and save kingdoms without proclaiming Yahweh to their monarch; and in the case of David and King Saul, *the latter* was full of often incongruous yahwistic zeal.

As for the Greek material, I have mentioned the Dionysian connections of Melampus: Pettazzoni[14] noticed that a story similar to that of Melampus and the daughters of Proitos was told of a Boeotian called Bakis, and that Bakis was the name of several such Greek heroes, for the term, like the term Sibylla, was in reality the common name of a class or type of diviners who divined when possessed or *entheoi*: and possession seems typical of the religion of Dionysos, whose "prophet" Melampus was according to Herodotus. So, outside the Bible, a tradition connects some charismatic healers with a specific religious "movement." As Dionysism, just like the Yahwism of the prophets, was, according to a rich mythology, persecuted by kings (such as the Pentheus I have quoted, or Proitus' brother Acrisius, or Lykourgos, who, as Pharaoh did with Moses, tried to kill Dionysos when the god was still a child), the great wonders worked by the prophet became both a revenge against the unbelieving monarch and a proof of the justness and power of the savior's "religion."

So, both in Greece and in Israel, some of the healers and saviors we have examined so far are not just men who possess more charismatic qualities than the detainers of political power: they also rank as religious or ideological innovators. In the light of this evidence, it is not surprising to note that many traits that we have so far seen to be typical of our (mythical and historical) "saviors" are also present in the (partly mythical) biographies of the first (historical or mythical) Greek "masters of truth" (Detienne[15]) and especially of the ones we can consider as the eponymous founders of Greek mysticism.

Like David, Orpheus invented the lyre (Timoth. Pers. 234–236 Wilamowitz); he wrote books about Healing Things (Suid. s.v.) and on purification (Plat. resp. II 364 E–365 A); like Melampus, he was a specialist in pacifying with music, and his relationship with the animals he charmed shoud be compared to that of Elijah.

A famous purifier was the Cretan Epimenides, who wrote books on mythological and ritual subjects, was a skilled diviner and lived 150 years, eating a special food he had been given by the Nymphs and kept in the hoof of an ox: but this food (Plat. leg. I 642 D–643 A) was rather a medicine, made of roots.

Once Epimenides fell asleep in a cave, slept for 60 years, and woke up being only 60 days older (Diog. Laert. I 115, quoting Theopompos). He purified various cities, among which was Athens (Paus. I 14.4). A terrible plague was raging in the city: Epimenides, summoned from Crete, saw that it was caused by the sacrilege committed by Kylon of the Alcmeonid *gene*, and ordered special sacrifices to be offered to the gods or two young Alcmeonids killed, thus saving the city.

The tradition that Epimenides spoke, in the cave of Zeus Diktaios, with Aletheia and Dike, resembles King Minos's meetings with Zeus in his Cretan cave and the oriental Sydyk and Misor; and it is not impossible to follow S. Mazzarino[16] in identifying the nymph Balte who was said to be his mother with the goddess Ba'alat (of Byblos?). It is more important, however, to note that all these are clearly "royal" traits, and form a strange contrast with the antitraditional and anti-Delphic ideology that has been recognized (again by Mazzarino) in his attitude toward the (guilty) Alcmeonids, in his denial of the (Delphic) Navel of the Earth, and, I would add, in his cooperation with Solon in rationalizing "excessive" burial rites.

Whether he was "oriental" or not, the healer and savior Epimenides was surely a religious innovator, and it is significant that his peculiar way of life may be compared to the life-style attributed to the prophets Elijah and Elisha, who wandered in "national" and foreign territory, were fed from Above and dwelt in the wilds. They too, as we have seen, were not devoid of "royal" traits and were critical of the religious establishment.

Pythagoras was born in Samos, and it is curious to note that during his lifetime he followed a geographical itinerary that was symmetrical and contrary to that of the physician Democedes I have discussed in section 3, for he moved from Samos to Croton in southern Italy, where his school flourished. He was forty, we are told, when, not being able to bear Polycrates' tyranny, he moved to Italy and settled in Croton, whence after many years he moved to Metapontus. His reason for emigrating is thus similar to Democedes' motivation in leaving Croton, where the physician's father was a harsh-tempered domestic tyrant.

The Orphic "connections" of Pythagoras agree with the fact that he was not only a diviner and a healer who could bite a venomous serpent to death (Apollon. mirab. 6.), but also a musician and an expert in musical theory. That his approach to music was not merely theoretic is shown by the fact that he cured and calmed people by having music played to them, and called such a cure a "catharsis" (Iambl. v. Pyth. 25). His powers over animals are not explicitly connected with music by the sources (especially Iambl. v. Pyth. 60–62), but we are told that once a white eagle flew to him and that he caressed it (Aelian. var. hist. IV 17), that he would speak to animals, and that he once caressed and fed with cakes the man-eating Daunian she-bear, who made him the same promise that the wolf of Gubbio made to Saint Francis of Assisi many centuries later.[17]

Though Pythagoras himself was considered divine by his followers, exhibited a golden thigh and was never mentioned by name by the Pythagoreans, he was hostile to tyrants, as we have seen, and was twice imprisoned by kingly authority: once by Cambyses, the crazy king who had tried to kill wise Croesus and who had captured Pythagoras in Egypt where he was living with the priests (Theol. Arithm. p. 52, 8 de Falco), after which the philosopher went to Babylon, where he was "initiated" to the local "mysteries"; and once by the cruel atheist Phalaris of Acragas, who put him in jail together with Abaris the wise Hyperborean, but was killed by a conspiracy on the very same day (Iambl. v. Pyth. 214–222).

Similar traits are also to be found in the biography of Empedocles of Acragas, a poet, physician (ἰατρός) and diviner (μάντις: Diog. Laert. VIII 51–77) who, according to Timaeus (fr. 81 FGH), was a disciple of Pythagoras. He was the author of a poem "on Nature" and of another poetic work called *Katharmoi* ("Purifications"), sharing the first title with the Ionian "philosophers," and the second with Orphic tradition, and also wrote books on medicine and on diet. Nikomachos (reconstructed from Porphyr. v. Pyth. 29 and Iambl. v. Pyth. 135) wrote that, like Pythagoras, Epimenides and Abaris, Empedocles was a great wonder-worker. We are told (Suid. s.v.) that once, when Acragas was damaged by a very strong wind that caused epidemics and rendered women sterile (Clem. Alex. strom. VI 30), he averted it by disposing the skins of donkeys around the city; and that, on another occasion, a certain young man, full of passion and fury, tried to kill Empedocles' host Ancytus, who had condemned his father to death, but was calmed by Empedocles who played on the lyre and sang an appeasing song (Iambl. v. Pyth. 113), just as David and Melampus did in the traditions we have examined. The young man, of course, became the most famous of Empedocles's disciples. In Herakleides' lost work on sickness (fr. 72 Voss) it was related that Empedocles had recalled to life a woman who had remained for thirty days without breathing (Diog. Laert. VIII 61): this, of course, should be compared to Elijah's and Elisha's miracles in I Kings 17:21 and II Kings 4:34–35.

The kingly and divine traits of Empedocles are well known. Clad in purple, wearing a golden crown and bronze sandals, with long hair and followed by his servants, he strode majestically "and seemed endowed with a nearly royal authority to those who met him" (Diog. Laert. VIII 73). He proclaimed in his verse that he would become a god (Philostr. v. Apoll. VIII 7), and the manner of his death, or rather of his "ascension," seems to confirm this.

According to some, he died a natural death during his exile in the Peloponnesus; but two other accounts are of great interest in the present context. According to one version, he disappeared during a banquet. He was searched for at dawn; the slaves were questioned but knew nothing; yet one of them declared that in the middle of the night a strong voice had been heard, calling Empedocles, and, getting up, he had seen a celestial light and the splendor of torches, then nothing more. His disciple Pausanias had Empedocles searched for without result, then declared that things had just happened worthy of prayer and that Empedocles should from then on receive the sacrifices due to one who had become a god (Diog. Laert. VIII 68). The same Pausanias denied another version, transmitted by Hippobotos (fr. 77 Voss), according to which Empedocles had thrown himself into the crater of the Etna in order to give credit to the belief that he had become a god: but the volcano spat out one of his bronze sandals (Diog. Laert. VIII 69).

If we consider the two last versions of Empedocles' end *together*, we shall note that each corresponds well to an aspect of Elijah's ascension, comprehensive of the light from Above, of the respectful and receptive presence of the faithful disciple, as well as of a more "distant" audience, and of the legacy of an object left behind, that in concordance with good biblical symbolic language was a mantle, not a sandal.

The contrast between such megalomanic attitudes (or such charismatic qualities!) and Empedocles' political tendencies towards *isotēs* (already attested by Neas of Cyzicos F.Gr.Hist. 84 F28 II 197) was already noticed by his ancient biographers (Diog. Laert. VIII 64, quoting Timaeus), who tell us that he refused the kingship that was offered to him (Aristot. fr. 66 Rose; Timaeus fr. 88a FHG 1214, both quoted by Diog. Laert. VIII 64), and that he once punished with death a prepossessing symposiarch, or denied the physician Acron a funerary monument for his father, who was also a famous physician (Diog. Laert. VIII 64–65).

5.a

If we now proceed to ask ourselves whether the connections we have noticed are a mere coincidence, and whether the data we have collected can be placed together to form a coherent picture, we will have to answer, first of all, by trying to construct a typology.[18]

Typologically, all the nonroyal healers and saviors we have examined so far form a rather compact unity, for the common traits seem both important and plentiful. First of all, our healers all possess *charisma:* the charisma kings have lost, as I suggested, and a charisma that is badly needed in times of crisis such as those they are placed in. This charismatic quality consists of the charismatic persons' special relationship with the supernatural, and this relationship is expressed, very concretely, by the working of miracles. Such practical aspect of the charismatic quality of our exceptional men is of course "a power," and this obviously means that *they detain power*, not potentially nor metaphorically, but actually. In a few, clearly mythical cases (Melampus, David) the healer-savior transforms that power into *institutional political power;* in other, more concrete cases he uses it to gain wealth (Democedes) or influence (dare we quote Pythagorism?); but often he is unable, or rather, unwilling, to transform (i.e., to rationalize) his power. Whether he is systematically employed (and even remunerated) by the center of political power, or lives at the margin of society, he remains consistently *"liminal,"* and his liminal quality is expressed, in the different contexts, in three different ways.

First of all, he often adopts *a way of life* that puts him aside from other men and women: he lives in deserts and flees to hills and forests, seeks shelter in caves, receives food from the nymphs or from animals, or follows a special, "pure" diet. Second, he *refuses* not only the kingdom that is offered to him (Empedocles), but even money and gifts (Epimenides, Pythagoras, Elijah, the "man of God" in I Kings 13:6–10). Third, averring the proverb *nemo propheta in patria sua*, he is practically always a *foreigner*.

Rich with a supernatural power that was by definition not institutional, and somehow "external," the charismatic persons we are dealing with here used their power to *save* society, sometimes even by curing the king; yet, as we have seen, a more or less open contrast with kingly and other authority was always present; and we could even speak of an intrinsic conflict with institutional power in general, or with the "status system," to use an expression shaped by V. W. Turner.[19] This apparently led them to (and at the same time did not keep them from) forming a series of small social groups of their own, in clanic or other form, organized hierarchically and mainly intended to allow the transmitting of specific crafts, lore, and doctrines; and this autonomous organization can well be seen as a further aspect of their liminality.

At this point we are confronted with the problem of *what* was transmitted by way of these groups, and of the doctrines that, as we have seen, some of them preached to others outside their circle.

It is immediately clear that, while the personalities and biographies we have studied share many traits and thus easily form an organic unity, their doctrines and beliefs differ much more, ranging as they do from prophetic Yahwism to Pythagorism and so on. At the same time, it is also obvious that the similarities we have observed in the personalities, real or mythical, and thus in the social meaning and function of the "saviors" we have studied, are bound to imply *some* set of common ideologies and beliefs.

It is only natural to think that the most common traits are to be sought among the beliefs most directly connected with the healing function of the wonder-workers who professed them. First of all, since what was required was the capacity for interpreting calamities and their causes, a common *guilt-culture* (E. R. Dodds[20]) may be presumed, and of course it was nothing new, for an international, highly complex system of guilt-research was well known to Bronze Age Near Eastern palace omen-bureaucracies. Secondly, since soothing was the aim, an ideology of purity, quiet and *katharsis* must be presumed, but also an ideology involving the knowledge, experience and control of phenomena like ecstasy, trance and possession. Finally, the "liminal" position of the powerful yet not integrated persons I have described must have involved some *ideology of liminality* present, if not in the persons themselves, at least in the traditions about them: an ideology of liminality, some implicit criticism or refusal of society as it was, that we must presume, and about which we can only state that it was probably connected with the guilt-culture I have mentioned, in the sense that liminality was bound to be felt as a sign of the (search for) freedom from guilt.

This seems to be a list, as good as possible, of the common traits that can be traced both in the (partly mythical) personalities and in the ideologies of our "nonroyal healers and saviors." The picture is rather vague, as will seem normal if we consider that our data cover a period of many centuries and a wide area. If we aim not at a mere typology but at historical comprehension, we should not stop at resemblances, but search for differences too, and try to explain what we find (if possible, diachronically). It is immediately obvious that an explanation can be sought along very different lines, for, as is always the case with any subject, very different approaches are possible and all possible approaches are useful. Of course, I have neither the competence nor the space here to solve the historical problems I have hinted at so far; yet I will try to present a broad outline of two such possible approaches.

5.b.1

In discussing my material with C. Zaccagnini (who teaches "Storia Orientale Antica" in the University of Bologna) I discovered that he had prepared an important research paper dealing with the patterns of mobility of specialized craftsmen in the ancient Near East from the Paleo-Babylonian to the Persian period, including diviners and physicians.[21] According to Zaccagnini, such specialized personnel were active mainly, if not exclusively, within the sphere of palace organizations. The craftsmen belonged to the court personnel, and both patterns of mobility singled out by Zaccagnini (first, movements from the central palace to peripheral units; second, exchanges in specialized personnel between different courts) excluded the craftsmen's own free initiative.

A third and entirely different pattern, possibly emerging in the course of the first millennium B.C.E. and especially in the Neo-Babylonian and Persian periods, is that of craftsmen autonomously moving from one center to another, presumably according to their own convenience, in a context that may suggest the beginning of some sort of labor market system. The third pattern was late and exceptional in the Near East, and it certainly did not supersede the other two patterns. But it seems to have been the rule in Iron Age Greece, where palace organization had ended with the fall of the Mycenean states, and some embryonic form of labor market involving specialized craftsmen such as poets, diviners, healers and artists is implied already by passages in the *Odyssey* (see esp. XVII: 382–386).

All this does not mean, of course, that the healers, diviners, and "prophets" of the early Iron Age in the areas quoted were nothing but specialized personnel pouring out from the palace into the wide world. On the contrary, one must suppose that at least some different figures and types of wonder-workers already operated at an inferior social level, and gradually emerged in the new context (and in the "new" texts: see section 1 of this essay): I think, for example, of Samuel, but also of the possessed "prophets" I shall deal with in the next section (5.b.2). What this means is that the function was the same, and that the "higher techniques" were first concentrated, and stopped, inside the palace, and then gradually, so to speak, "commercialized."

The "new" idea that healers must not be detained at court seems to me to be expressed very clearly, though of course in the usual narrative form, by Herodotus in the shape of two stories. In III 134–149, a passage I have already briefly quoted, he tells how Democedes' desire to escape from the Persian court where he was being held against his will ended up by causing the Persian wars that were such a disaster for the Orientals; and in III 1 he explains the Persian conquest of Egypt as a consequence of the fury of an Egyptian physician sent by his king Amasis as a present to Cambyses and thus separated from his wife and children.

I shall venture to add that a further step along this path is probably to be seen in the sale of texts relating to divination and purification. Plato is not detailed in his denounciation of Orphic charlatans and of their books, studied by F. Adorno;[22] but the Roman tradition about King Tarquinius' purchase of the Libri Sibyllini at a great price (Dion. Hal. IV. 62; Lactant. Div. Instit. 1, 6) is well known and clear in its historical implications. In the new context the wisdom embodied in the professional "savior" (healer or diviner) can be, so to say, detached, put in writing, and even sold.

It is interesting to note the R. Bloch[23] has recently connected the tradition about the Libri Sibyllini to an early hellenistic Etruscan mirror from Volsinii showing the seer Cacus playing the lyre and probably singing prophetic verse while a young assistant, Artile, is sitting near him, holding a written dyptic: the transition from the inspired song of the archaic *maître de vérité* to the written text is shown here in a fascinating synthesis.

To conclude: The pattern consisting of the concentration of healers and diviners (and also of texts on such special crafts) at court is dominant before the Iron Age. The crisis or collapse of the ancient Oriental palace organization implies that the healers and diviners are "free" to move about and to offer their services on "the market." It is this new situation that accounts for the figures I have described so far, and of course for the typology I have tried to reconstruct in section 5a, for only in the new Iron Age situation are the "healer-saviors" at the same time "free" and unattached, and "liminal" in the sense that their special skill and power set them apart in the way I have shown.

A study in just this context of the scene in Sophocles' *Oedipus Rex* (vv. 316–462) where Oedipus and Teiresias fight would be instructive. The diviner is accused of being dishonest and of having sold himself out to Oedipus' enemy Creon; in turn Teiresias admonishes Oedipus that diviners such as he are the equals of kings in virtue of the power of Apollo, whose prophet he proclaims himself to be. Two aspects of my healer-savior figures, the "mercenary" quality and the authority that comes from religious power, are dialectically opposed in this passage, and it is important to observe that once more such a power comes from a special relationship with a given god.

Of course, the "Orphic," "Pythagoric" and other Greek healer-saviors I have examined in section 3 are to be connected with the final pattern of the sequel I have just described. Orphism, in Bianchi's[24] words, is first of all a *literature*. This means that truth and thus salvation can now be found (and bought!) in written texts.

The process I have briefly hinted at in these few words seems to me to lead to *one* of the preliminaries not only of Greek mysteriosophy, but also of many other later soteriological religious phenomena. That salvation can be acquired, at least in principle, by all the members of a community of equals who choose to seek it (which is to say, by all who can afford it) begins to be true only when the detainers of the knowledge that leads to salvation leave the "Oriental" palace and cross over to the square, if not actually to the market square. That a god can be preferred to all others and followed as the true saving one, that a religion can be "founded" by an innovator, that it can be "spread" through books, that conversion can take place, and the very idea that initiation may be *freely* undertaken, all this can only be imagined in the new situation, for all this implies that *the believers choose.* Since at least some of these elements occur in later soteriologies, and in most of the Hellenistic-Oriental soteriological religions of the Roman Empire, we may venture to reverse the *locus communis* by asserting paradoxically that the roots of those soteriologies are buried in the *humus* of post-Oriental (or even "anti-Oriental" in the sense in which Greece and Israel, for instance, are "anti-Oriental") cultures and religions.

5.b.2

As H. B. Huffmon[25] has shown, possession-prophecy existed in the Near East, and especially in Western Mesopotamia and in Syria, before biblical times. It was a "popular" phenomenon, different from "technical divination," and was *used,* but never totally controlled, by the palace. It obviously "exploded," at least in Palestine, during the crisis of the early Iron Age, and emerged strongly (see the beginning of my section 2) in connection with the collapse of the palace system. In ancient Israel, as I have shown in section 3, the (mythical or "historical") charismatic seers, healers and "saviors," who were often "possessed," were connected by tradition with early Yahwism; while at least some of the more archaic Greek (mythical or, possibly, "historical") charismatic "saviors" were connected in a similar way with the cult of Dionysos or of Apollo.

It would be absurd to try here to compare the two religious movements; but it is possible to note that both Dionysism, and early Yahwism as presented in the Bible, react against a polytheistic environment in the name of the totalitarian relationship with one specific god, often involving possession (for Dionysism, this has been acutely, if briefly, noted by J. P. Vernant[26]). The Dionysian and Yahwistic healers and "prophets" I have quoted can make miracles and cure possession but are often possessed, for they seem to be part of an atmosphere of what I. M. Lewis[27] calls Ecstatic Religion.

Now, H. Jeanmaire[28] has criticized E. Rohde's[29] somewhat naive old theory of the origin of the ecstatic religion of Dionysos. But Rohde was surely right in interpreting the widespread phenomena of ecstasy and possession that were typical (but not exclusive) of Dionysism and were endemic, and at times "epidemical," in ancient Greek society, as a response to a crisis that was of course a social crisis, and even as a form of social rebellion. The same can be said of the early charismatic and "prophetic" movement in Israel: its social as well as its "psychological" aspects have been studied by many, and already by H. Gunkel.[30]

The Dionysian and Yahwistic "healers" present themselves as "masters" and controllers of disturbances and as pacifiers, if not of the crisis, at least of its symptoms, for they "belong" to the god that causes possession, but they can treat it. Their ambiguous position gives them a power the institutional power (the king) does not possess, for at times (Saul) the king is also possessed against his will. The fact that all this does not imply the "success" of the two religious movements (and surely there was no such success, for the possible Bacchic sympathies of some *tyrannoi* or the short-lived religious attempts of kings like Jehu were nothing more than exceptional episodes) clearly indicates that the great crisis that is behind the possessions is being dealt with, i.e., that society is being rationalized, along different lines, for the "total" religious demands of Yahwism and Dionysism provide forms of escape, but no solution. In Greece the *polis* and its coherent polytheism, in Israel monarchy and its "official syncretism" (Soggin[31]) that is nearer than most scholars would like to think to the traditional religion of the rural masses, provide answers, furnish society with an ideological unity.

It would be easy but wrong to follow Rohde and Pettazzoni[32] in explaining Orphism as a "development" of Dionysism into the mystical ideology of small sects, parallel (in Pettazzoni's view) to the transformation that led from the archaic "ecstatic" nabism to the prophetic movement in Israel. This is not feasible for a series of reasons illustrated by Jeanmaire and, more recently, also by Detienne[33] and by Bianchi,[34] who is right in insisting that "non si dovrà immaginare un rapporto necessariamente e sempre diacronico (o, peggio, evoluzionistico) tra dionisismo entusiastico-orgiastico e dionisismo orfico-misteriosofico. Dovette trattarsi infatti di correnti in parte parallele. . . ." Yet it cannot be denied that the "prophets" and healers of Orphism and Pythagorism as well as the later $n^e bi'im$ were somehow similar, in their form and function, to the archair "healers and saviors," and that their doctrines were connected respectively to the religion of Dionysos (as Bianchi[35] reminds us) and to archaic Yahwism.

The differences were of course many, and we cannot deal with them here. One novelty (the written texts) I have discussed in the previous section (5.b.1); I will mention only one other novelty, quoting Plato who (resp. II 364 E) wrote that the books of Orpheus and Musaeus convinced whole cities that purifications should and could be offered by *poleis* and by individuals, both for the living and for the dead, because they freed from the sufferings of the Netherworld, while terrible sufferings awaited those who had not offered sacrifice.

The salvation offered by the Orphic healers was thus no more a salvation of the type I have described at the beginning of this chapter, for the Orphic books taught, in Dodds'[36] words, that "the body is a prisonhouse of the soul; and that the unpleasant consequences of sin, both in this world and in the next, can be washed away by ritual means."

It would be "evoluzionistico" (in the sense in which the word is used by

Bianchi in the passage I have just quoted) to state that this attention to Afterlife and this negative attitude toward the body are an ultimate consequence of the intrinsic incapability of the charismatic healer to rationalize and thus to heal the very crisis that produced him. Yet it should be possible to see the Orphic religiosity that stems from such beliefs as the final outcome of a historical process involving the Eastern Mediterranean, that could be described as twofold—consisting of the rise of forms of "ecstatic religion" and of what we have called "nonroyal healer-saviors" in a period of crisis (the economical and social "revolution" of the early Iron Age), and of the new meaning and function acquired not so much by "saviors" as by *the very concept of salvation* in increasingly "rationalized" societies.

6

All this (sections 5.b.1 and 5.b.2) is merely hypothetical, and each paragraph presents one only of the many possible approaches. But A. Brelich[37] has listed the phenomena that, in spite of *communis opinio*, can *not* account for the rise of soteriology (in the more specific sense of the term, defined by Brelich himself in the same context): *not* cosmogonical myths, *not* "dying gods," *not* sacral kingship, but rather "nuovi orientamenti culturali estranei al politeismo." The question, I think, is open; and any reasonable hypothesis or approach is, I hope, useful.

NOTES

1. D. Sabbatucci, *Saggio sul misticismo greco* (Rome, 1968).

2. U. Bianchi, *Initiation, mystères, gnose:* AA. VV., *Initiation* (Leiden, 1969).

3. J. Teixidor, *The Pagan God, Popular Religion in the Graeco-Roman Near East* (Princeton, 1977).

4. M. Liverani, *La Royauté syrienne de l'Age du Bronze Récent:* AA. VV., Le Palais et la Royauté (Archéologie et Civilization), Actes de la XIX Rencontre Assyriologique Internationale (Paris, 1971), 329–356; idem, *Sydyk e Misor:* Studi E. Volterra, VI, s.l. 1969, 57–74.

5. F. M. Heichelheim, *An Ancient Economic History*, I (Leiden, 1968), 193–212.

6. G. Buccellati, *Cities and Nations of Ancient Syria* (Rome, 1967).

7. C. Grottanelli, *Possessione carismatica e razionalizzazione statale nella Bibbia ebraica:* SSR I (1977), 263–288 (chapter 5 in this volume).

8. J. Pedersen, *The Role Played by Inspired Persons among the Israelites and the Arabs:* AA. VV., *Studies in Old Testament Prophecy (Festschrift Robinson)* (1950), 127–142.

9. G. Fohrer, *Geschichte der Israelitische Religion* (Berlin, 1968).

10. Ibid. I quote from D. E. Green's English translation (London, 1973), 233.

11. J. Morgenstern, *The Fire upon the Altar* (Leiden, 1963).

12. C. Grottanelli, *Spunti comparativi per la storia biblica di Giuseppe:* "Oriens Antiquus" XV (1976), 115–140.

13. C. Grottaneli, *Aesop in Babylon: Actes de la XXVII Rencontre Assyriologique Internationale* (Berlin, 1978).

14. R. Pettazzoni, *La religione della Grecia antica fino ad Alessandro* (Turin, 1953, 2nd ed.), 105–106.

15. M. Detienne, *Les Maîtres de Vérité dans la Grèce Archaïque* (Paris, 1973, 2nd ed.).

16. S. Mazzarino, *Il pensiero storico classico*, I (Bari, 1966), 23–51, 532–533.

17. See G. Camassa's intervention in the discussion published in AA. VV., *Orfismo in Magna Grecia, Atti del XIV Convegno di Studi sulla Magna Grecia* (Naples, 1975) 164–171.

18. For a similar attempt, involving Greek sources only, see L. Bieler, Θεῖος ἀνήρ (Darmstadt, 1967, 2nd ed.; Vienna, 1935).

19. V. W. Turner, *The Ritual Process: Structure and Anti-Structure* (Chicago, 1969).

20. E. R. Dodds, *The Greeks and the Irrational* (Berkeley, 1951).

21. C. Zaccagnini, *Patterns of Mobility among Near Eastern Craftsmen:* Journal of Near Eastern Studies 42 (1983), 245–264 Cf. also M. Liverani, "Il modo di produzione," in S. Moscati (ed.), *L'Alba della Civiltà*, II (Turin, 1976), 33–34. Cuneiform material has been published by E. Edel, *Ägyptische Ärtzte und ägyptische Medizin am hethitischen Königshof. Neue funde von Keilschriftsbriefen Ramses' II. aus Bogazköy* (Opladen, 1976).

22. F. Adorno, *Da Orfeo a Platone. L'Orfismo come problematica filosofica:* AA. VV., Orfismo in Magna Grecia, Atti del XIV Convegno di Studi sulla Magna Grecia (see note 17), 9–32.

23. R. Bloch, *Les prodiges dans l'antiquité classique* (Paris, 1963), fig. 2.

24. U. Bianchi, *Prometeo, Orfeo, Adamo. Tematiche religiose sul destino, il male, la salvezza* (Rome, 1976), 130, 134.

25. H. B. Huffmon, *The Origins of Prophecy*, in F. M. Cross, W. E. Lemke and P. D. Miller (eds.), *Magnalia Dei: The Mighty Acts of God: Essays on the Bible and Archaeology in memory of G. E. Wright* (New York, 1976); contra: H. Orlinsky, *The Seer in Ancient Israel:* "Oriens Antiquus" 4 (1965), 153–174.

26. J. P. Vernant, *Mythe et pensée chez les Grecs: Etudes de psychologie historique* (Paris, 1965) (chapter 6: "Aspects de la personne dans la religion grecque").

27. I. M. Lewis, *Ecstatic Religion* (Harmondsworth, 1975, 2nd ed.).

28. H. Jeanmaire, *Dionysos: Histoire du culte de Bacchus* (Paris, 1951).

29. E. Rohde, *Psyche, Seelencult und Unsterblichkeitsglaube der Griechen* (Freiburg in Brisgau, 1890–1894).

30. H. Gunkel, *Die Propheten* (Göttingen, 1917).

31. J. A. Soggin, *Der offiziel gefördete Synkretismus in Israel wärend des 10. Jahrhundert:* "Zeitschrift für die Alttestamentliche Wissenschaft" 78 (1966), 179–204.

32. R. Pettazzoni, *La religione della Grecia antica fino ad Alessandro* (see note 14), 104–126.

33. M. Detienne, *Dionysos mis à mort* (Paris, 1977), 163–217.

34. U. Bianchi, *Prometeo, Orfeo, Adamo* (see note 24), 92.

35. Ibidem, 132.

36. E. R. Dodds, *The Greeks and the Irrational* (see note 20), 149.

37. A. Brelich, *Politeismo e soteriologia: The Saviour God. Comparative Studies in the Concept of Salvation presented to E. O. James* (S. G. F. Brandon, ed.) (Manchester, 1963), 37–50.

8

BIBLICAL NARRATIVE AND
THE ANCIENT NOVEL
Common Motifs and Themes

1. Oriental Narratives and the Ancient Novel

The recovery of a vast quantity of Near Eastern texts, belonging to different linguistic, cultural and political contexts but forming a continuum across the boundaries of time, space, and literary genres, has enabled specialists of Greek and Roman history and cultures to look at their materials in a new way. To quote but one example, the formation of Greek society and religion in the eighth and seventh centuries B.C.E. has been profoundly revised by Walter Burkert in the light of the contemporary, and of some older, Near Eastern data, by acknowledging and reviewing the Oriental influences on the Greek world during the so-called Orientalizing period.[1] Though vaguer and less scholarly attempts to assess that influence had already been produced in great quantity throughout the history of Greek studies, Burkert's painstaking, meticulous and critical survey is indeed pioneering work and a truly seminal achievement. Surely further research in this direction is forthcoming, and it shall alter our views of the ancient Greek world still more.[2]

In the light of these same data, and especially of Near Eastern "literary" texts (variously labeled as "epics," "myths," "tales," "historical" texts,[3] but also forming a continuum), the literatures of Greece and Rome are also being profoundly revised. The connections between Hesiod's cosmogonical poem, the *Theogony*, and the cosmogonic, often poetic, texts of the Near East are well known, and have been explored by many specialists;[4] Homer and the Bible have also been studied together.[5] At the other end of the literary history of Greece, the Hellenistic novel of the Eastern Mediterranean, and its Latin counterpart of the first and second centuries C.E., are also being placed against their ancient Near Eastern background. The Oriental roots of the Hellenistic novel were not unknown to scholars such as Kerenyi[6] and Braun[7] in the late twenties and in the thirties; but only in the light of the enormously rich literatures revealed since then by the discovery of clay tablets and papyrus scrolls is the significance of these roots really apparent. To A. Lesky[8] we owe the first critical assessment of that importance, and J. W. B. Barns[9] and B. P. Reardon[10] have insisted on ancient Egyptian parallels. But G. Anderson's book on ancient fiction[11] has now proved beyond doubt that the Oriental roots of the

Hellenistic novel go back to the earliest known Near Eastern civilizations, and that the ancient narrative tradition of the Near East provides the bulk of the material for the sophisticated stories we find in the Greek and Roman novels. The genre is thus not a mere product of the Hellenistic age; the importance of the questions of development and relative chronology of the novels becomes less, while the work of the novelists is seen to consist less of inventing original narrative structures than of modifying or reshaping a millennial tradition.

Anderson's work is based mainly upon Mesopotamian texts, but it also includes some Ugaritic, Egyptian and even some biblical parallels to the Hellenistic narratives. In a way the use of the most recently discovered material seems, in Anderson's book, to have replaced or shadowed the possible use of other, traditionally well known Oriental literatures. Thus, the Ahiqar tradition is used but scarcely; the better known Egyptian stories of Lefebvre's collection[12] are rarely mentioned, though they may have helped to solve many problems posed by Anderson's Hellenistic material. Though the *Arabian Nights* and other medieval and later Oriental narratives are used, and seen as a continuation of the ancient Near Eastern narrative traditions, some genuine ancient texts such as the Hittite-Hurrian tales[13] are never quoted. But what seems most striking to me is the fact that the Hebrew Bible, with its great wealth of narrative material comparable to the Hellenistic stories discussed by Anderson, is very rarely exploited. This is particularly surprising because one important link between the Hellenistic novel and Near Eastern narrative traditions is provided precisely by an early romance, which was written in Greek and found in Egypt, based upon a biblical episode. I refer, of course, to the text called *Joseph and Aseneth*.[14]

This limited use of biblical parallels may be explained by considering the traditional status of the Hebrew Bible: a sacred text for many of us, and thus often seen as separate and unique. But even the most traditional biblical scholarship now accepts a view of the Bible as a Near Eastern text that has to be studied together with all the other texts of the ancient Orient:[15] indeed, the narrative sections of the Hebrew Bible are one specific strand in the complex texture of Near Eastern narrative tradition; when treated as such by students of that tradition, they have always repaid researchers very generously.

2. The Joseph Story and the Life of Aesop

A fundamental text in the study of the origins of the Greek and Latin novel is the Aesop Romance or *Vita Aesopi*, a narrative about the life of the culture-hero, storyteller and sage Aesop. It was known to medieval and modern European culture through a manuscript tradition that has been studied by B. E. Perry[16] and goes back to the second or third century C.E. According to Perry, however, the prototypes of the known texts may go back to a period between the first century B.C.E. and the second century C.E.; but the archetype of all the texts discussed was probably not the earliest form in which the biography of Aesop had appeared, but may have been derived in part from a written tradition reaching back as far as the fifth century B.C.E. A. Momigliano[17] also proposed that anecdotes about Aesop and the Seven Sages circulated widely in Greece around that same century and were connected to the birth of Greek biography, and A. Lesky[18] went even further than this, and imagined that a *Greek Story of Aesop* was formed, in the manner of the Oriental story of Ahiqar, in the sixth century B.C.E.[19]

As is well known,[20] the central part of the Aesop Romance, the part that places the storyteller in Babylonia and in Egypt, while having no precise Greek equivalent, corresponds to the well-known Near Eastern story of the Sage Ahiqar. Not only is Aesop, like Ahiqar, presented as a sage counselor of the kings of Mesopotamia and of Egypt, but the two narratives share an identical plot, the only difference being that in the Near Eastern story Ahiqar, a wise royal chancellor, takes the place of Aesop, and Sennacherib and Esarhaddon, kings of Assyria, that of Lykeros the Babylonian in the Aesop Romance, while Nadin, Ahiqar's adopted son, and an anonymous king of Egypt correspond to Ainos, Aesop's adopted son, and to Nectenabo, the king of Egypt, respectively.

Now, the story of Ahiqar was known in several versions written in Syriac, Arabic, Ethiopian and Slavonic. These were carefully edited in the last century and translated into English in 1898; but in 1907 a papyrus was found in Elephantine in Egypt that contained an Aramaic version of the story going back to the fifth century B.C.E. In all probability the story itself is somewhat older than this, and may go back to the seventh century.[21]

I shall not deal here with the complex problem of the relationship between the Aesop Romance and the Story of Ahiqar.[22] I have dwelt on the problem in my essay quoted in note 20 above, and I still think that both stories were created at the same time in the context of an Eastern Mediterranean *koinē*, and by using a complex narrative repertoire. What is more important in the present context is the fact that narrative motifs that are well known in the Near East are found not only in the Babylonian and Egyptian parts of the Aesop Romance, which correspond to the Ahiqar texts, but also in the more "Greek" parts. For instance, as I noticed in my earlier essay, the motif of the sacred cup hidden among Aesop's belongings by the hostile Delphians is present in Genesis 44, where the patriarch Joseph hides his divination cup in his brother Benjamin's luggage and then orders it to be found and detains the boy, accusing him of the theft.[23]

Though the motif is exactly the same (and we shall return to it in the next section of this essay), its context and function within the two narratives are profoundly different. In the Aesop Romance, the hero of the story is also the victim of the false accusation: the Delphians, criticized and offended by Aesop, plant the cup on him and thus manage to arrest him and to execute him. In the biblical Joseph story, the protagonist is the author, not the victim, of the deceitful deed; he acts thus in order to detain his youngest brother, Benjamin, who is the most beloved son of Jacob, and to obtain control of, and to punish, his brothers who had been hostile to him. This different use of a common motif is, however, more than just different. It is clearly a neat structural reversal. The authors of the two stories have used a traditional motif in two ways that are geometrically opposed. This symmetry points to a connection, though probably not to a direct one, and encourages us to consider the two narratives together.

If we compare the biblical Joseph story to the oriental section of the Aesop Romance, we notice immediately that the relationship between the two narratives is not one of diversity or of opposition, as in the use of the "stolen cup" motif in the two texts, but rather one of similarity, though of course not of identity as in the case of the relationship between the Aesop Romance and the Story of Ahiqar.[24] For in both stories, the hero is a foreigner and a slave. In both stories, the protagonist is a wise yet lowly man, promoted by king(s) because of his wisdom and knowledge. In both stories, the hero is unjustly accused and hated, imprisoned and almost killed, then sought for by a king whom he saves, and exalted by the monarch. Both stories contain a *Scheintod* motif: Joseph is thought to be dead at the beginning of his adventure, while Aesop is condemned to death and hidden away in an empty tomb and secretly nourished by Hermippus, the official who had been charged with his execution. Even some of the differences between the two stories are clearly different motifs within a common theme: thus Aesop solves riddles for his Egyptian king, while Joseph interprets dreams; Aesop is hidden in an empty tomb, while Joseph is first thrown by his brothers in a dry cistern (Hebrew *bôr*), and later imprisoned by order of Pharaoh in a dungeon. In one case, the differences between the Joseph story and the Aesop Romances are bridged over by the Aramaic narrative about Ahiqar: Jacob believes Joseph is dead because the brothers show him Joseph's dress reddened by the blood of a kid they have killed for the purpose; though there is no clear parallel for this in the Aesop Romance, the Aramaic Ahiqar text presents a pretended capital execution of the disgraced official simulated by killing, not the animal of modern folk tales and of the story of Joseph and his brothers, but a eunuch slave.[25] Here, as in the case of the "stolen cup" motif, we have a reversal, for the simulated death of Joseph is a terrible blow to his father, while the death of Ahiqar must be simulated in order to satisfy the king who wants Ahiqar killed.

The Joseph story, which resembles the Aesop Romance so closely,[26] has recently been the object of much attention on the part of biblical scholars. D. B. Redford[27] has insisted on the importance of its Egyptian setting and suggests a date in the seventh, sixth or fifth centuries B.C.E. for its composition. In spite of A. Kitchen's[28] important criticism of Redford's book, the late date proposed by Redford has much to recommend it.[29] Indeed, even if G. W. Coats[30] is right against Redford in seeing the Joseph story as an integral part of a firmly structured unit, the patriarchal narrative of the book of Genesis, Coats' Solomonic dating of the Genesis stories must be discarded in the light of recent research on the origin and nature of biblical "historical" narrative (including Genesis), which has been shown to be no earlier than the sixth century B.C.E.[31] So, whether or not the story of Joseph is an integral part of the original Genesis narrative, the date of its composition is probably not too far removed from the date of the formation of the Story of Ahiqar and of the most ancient versions of the Aesop Romance. The three stories were probably shaped in the Eastern Mediterranean in a period ranging from the seventh to the fifth century B.C.E.

In spite of its probably late date, the story of Joseph (just like the Hellenistic novel in the light of Anderson's contribution) contained a large deal of ancient narrative material. In particular, it derived from traditions of the type attested by the Egyptian story of the two brothers, a popular narrative of the Nineteenth Dynasty.[32] The protagonists of that story, Anpu and Bata, were two gods of the Egyptian pantheon; but the narrative treats them as human beings, turning them into a married peasant and his unmarried younger brother. The transformation of myths about gods into novels about men, which has often been recognized in the background of the Hellenistic novel, is already at work in this ancient text; it is complete in the writing of the Joseph story, a tale that uses mythological motifs in a new, and totally earthly, setting.[33]

Since the Story of Ahiqar and the Aesop Romance also contain narrative motifs (see above, note 20) that can be traced to previous Near Eastern (and, more specifically, Egyptian) tales, the analogy between the three texts that has been described so far is not only a similarity in content and in date, but also the result of a common dependence on a rich and ancient narrative tradition.[34] In the light of this complex relationship, the fact that both Joseph and Aesop were culture-heroes whose funerary monuments were famous landmarks placed in sites (Delphi, Shechem) known as important (cultic) centers, and the similarity of their very names, may be seen as the trace of a common background that goes beyond the level of narrative tradition. We should consider the fact that, though Joseph's name has a good Semitic structure and at least one convincing Semitic etymology, Aesop's name is unique and strange in its Greek context.[35] But this is a different problem, which may perhaps be solved elsewhere; here we should be content with the discovery of a complex relationship between the Aesop Romance, which plays such an important part in the history of Greek narrative and in the origin of the Hellenistic novel, and the biblical Joseph story.

3. The Stolen Cup Motif

If we turn to a more detailed analysis, we shall find that the relationship we have described so far is only one specific aspect of a much wider series of connections binding the biblical Joseph story to novels and other narrative texts of Hellenistic and Roman times. In particular, one should pay attention to the fact that a number of Hellenistic and some later narrative texts contain motifs or structural aspects that occur in the biblical story. I shall present only a couple of examples, but there are sufficient, I hope, to point to a more complex picture and to justify some generalizations.

Let us examine the "stolen cup" motif I mentioned above as being present, in reversed positions, in both the Joseph story and the Aesop Romance. The Bible (Gen. 44:1–6) presents the motif as follows:

(Joseph) commanded the steward of his house, saying: "Fill the men's sacks with grain, as much as they can carry, [and put every man's money in his sack's mouth]. And put my cup, the silver cup, in the sack's mouth of the youngest [with his corn money].[36] And the steward did according to the words that Joseph had spoken. As soon as the morning was light, the men were sent away with their asses. When they had gone but a short distance from the city, Joseph said to his steward: "Up, follow after the men; and when you overtake them, say to them: —Why have you returned evil for good? Why have you stolen my silver cup? Is it not from this that my lord drinks, and by this that he divines? You have done wrong in so doing. —." When he overtook them, he spoke to them these words. The brothers declare themselves innocent, and add: "With whomever of your servants (the cup) be found, let him die, and we also will be my lord's slaves." Then every man quickly lowered his sack to the ground, and every man opened his sack. And he searched, beginning with the eldest and ending with the youngest; and the cup was found in Benjamin's sack. Then they rent their clothes, and every man loaded his ass, and they returned to the city.

The Greek Septuagint text calls the cup a κόνδυ in this passage; one should also note the presence of asses carrying grain sacks. The Aesop Romance speaks of a φιάλη χρυσῆ, and no details are given of Aesop's departure from Delphi and of his capture: we are told only that Aesop is caught with the cup that the Delphians had placed among his belongings, arrested and sentenced to death as a *hierosylos*.

The episode is told in ways that are very similar in the two main recensions of the Aesop Romance, Perry's G and W texts.[37] The G text, however, contains a detail that is absent from the W recension, but present in the biblical Joseph narrative: when accused of the theft, Aesop declares, just like the brothers do in Genesis 44, that he is ready to die, if the golden cup is found in his possession (ἀπολέσθαι θέλω, ἐάν τι τοιοῦτον εὑρεθῇ εἰς ἐμέ).[38] A clearer expression of his good faith could hardly be imagined. The detail has good parallels both in Greek narrative tradition[39] and in the Bible (in the Book of Genesis 32, Laban accuses Jacob of having stolen his sacred *teraphim*, and Jacob, not knowing that they have indeed been stolen by his wife Rachel, who is with him, exclaims: "With whomever you find your gods, let him not live"; it is probably for this reason that Rachel died in giving birth to Benjamin years after having escaped detection by Laban).

In the Aesop Romance only Aesop's σχεύη are mentioned, and there is no trace of the grain sack containing the precious, indeed the sacred, object. This sack is probably an Egyptian trait, for we find such a sack in one of the Middle Kingdom "folktales" contained in the Westcar papyrus.[40] Three children are born together to the god Re from the priestess Redjeddet; the woman is assisted in childbirth by the potter-god Khnum and by the goddesses Isis, Nephtys,

Meskhent and Heqet. The divine midwives give the children their names according to specific birth episodes, and their destinies are fixed together with their names: they are to be the first kings of the Fifth Dynasty. Redjeddet offers the helpful deities a sack of barley as a parting gift: they should take it home with them but, instead of giving it to their bearer to carry, they place three kingly crowns inside it, and hand it to Redjeddet's servants. The sack is thus placed in an empty, sealed room, and when, fourteen days later, it is fetched because barley is needed to make beer, kingly and festive sounds miraculously fill the sealed room, and the sack's supernatural contents are revealed.

Whether one accepts the (sixth through) fifth century B.C.E. date for the origin of the Aesop Romance or not, the "stolen cup" motif of that narrative is probably rather ancient. Herodotus (II 134) says that Aesop was unjustly killed by the Delphians, and gives no details; but in a lost work, the fourth-century author Herakleides of Pontus, a disciple of Aristotle, explicitly mentioned the fact that a golden cup had been placed in Aesop's luggage, and that he was condemned to death as a sacrilegious thief. A scholion to Aristophanes' Wasps 1446 recounts that the Delphians, having been criticized by Aesop, hid a sacred cup among his belongings, caught up with him on the way to Phocis, and pretended to catch him red-handed. In his De sera numinis vindicta 12, Plutarch is less specific, and says that Aesop was accused of a sacrilegious deed.[41]

Just like the "stolen cup" motif in the Aesop tradition, the corresponding episode in the Joseph story also has its starting point. The biblical description of the framing and capture of Benjamin is repeated by many later Jewish writers who, both in Palestine and in the Hellenistic world of the Diaspora, dealt with the Joseph story, either to comment upon it in Midrashic fashion or to present it to a Greek-speaking (but often still Jewish) world.[42] In his Jewish Antiquities (II.vi.7), Flavius Josephus expands upon the biblical narrative[43] by adding new details:

> But after the supper, when [Joseph and his brothers] had retired to rest, he ordered his steward to give them their measures of corn, and again to conceal the purchase-money in their sacks, but also to leave deposited in Benjamin's pack his own favourite drinking cup. This he did to prove his brethren and see whether they would assist Benjamin, when arrested for theft and in apparent danger, or would abandon him, assured of their own innocence, and return to their father. The servant executed his orders and, at daybreak, all unaware of these proceedings, the sons of Jacob departed along with Simeon doubly delighted both at having recovered him and at bringing back Benjamin to their father in accordance with their promise. But suddenly they were surrounded by a troop of horsemen, bringing with them the servant who had deposited the cup in Benjamin's pack. Confounded by this unexpected attack of horsemen, they asked for what reason they assailed men who had but now enjoyed the honour and hospitality of their master. The pursuers retorted by calling them scoundrels, who, unmindful of that very hospitality and benevolence of Joseph, had not scrupled to treat him ill, carrying off that loving-cup in which he had pledged their

healths . . . The brothers protest that they are innocent, and the cup is found in Benjamin's sack. The brothers groan, mourn and rend their clothes, blaming themselves for Benjamin's plight. "So the horsemen arrested Benjamin and led him off to Joseph, the brothers following."

Though the asses are never mentioned in this version of the narrative, Benjamin's sack, which contains the cup, is said to be a part of Benjamin's pack, the term for pack, φορτίον, being the usual name of the pack carried by pack animals. Joseph's drinking- and divination-cup becomes "the loving-cup with which he had pledged [his brothers'] health." Joseph is said to have laid the trap for Benjamin in order to test his brothers' fidelity to their sibling and father. Finally, a troop of horsemen, of whom the Bible knew nothing, suddenly appears upon the scene and apprehends the brothers.

These horsemen, obviously an addition by Josephus, point to the fact that the Joseph story could be expanded upon very freely even by an author for whom the narrative contained in Genesis 44 was a sacred text. This, however, will cease to surprise us if we consider that it was precisely through such gradual additions of details, glosses, and parts that the biblical texts were formed in the first place. What is more striking is the fact that such horsemen appear, in a very similar context, in two of the best-known novels of the Hellenistic world, both probably later than Josephus' text by less than a century.

The Greek *Ass Novel*, attributed to Lucian of Samosata,[44] contains the following episode. The hero, Lucius, who had been magically turned into an ass, is bought by a group of castrated followers of the Syrian goddess, who beg their way through the countryside, and perform various strange "religious" feats in the villages. On one occasion, they reach a large and populous village, "where they introduced a fresh monstrosity by insisting that the goddess should not stay in the house of a human but take up residence in the temple of the local goddess held in most honour amongst them." This is gladly accepted by the villagers, and after many days, the protagonist adds,

> my masters wished to leave for the nearby city, and asked the goddess back from the local people. They entered the sacred precinct themselves, carried her out, put her on my back and rode off. Now when the impious fellows entered that precinct, they stole a golden bowl (φιάλην χρυσῆν), a votive offering (ἀνάθημα). This they carried off concealed in the person of the goddess. When the villagers discovered this, they gave immediate pursuit; then, upon drawing near, they leapt down from their horses and laid hold of the fellows on the road, calling them impious and thieves of sacred objects (δυσσεβεῖς καὶ ἱεροσύλους), and demanding the return of the stolen offering. They searched everywhere and found it in the bosom of the goddess. They therefore tied up the effeminate fellows, dragged them off and threw them into prison; the goddess whom I had carried they took and gave to another temple, while the golden vessel (τὸ χρυσίον) they gave back to their local goddess.

The corresponding episode in Apuleius' *Golden Ass*[45] is practically identical: the "local goddess" of the Greek text becomes the Phrygian *Mater Deum*, another oriental deity; the sacred vessel is an *aureum cantharum*; the castrated Galli leave at dawn, like Josephs' brothers in the Bible and in Josephus' account—but of course, they leave early (*luce dubia*) to avoid being detected. The story is told with greater ability: as in Josephus' account, the horsemen appear upon the scene suddenly, and the effect is greater still, for nothing has been said so far to explain their presence: *Et ecce nobis repente de tergo manus spiculis armati supercurrunt equites aegreque cohibita equorum curruli rabie Philebum ceterosque comites eius involant avidi colloque constricto et sacrilegos inpurosque compellantes interdum pugnis obverberant.* . . . The golden cup is found *in ipso deae gremio* and the thieves minimize their own guilt while they are bound, brought back to the village and thrown in the local *tullianum*. The divine image and the vessel are reconsecrated and given to the local temple.

Now, we know that there probably were other Greek *Ass* narratives, one of which was extremely similar to Lucian's text, while according to Anderson another, probably shorter, *Ass Tale* was translated into Latin by L. Cornelius Sisenna in the first century B.C.E. and goes back to the second century B.C.E.[46] Therefore, it is impossible to establish a precise date for the Hellenistic novel or tale containing this episode, and so to determine the relative chronology of such a narrative in connection with Josephus' enlarged version of the framing of Benjamin. The same is true of the relationship between the biblical episode and the corresponding one in the Aesop Romance; and it is also difficult to determine whether some direct connection exists between the *Ass Tale* episode and the story of Aesop's mishap in Delphi.[47]

While we are unable to trace the history of the motif, we do possess material for a comparative study of its function and meaning, and of its form and specific details, in the various texts we have examined. Thus, in respect to the function and meaning of the motif within its *wider* context, we must classify the Joseph and the Aesop narratives together, for they present the episode as the capture and punishment of an innocent person who has been trapped into a dangerous position. Moreover, the ambiguous position of Benjamin, who is chosen as a scapegoat precisely *because* he is "chosen" by his father Jacob as the favorite son, may be connected with the suggested Egyptian derivation of the motif, that is clearly the symbol of divine election and kingly power in the Westcar papyrus: we should not forget that just before the silver cup episode, during Joseph's meal with his brothers, Benjamin had received from Joseph's table a portion that was five times as much as any of theirs (Genesis 43:34): a clear symbol of kingly election, as shown by other biblical texts dealing with the Benjaminite king Saul.[48] On the other hand, the motif has, in the two versions of the *Ass Tale*, the opposite function of bringing to grief a group of impious scoundrels; and their reaction when caught contrasts strangely and ironically with the simple words of Joseph's brothers or of Aesop. We have also seen that the similarity between the Joseph and the Aesop versions of the motif does not exclude, indeed, that it points to a profound difference, which must be considered a structural reversal.

Some important details of the motif seem to tie the various episodes to one another in ways that are totally independent of this classification according to function and meaning. Thus, the stolen vessel is a silver cup in the Joseph story, and a golden cup in all other texts; it is a drinking and a divining cup belonging to the powerful vizier Joseph in the biblical narrative, only a drinking cup belonging to Joseph in Josephus' account, and a holy cup belonging to a sanctuary in all other narratives.[49] The donkeys carrying luggage appear in the biblical episode, and only implicitly in Josephus; there is no such animal in the Aesop traditions, but an ass is prominent in the *Ass Tale* episode. Aesop's declaration of innocence in the D recension of the Aesop Romance is similar to the brothers' declaration of innocence in Genesis, while the departing group with asses are overtaken by horsemen in the account by Josephus and in the *Ass Tales*,[50] and the way the detail in question is treated by the Latin text is surprisingly similar to the treatment of the corresponding detail by Josephus.

All these complex and apparently contradictory typological connections point to a rich context of widespread narrative traditions, both Oriental and Greek, underlying the narratives we have compared: no other hypothesis could account for the criss-crossing of differences and similarities across time and space. These texts are the tip of an iceberg. Moreover, some futher correspondences are not immediately evident: they must be found. I give only one example.

We have seen that the asses carried corn sacks in the biblical Joseph story, and that corn sacks were still important in Josephus' version, in spite of the obliteration of the donkeys. We have also seen that the sack containing grain and a silver cup could well be derived from a sack containing barley and three royal crowns in an Egyptian narrative. Now, the ass, as we have shown, reappears to carry the cup in the Greek and Latin versions of the *Ass Tale*; but the cup is not hidden in a sack: it is inserted in the bosom (in the folds of the tunic) of a statue, carried by the ass. But we shall now observe that the grain does not disappear. In the Greek *Ass Tale*, we are simply told that the holy beggars receive various types of cereal food, and specifically barley for their ass and wheat for themselves. But Apuleius expands upon this, and adds that the *cinaedi* received *farris et siliginis aliquid et . . . hordeum deae gerulo*: they put all this into sacks and placed the sacks on the ass's back, so that the animal carried both the goddess and the grain, being a temple and a granary at the same time (*et horreum simul et templum incederem*).[51] The position of the stolen cup has changed; but the function of the ass, which carries it, as a movable granary, has remained the same, and entails the association of a sacred, precious vessel with cereal food.

4. The Scheintod Motif

A wide series of specific aspects, episodes and details diversify the Joseph story sharply from the Aesop Romance we have compared it with so far. In particular, Joseph is no laughing-stock, no intelligent but ugly misfit: he is a seductive young man who achieves success through many adventures, and is finally re-united with those he loves.[52] Precisely this distinctive quality of the Joseph story, as the tale of a charming hero who reaches promotion, and finally happi-ness, after a touching scene, during which he is recognized by the family he had lost at the beginning of the narrative, makes the Joseph story surprisingly similar to some "typical" Hellenistic novels. In this respect, the biblical Joseph story is more "Hellenistic" than the Aesop Romance; more "Hellenistic," even, than the Hellenistic novel of *Joseph and Aseneth*.

I have shown above that both the Aesop Romance and the Aramaic Story of Ahiqar and its later versions contained a motif that was frequent in Greek nov-els: the *Scheintod* motif. We have also noticed that comparable episodes ap-peared twice in the biblical Joseph story: once at the beginning of the story (Gen. 37), and again at the beginning of Joseph's adventures in Egypt (Gen. 39–40). A more detailed comparative analysis of the texts in question shows that, as happens with the general structure of the plot, in the treatment of the motif the Joseph story of Genesis has more in common with the Hellenistic novels containing the *Scheintod* motif than the other two narrative traditions have.

The texts containing the stories of Aesop and of Ahiqar present the *Schein-tod* motif as follows: the hero, a wise minister of an Oriental king, is unjustly accused of some misdeed, and the monarch sentences him to death; but the man charged with the execution hides the hero away (in an empty tomb),[53] and pretends he has killed him. The king is suddenly faced with some difficult problem and realizes that only the wise minister he has sentenced to death could save him; the wise man suddenly appears upon the scene and solves the problem. This episode, as I have shown elsewhere, is paralleled in some bibli-cal narratives and in Herodotus;[54] in the Joseph story the corresponding episode shows Joseph unjustly accused by Potiphar's wife, imprisoned and des-tined to die, then saved because he can interpret Pharaoh's dreams, and finally promoted.[55] So the Joseph story contains an episode that corresponds well to the *Scheintod* episode of the narratives about Aesop and Ahiqar (and in that episode of the Joseph story the hero is imprisoned in a space that corresponds to the underground place of the Ahiqar narratives); but the biblical episode does not contain a proper *Scheintod*.

The *Scheintod* appears, associated with the term *bôr*[56] (here: an empty cis-tern) in the episode of the attempted murder and sale of Joseph in chapter 37. Joseph is first cast into the pit by his brothers (at Reuben's suggestion), then lifted out of the pit and sold into slavery (at Judah's suggestion). Reuben, knowing nothing of the sale, returns to the cistern, "and behold, Joseph was not in the pit; and [Reuben] rent his clothes (in despair, and as a sign of mourning). And [Reuben] returned to his brothers, and said: 'The child is not in the pit; and I, where shall I go?' And they took Joseph's robe, and killed a kid of the goats, and dipped the robe in the blood, . . . and brought it to their father, saying: 'We have found this; see now whether it is your son's robe or not.'" As noticed above, the use of an animal's blood corresponds well to a gruesome detail of the Ahiqar *Scheintod* scene.[57]

In this episode we have the *Scheintod* within a narrative context that corresponds in part both to the *Scheintod* episodes of the Aesop and Ahiqar traditions, and to the episode of Joseph's imprisonment in Egypt. But this episode is different from the others: its function is to divide Joseph from his family, to prepare his move to Egypt, and to start his adventures off. So the content of the single *Scheintod* episodes in the traditions about Aesop and Ahiqar is, so to say, divided among the two similar episodes of Joseph's career: the second (Gen. 39–40) contains the slander-unjust punishment-recovery-salvation sequence, the first (Gen. 37) contains the *Scheintod*.

Now, precisely the aspects of the *Scheintod* scene in Genesis 37 that are *not* paralleled in the Aesop and Ahiqar narratives correspond well to aspects of the *Scheintod* scenes in many Hellenistic novels.[58] More specifically, the *Scheintod* scene at the beginning of the Joseph story resembles the *Scheintod* scene at the beginning of the novel known as *The Adventures of Chaireas and Callirhoe*, by Chariton of Aphrodisias in Caria, commonly dated to the first century C.E.[59]

The protagonists of that novel are a young married couple living in Syracuse. Shortly after their marriage, Chaireas is overtaken by jealousy and hits beautiful Callirhoe; the young woman is thought to be dead, and buried. A band of robbers steals into the tomb to rob it of its rich contents just as Callirhoe is reviving, they capture her and take her with them to Asia Minor, where they sell her as a slave. Chaireas comes to his wife's sepulchre to celebrate the proper funerary ceremonies, and finds the tomb open and empty. His reaction is one of pure despair.[60]

The resemblance between the two scenes need not be stressed: it includes the jealousy (though of course the brothers' jealousy in the Joseph story and Chaireas' jealousy are very different), the supposed murder, the real or symbolic burial in an underground chamber or cavity. In both narratives a man returns to the burial or cistern only to find it empty, and reacts with despair. In both cases the supposedly dead hero or heroine is lifted out of a tomb or pit by a band of adventurers and sold by them as a slave in a distant land.

This resemblance is no mere relationship between two different uses of a traditional motif in different contexts, as in the case of the presence of the "stolen cup" motif in the stories of Joseph and Aesop and in the *Ass Tale*. Nor is it a relationship between two episodes, each of which contains a part of the contents of a motif found in a third episode, as in the case of the *Scheintod* scenes in the Joseph story and in the traditions about Aesop and Ahiqar. This resemblance is a specific aspect of a deeper structural correspondence between two narratives. For the two similar episodes, containing the *Scheintod* motif, insert that motif within similar narrative structures and confer upon it functions that are also similar. This shall be clear in the following schematic presentation of the two plots:

Joseph Story	*Chaireas and Callirhoe*
Being jealous the brothers decide to kill Joseph	Being jealous Chaireas hits his wife Callirhoe
and their father Jacob believes he is dead.	and thinks he has killed her.
Joseph is thrown in a dry cistern, alive,	Callirhoe is buried in a tomb, alive,
but then lifted out of it and taken by the Midianites/Ishmaelites	but discovered by a band of robbers and taken by them
to Egypt, where he is sold as a slave	to Asia Minor, where she is sold as a slave
to a powerful master.	to a powerful master.
One of the brothers comes to the dry cistern,	Chaireas comes to the tomb,
finds it empty, and is desperate.	finds it empty, and is desperate.
In the meantime Joseph is loved by his master's wife who tries to seduce him,	In the meantime Callirhoe is loved by her master who wants to marry her,
but he remains chaste,	so she accepts him,
and, after many adventures, ends up at the Egyptian court,	and, after many adventures, ends up at the Persian court (in Babylon)
where he is promoted by the king.	where she is loved, but respected, by the king.
Joseph and the brothers meet again, in a touching scene;	Chaireas and Callirhoe meet again, in a touching scene;
the brothers are forgiven	Chaireas is forgiven
and they all live happily.	and they all live happily.
The Israelites shall go back to their land, taking Joseph's bones with them.	The two go back to their city.

The similarity between the two narratives does not, of course, exclude many differences in both detail and structure. A good example is the different attitude towards foreign lovers: Joseph rejects Potiphar's wife because she is his master's spouse, but in the end marries Potiphera's daughter; Callirhoe, though she is married to Chaireas, agrees to marry her master Dionysios. For obvious reasons of context, Joseph's moral standards must be higher than Callirhoe's, but both end up by marrying an important foreign person, for the marriage is connected with their promotion and must be accepted in spite of the fact that it does not agree with their superior allegiance to their nation, god, or spouse. Another example is the difference in structure deriving from the fact that one story is about siblings, and the other about a young married couple: while Callirhoe goes through adventures similar to Joseph's, Chaireas can, indeed must, be presented as the active and brave hero of more manly and warlike deeds (and, incidentally, this brings Egypt into the picture). But even the differences can be explained as variations upon similar themes. The plots of the Joseph story and of Chariton's novel are profoundly similar; and the aspects they share (*Scheintod*, sale into slavery, success in an Oriental court, final reunion, happy ending, and many others) are the qualifying traits of the Hellenistic novel.

If we consider it as the story of a wise vizier who saves an Oriental king, the biblical Joseph story is similar to the narrative traditions about Ahiqar and to the Aesop Romance. It shares motifs with these traditions and texts as well as with other ancient novels, both Greek and Latin. But the complete story of the adventures of beautiful Joseph of Shechem is a perfect "Hellenistic novel" in its own right, though it pays less attention to *erotika*, and slightly more attention to the divine sphere, than the average Hellenistic novel. This means that not only the raw matter but the structure itself of the Hellenistic novel is present in the Book of Genesis; and if we examine one of the ancient prototypes of the Joseph story, the Egyptian tale of the Two Brothers, from this perspective, we shall notice that the older narrative differs from the biblical story precisely in its degree of "rationalization," being halfway between the level of myth and fairy tale and the level that the Joseph story shares with the average Hellenistic novel.[61]

5. Bible and Novel

The comparative study of the Joseph story and of the Greek and Latin novel shows how important it is to turn also to the biblical narratives when studying the Oriental "roots" of ancient fiction. But that study also shows that the turning-point in the historical process leading from a series of mythical narratives to the construction of comparable, but "rationalized" and down-to-earth stories had already been reached by the biblical authors and redactors who created stories such as the adventures of Joseph. These narratives differed both from the Oriental myths they have often been compared to and from the wonderful tales of Egyptian and other literatures because they were human stories about humans, where the divine sphere was important but clearly distinct from the sphere of the mortal protagonists.[62] In this, however, the biblical narratives were neither alone nor entirely new, as shown by some Mesopotamian and Egyptian "wisdom" tales, and by traditions such as the Aramaic one of Ahiqar and the many "oriental" stories we find in Herodotus. On the other hand, the writing of such biblical narratives continued for many centuries after the Exile, and some of the narratives, such as the stories of Daniel, of Tobit, and of Esther, surely belong to a wholly Hellenistic milieu, so that the romance *Joseph and Aseneth* finds its place in an uninterrupted tradition of storytelling.

Since direct contacts between the Hebrew and the Greek world were scarce before the Christian era, and rarely reached levels higher than those of mercenary troops and of petty commerce, one should refrain from imagining an influence of the Bible on Greek culture—though some Greek influence on the beginnings of biblical narrative can be accepted.[63] Probably, a common repertoire of motifs and tales, widespread in an Eastern Mediterranean *koinē*, was modified in similar ways independently by Greeks, Arameans and Jews around the middle of the first millennium B.C.E. and gave rise to the new type of narratives. Thus the Hebrew Bible with its characteristic narrative style and the Greek narrative traditions whose first representatives were authors such as Herodotus, Xenophon, Ctesias and Xanthus of Lydia, and whose final product was the Greek novel, arose from similar but autonomous transformations of a common tradition of myths, legends and fairy tales.

But, though they are similar in their origin and in their earthly quality, the Greek, Hellenistic, and Roman stories and novels and the biblical narratives differ profoundly in their ultimate meaning and function. While the former gradually lose their historical value and are finally only meant to entertain, and are presented as fictitious, the latter are believed to be true. This quality of truth that is consistently attributed by authors and readers to the biblical narratives is central both on the level of their literal faithfulness to historical events, and on the level of their symbolic value. The biblical narratives are sacred texts: as such, they should be compared to myths (e.g. to Greek myths) for they share with mythical narratives the function of providing sacred warrants and perennial charters for behaviors, beliefs, and institutions.[64] Hellenistic culture (and Greek culture before it) produced desacralized history along with mere fiction; the Hebrews told similar demythicized stories about their ancestors and founding heroes, but the stories they had demythicized and rationalized never became desacralized history or desacralized and dehistoricized fiction. In this respect, the ancient novel is not paralleled in any biblical text.[65]

Narrative traditions such as the Ahiqar complex show that in the Near East, but outside the Bible, a totally "lay" literary production similar to the Hellenistic novel was beginning to take shape around the middle of the first millennium B.C.E. On the other hand, the Greek literature of the Roman imperial age contains demythicized narratives that, in spite of the fact that they have been "rationalized," still keep their sacred quality and their function as foundation- and charter-myths. If we turn to the *Story of Combabos*, the virtuous vizier and pious eunuch who, according to the Greek treatise *De dea Syra*, had founded that goddess's sanctuary in Hierapolis, we shall find that many of the motifs we have examined in this article appear in a court tale that is at the same time a sacred narrative, told in an Oriental sanctuary. But this, as a famous modern writer of "Oriental" novels would say, is another story.

NOTES

I am grateful to my friends Giovanni Garbini, Lucio Milano, Frederick Mario Fales, Eleonora Tagliaferro, and Luigi Enrico Rossi for reading the manuscript and helping with useful criticsm and suggestions. Special gratitude is due to Riccardo Contini for information, encouragement, and suggestions.

1. Walter Burkert, *Die orientalisierende Epoche in der griechischen Religion und Literatur* (Heidelberg, 1984).

2. On the problems of the formation of aristocracies and of international trade in the Mediterranean during the Orientalizing period one should see the periodical *Opus, Intern. Journ. for Soc. and Econom. Hist. of Antiquity* 3/2 (1985), with articles on Assyria, Cyprus, Greece, Italy, Sardinia and Spain in the eighth through seventh centuries B.C.E.

3. For a perspective on the "historical" texts of the ancient Near East one should see M. Liverani, "Memorandum on the Approach to Historiographic Texts," *Orientalia* 42 (1973), pp. 178–194.

4. P. Walcot, *Hesiod and the Near East* (Cardiff, 1966); M. L. West, *Hesiod, Theogony*, edited with prolegomena and commentary (Oxford, 1966); also H. Schwabl, "Die Griechischen Theogonien und der Orient," in the volume by various authors *Eléments orientaux dans la religion grecque ancienne* (Paris, 1960), pp. 39–59.

5. C. H. Gordon, "Homer and the Bible. The Origin and Character of East Mediterranean Literature," *Hebrew Union College Annual* 26 (1955), pp. 43–108; idem, *Before the Bible: The Common Background of Greek and Hebrew Civilizations* (London, 1962). But one should beware of Gordon's peculiar brand of "pansemitism."

6. K. Kerenyi, *Die griechisch-orientalische Romanliteratur in religionsgeschichtlicher Beleuchtung* (Tübigen, 1927).

7. M. Braun, *Griechischer Roman und Hellenistische Geschichtsschreibung*, Frankfurter Studien zur Religion und Kultur der Antike 6 (Frankfurt, 1934); idem, *History and Romance in Graeco-Oriental Literature* (Oxford, 1938).

8. A. Lesky, *Geschichte der griechischen Literatur* (Bern, 1971, 3d ed.), pp. 957–969. Lesky also points to a series of other forerunners of the ancient novel, but insists on a profound difference between the two genres *Novelle* and *Roman*, and so denies that a genetic link between the two genres may be reconstructed. This distinction is not convincing.

9. J. W. B. Barns, "Egypt and the Greek Romance," in *Akten des 8. Kongress für Papyrologie*, Mitteilungen aus der Papyrussammlung der Oesterreichl. Nationalbibliothek n.s. 5 (1956), pp. 29–36 (ed. H. Gerstinger).

10. E. P. Reardon, *Courants littéraires grecs des IIe et IIIe siècles après J. C.* (Paris, 1971).

11. G. Anderson, *Ancient Fiction. The Novel in the Graeco-Roman World* (London, 1984).

12. A. Gardiner, *Late Egyptian Stories*, Bibliotheca Aegyptiaca I (Brussels, 1932); G. Lefebvre, *Romans et contes égyptiens de l'époque pharaonique* (Paris, 1949); see already G. Maspéro, *Les contes pop. de l'Ég. anc.*, Paris, 1911); M. Pieper, *Das ägyptische Märchen* (Leipzig, 1935), is a good study of the tales.

13. For a "folkloric" approach to a Hittite story see C. Grottanelli, "Observations sur l'histoire d'Appou," in *Actes de la XXIVe R.A.I.*, *Les Hourrites, Revue Hittite et Asianique* 35 (1978), pp. 49–57.

14. On the novel *Joseph and Aseneth*, see M. Philonenko, *Joseph et Aséneth, introduction, texte critique, traduction et notes* (Leiden, 1968) (prefers the shorter recension). See also E. Peterson's article "Aseneth" in the *Enciclopedia Cattolica*; A. D. Nock, *Essays in Religion and the Ancient World* 2 (Oxford, 1972), p. 900 n. 14: both authors think the novel is a Christian book; *contra* A. Momigliano, *Alien Wisdom: The Limits of Hellenization* (Cambridge, 1975). More recently S. West, "Joseph and Asenath: Neglected Greek Romance," *Class. Quart.* n.s. 24 (1974), pp. 78–81; C. Burchard, "Joseph and Aseneth, a New Translation and Introduction," in J. H. Charlesworth, *The Old Testament Pseudepigrapha* 2 (London, 1985). Burchard provides further bibliography, to which one must add M. Philonenko, "Joseph et Aséneth: Questions actuelles," and C. Burchard, "Joseph et Aséneth: Questions actuelles," in W. C. van Unnik (ed.), *La littérature juive entre Tenach et Mischna: Quelques problèmes* (Leiden, 1974), pp. 73–100; Marina Cavalli, *Storia del bellissimo Giuseppe e della sua sposa Aseneth*, (Palermo, 1983) (Italian translation of Philonenko's text, with a note by Dario Del Corno); J. Schwartz, "Cléopatre et Aséneth," *Rev. hist. et philos. relig.* 65 (1985), pp. 457–459. The "common material" adapted by the novel *Joseph and Aseneth* is also found, as Burchard has rightly stressed, in the ancient novels *stricto sensu* as well as in "the whole range of ancient romance in the wider sense of the term, which also includes such writings as *Ahiqar, Judith, 3 Maccabees, Daniel* chapters 1–6, certain passages from Josephus, the *Life of Alexander*, the *Life of Aesop*, the *Pseudo-Clementines*, or the apocryphal *Acts of the Apostles*, and the Greek novella." One should, of course, mention also some parts of the so-called Apocrypha of the Old Testament. It is also important to know that there were (ancient) versions of the novel in question into Syriac, Armenian, Latin, Slavonic, modern Greek, Rumanian, and Ethiopian (possibly also Arabic?): the same languages into which Ahiqar was transmitted (Greek and Latin, in this case, are represented by the Aesop tradition: see below).

15. J. B. Pritchard, *Ancient Near Eastern Texts Relating to the Old Testament*, (Princeton, 1969, 3rd ed.) (ANET), is the best proof that this view is correct.

16. B. E. Perry, *Aesopica* (Urbana, 1952); idem, *Studies in the Text History of the Life and Fables of Aesop* (Hanford, 1936).

17. A. Momigliano, *The Development of Greek Biography* (Cambridge, Mass., 1971).

18. A. Lesky, *Geschichte der griechische Literatur* (see above, note 8).

19. The most recent translator of Aesop's *Vita*, L. Daly, suggests a date in the fifth century B.C.E.: L. Daly, *Aesop without Morals* (New York, 1961), pp. 21–22. The date of the Aesop tradition, and the existence of a *Volksbuch* containing a *Life of Aesop* already in the second half of the sixth century B.C.E., are discussed by M. L. West, M. Adrados and M. Lasserre in the volume by various authors (R. S. Falkowitz, G. U. Thite, F. Lasserre, M. L. West, F. R. Adrados, J. Vaio, M. Nøjgaard, F. P. Knapp), *La fable*, *Entr. Hardt* XXX (Vandoeuvres-Genève, 1984), pp. 129–136. M. L. West is surely right in denying the existence of such a *Voksbuch*; and he is probably right in imagining a fifth century B.C.E. text containing a *Life of Aesop*, though as he notes (in his contribution, "The Ascription of the Fables to Aesop in Archaic and Classical Greece" in the same volume, p. 125), "this is a conclusion based on subjective judgement rather than upon hard evidence."

20. I have dealt with this problem: C. Grottanelli, "Aesop in Babylon," in *Akten der XXV Rencontre Assyriologique Internationale, Mesopotamien und seinen*

Nachbarn, hrsg. von H. J. Nissen und J. Render (Berlin, 1982), pp. 471–482. Some of the comparative suggestions I made in the article are to be found already in the long essay by A. La Penna, "Il romanzo di Esopo," *Athenaeum* 40 (1962), pp. 264–313, which is still the most important study of the connections between the Aesop tradition and the Ahiqar texts. The innovative and suggestive article by F. R. Adrados, "The 'Life of Aesop' and the Origins of Novel in Antiquity," *Quad. Urb.* n.s. 1 (30)(1979), pp. 93–112, was published a year after the Berlin Rencontre, so I could not use it. Many of the suggestions contained in my 1978 essay, which was published in 1982, are found, quite independently, in Adrados's article: notably, the suggested connection between the Aesop-Xanthus contrast and the Boeotian ritual contrast between Xanthus and Melanthion studied by Usener and by Nilsson. La. Penna's contribution was unknown to me in 1978; it may have escaped even the attention of G. Anderson, who does not quote it in his *Ancient Fiction*. The contributions and discussion published in the collective volume *La Fable* (quoted above, n. 19), shed more light on this complex problem: see especially F. Lasserre, "La fable en Grèce dans la poésie archaïque," pp. 61–96; M. L. West, "The Ascription of Fables" (quoted above), pp. 105–128; F. R. Adrados, "Les collections de fables à l'époque hellénistique et romaine," pp. 137–186. M. L. West has shown in his contribution to the volume that even the earliest evidence about Aesop belongs "to the realm of legend." The legend became a "fully fledged novella" in the fifth century, and probably in Samos. This agrees with my suggestion of a mythic quality of the figure Aesop in my 1978 essay. But in the preface to the volume Aesop is presented as a "personage . . . peut-être mythique, mais plus probablement historique." The faith in the historicity of meaningful figures is hard to kill.

21. J. Rendell Harris, F. C. Conybeare, A. Smith Lewis, *The Story of Ahiqar, from the Syriac, Arabic, Armenian, Ethiopian, Greek and Slavonic versions* (Cambridge, 1913, 2nd ed.); R. H. Charles, *The Apocrypha and Pseudepigrapha of the Old Testament* II (Oxford, 1913), pp. 715–784; F. Nau, *Histoire et sagesse d' Ahiqar l'Assyrien. Traduction des versions syriaques avec les principales différences des versions arabes, arménienne, grecque, néo-syriaque, slave et roumaine* (Paris, 1909). An Italian translation and a good recent bibliography: F. Pennacchietti, "Storia e massime di Ahiqar," in P. Sacchi, *Apocrifi dell'Antico Testamento*, (Turin, 1981), pp. 51–95. For the fifth century B.C.E. Aramaic text from Elephantine (Egypt) one should see E. Meyer, *Der Papyrusfund von Elephantine* (Leipzig, 1912); A. E. Cowley, *Aramaic Papyri of the Vth century B.C. from Oxford* (1923; repr. 1967); ANET, 3rd ed., pp. 491–493, with bibliography. J. M. Lindenberger, *The Aramaic Proverbs of Ahiqar* (Baltimore, 1983); R. Degen, "Achikar," in *Enzyklopädie des Märchens* I (Berlin, 1977), coll. 53–59. A new English translation and further bibliography is to be found in "Ahiqar (Seventh to Sixth Century B.C.). A New Translation and Introduction by J. M. Lindenberger," in J. H. Charlesworth (ed.), *The Old Testament Pseudepigrapha* 2 (quoted above, n. 14), pp. 479–507. On the Near Eastern context of the Aramaic Ahiqar text, see J. C. Greenfield, "The Background and Parallels to a Proverb of Ahiqar," in *Mélanges A. Dupont-Sommer* (Paris, 1971), pp. 49–59, and idem, "Ahiqar in the Book of Tobit," in *De La Torah au Messie. Mélanges H. Cazelles* (Paris, 1981), pp. 328–335. On Ahiqar see M. Küchler, *Frühjüdische Weisheitstraditionen* (Frankfurt-Göttingen, 1979), pp. 317–413.

22. I still believe what I wrote in my 1978 essay: "It is . . . realistic to think that the personalities of both Aesop and Ahiqar were created at the same time around a common set of proverbs, fables, maxims and narrative motifs and tradi-

tions in a highly cosmopolitan milieu such as the Eastern Mediterranean surely was around the sixth or fifth centuries B.C.," though J. M. Lindenberger is probably right in suggesting an earlier date for the origin of the Ahiqar story in his introduction to the 1985 translation (see above, n. 21). The problem of the relationship between Aesop and Ahiqar is still debated. Q. Cataudella, "Aristofane e il cosiddetto 'romanzo di Esopo,' *Dioniso* 9 (1942), pp. 5–15, thought he possessed the proof that the Ahiqar tradition was known in Greece, and had been used to shape the Aesop tradition, already in the fifth century B.C.E.; but La Penna in *Athenaeum* (quoted above, n. 20), pp. 289–290, denied that Cataudella's argument was valid and insisted on the name of the king of Egypt, Nectanebos in the Aesop tradition, as a *terminus post quem* sicuro," dating after the fourth century B.C.E. But the names of the characters, as shown by the very development of both the Ahiqar and the Aesop tradition, are the most mobile element of the whole traditional complex, so they cannot be a terminus for the story, but only for a specific version, redaction or recension. On the other hand, Cataudella's sources and reasoning seem sound; and the fact that "il pezzo babilonese è quello che più chiaramente si mostra come intruso" may be explained with my remarks on the "two Aesop figures" (in the Greek and in the Near Eastern contexts) in my essay quoted above in n. 20 (pp. 561–563). For these reasons, I think La. Penna's arguments for a late addition of the "Babylonian" section to the Aesop narrative tradition are not convincing; and I tend to agree with F. R. Adrados, *Quad. Urb.* (quoted above, n. 20), who writes that "the stories of Ahikar and Aesop had something in common; the Aesop who from the fifth century uses fables in his arguments to the Delphians, the Aesop who perhaps at the same date . . . advises the Samians with a fable, clearly has some elements in common with Ahikar. Not only did the writer of the Life of Aesop of the first century A.D. know the life of Ahikar which he used freely, but it is very likely that from the fifth century (B.C) onward the name of Aesop was used as a Greek name of Ahikar, and that his legend was, at least in part, the result of transferring the oriental legend to the Greek world. It is clear that these legends were transferred, and the names adapted, as we have the example of the Hittite myths found hellenized in Hesiod" (p. 98), or that "(Aesop's) relationships with the Delphians can be compared with those of Ahikar with Sennacherib. There must have been two different moments in which the oriental story influenced the Greek one" (p. 100). I would go somewhat further than this; but surely Adrados is very near the mark. For more recent discussions on the relationship between Aesop and Ahiqar see the volume *La Fable* (quoted above, n. 19), pp. 130–134 (especially the remarks by R. S. Falkowitz, F. R. Adrados, M. L. West).

23. On this episode (Genesis 37) and on similar episodes in Near Eastern and in ancient Greek narratives, one should see G.R.H. Wright, "Joseph's Grave under the Tree by the Omphalos at Shechem," *Vetus Testamentum* 22 (1972), pp. 476–486; C. Grottanelli, "Spunti comparativi per la storia biblica di Giuseppe," *Oriens Ant.* 15 (1976), pp. 115–140, with further bibliography quoted in nn. 13 and 20. See also below, section 4, "The *Scheintod* Motif," and nn. 53 and 56.

24. See infra pp. 18–25.

25. Ahiqar columns III, IV and V.

26. The connections between the story of Joseph and that of Aesop were noticed already by A. La Penna (quoted above n. 20), p. 296, who discusses the similarity between the slandered Ahiqar and the slandered Joseph, but adds that "precisare le vie del rapporto è impossibile." In this study of the Aramaic Ahiqar (1985),

J. M. Lindenberger (quoted above, n. 21, p. 484 n. 34) observes that "there is some evidence that parallels between Ahiqar, Aesop and Joseph were observed in Antiquity. One of the Syriac MSS of Ahiqar also contains a collection of Aesop's fables attributed to 'Josephus': F. C. Conybeare et al., *The Story of Ahiqar*, Cambridge 1913[2], p. xxx, p. 2." But the mention of Joseph that Lindenberger sees in the Syriac text is the result of a misunderstanding, for Josipon was, in medieval Near Eastern texts, the name of the Greek storyteller Aesop: see B. E. Perry, "The Origin of the Book of Sindbad," *Fabula* 3 (1959), pp. 21, 31 n. 62. Perry's article is a mine of information on the later development of the traditions about Aesop, Ahiqar, and even Joseph (see p. 51 n. 104) in antiquity and in the Middle Ages. I have mentioned connections between the stories of Joseph and of Aesop in my articles quoted in nn. 20 and 54.

27. D. B. Redford, *A Study of the Biblical Story of Joseph* (Gen. 35–70) (Leiden, 1970).

28. *Oriens Ant.* 12 (1973), pp. 233–242.

29. For a late date see also J. J. Collins, "The Court-Tales in Daniel and the Development of Apocalyptic," *Journ. Bibl. Lit.* 94 (1975), pp. 218–234; A. Meinhold, "Die Gattung der Josephgeschichte und des Estherbuches: Diasporanovelle I," *Zeitschr. f. Alttestamentliche Wissens.* 87 (1975), pp. 306, 324; idem, "Die Gattung . . . Diasporanovelle II," ibid. 88 (1976), pp. 72–93.

30. G. W. Coats, *From Canaan to Egypt, Structural and Theological Context for the Joseph Story* (Washington, 1976).

31. A. Van Seters, *In Search of History. Historiography in the Ancient World and the Origins of Biblical History* (London, New Haven, 1983).

32. *Papyrus Orbiney*, British Museum N. 10 183. A. H. Gardiner, *Late Egyptian Stories*, Bibliotheca Aegyptiaca 1 (Brussels, 1932), pp. 9–29; G. Lefebvre, *Romans et contes égyptiens de l'époque pharaonique* (quoted above, n. 12), pp. 137–158.

33. On this theme one should consult the articles quoted in n. 23 above, and also Redford's volume quoted in n. 27 above. A mythical narrative of the "dying god" type has been thought to lie "behind" the Joseph story by some scholars during the first two decades of this century; but that theory is now abandoned. In more recent times, it has been defended by H. G. May, "The Evolution of the Joseph Story," *Am. Journ. of Semitic Lit.* 47 (1931), pp. 83–93; and by M. Astour, *Hellenosemitica* (Leiden, 1969). For a somewhat similar treatment of the Aesop tradition (but along more convincing lines) see Adrados's article quoted above, n. 20. See also my criticism of the "fertility" interpretations of the Joseph story in C. Grottanelli, "Spunti comparativi per la storia biblica di Giuseppe" (quoted above, n. 23), pp. 137–139 (section 4.3 *Il rapporto con la fertilità*).

34. The connections between the Ahiqar and the Joseph stories are well known; both stories are studied as examples of a folkloric motif ("Aarne-Thompson's motif 922," A. Aarne, S. Thompson, *The Types of the Folktale*, Folklore Fellows Communication 184, [Helsinki, 1964, 2nd ed.] by S. Niditch, R. Doran, "The Success Story of the Wise Courtier: A Formal Approach," *Journ Bibl. Lit.* 96/2 (1977), pp. 179–193. These connections have been noticed now by G. Anderson, who writes that "the material of the Joseph legend can be presented equally easily as popular love-romance (Joseph and Asenath) with a religious message or as a frame for elementary moral instructions (Ahiqar)" (*Ancient Fiction*, quoted above, n. 11, p. 52). For the relationship between wisdom literature and the biblical Joseph story, see G. von Rad, "Josephgeschichte und ältere Chokma," *Vetus Testamentum*

Supplement 1 (1953), pp. 120–127; R. N. Whybray, "The Joseph Story and Penta-teuchal Criticism," *Vetus Testamentum* 18 (1968), pp. 512–528; G. W. Coats, "The Joseph Story and Ancient Wisdom: An Appraisal," *Catholic Bibl. Quart.* 35 (1973), pp. 285–297.

35. Aesop's name has been compared to that of a river on Phrygia (F. R. Adra-dos, A. La Penna), Αἴσηπος. On the ancient etymology (transmitted by Eustathius) of Aesop's name as "shining-eye" (or, possibly, "black face"), which would identify his name with the name Aithiops, see Nau, *Ahiqar l'Assyrien* (quoted above, n. 21), p. 128. This etymology is usually not accepted by modern scholars; for a modern et-ymology (*Aîs-ōpos* = "having the look of baseness"), see G. Nagy, *The Best of the Achaeans* (Baltimore, London, 1979), pp. 315–316. Nagy's etymology is based upon a convincing study of the story of Aesop's mishap in Delphi, which should be taken into account by all who study the Aesopic tradition. For Joseph's name, see C. Grottanelli, *Oriens Ant.* (quoted above, n. 23), pp. 138–139; Andrzej Strus, *Nomen-Omen. La stylistique sonore des noms propres dans le Pentateuque* (Roma, 1978), pp. 61, 136–152; E. C. B. MacLaurin, "Joseph and Asaph," *Vetus Testamentum* 25 (1975), pp. 27–45. The two roots that have to be considered are *'sp*, "to increase, to add," and *ysp*, "to collect."

36. The fact that Joseph places his brothers' money in their sacks is probably a somewhat unneccessary later redactional addition to the Jewish text, for the same motif had already appeared in Genesis 42, and nothing further is said about the money in what follows. This has been noticed by several scholars, among them G. von Rad, *Das Erste Buch Mose, Genesis, Das Alte Testament Deutsch* 2–4 (Göttin-gen, 1949).

37. Perry, *Aesopica*, p. 74 (G recension); p. 105 (W recension).

38. Ibidem, p. 74 (§128).

39. I might quote here Hermes' more moderate, but less honest oath, ὡς ὄλβιος εἴην, when he swears he has not stolen Apollo's cattle in the *Homeric Hymn to Hermes*, which I have compared to another oath, *sic oculi extillescant mei si vidi aut tetigi*, sworn by another thief in Phaedrus' fable *Pompeius et Miles* (the 113th of Brenot's Belles Lettres Edition), in my article "Tricksters, Scapegoats, Champions, Saviours," *Hist. of Relig.* (1983), pp. 125–128.

40. *Papyrus* 3033 of the Berlin Museum: A Erman, "Die Märchen der Papyrus Westcar," *Mitt. Orient, Samml. Königlischen Museum* 5–6 (Berlin, 1890); M. Pieper, *Das ägyptische Märchen* (Leipzig, 1935), p. 15; G. Lefebvre, *Romans et con-tes égyptiens de l'époque pharaonique* (quoted above, n. 12), pp. 70–90; S. Dona-doni, *Storia della letteratura egiziana antica* (Milan, 1957), pp. 145–147.

41. See E. Chambry, *Ésope, Fables* (Paris, 1967), pp. xvii–xix.

42. On the treatment of the Joseph story in Hellenistic and in "Palestinian" Ju-daism see most recently F. Manns, "Une nouvelle source littéraire pour l'étude du Judéo-Christianisme," *Henoch* 6 (1984), pp. 168–176 (especially the section "La fig-ure de Joseph le Patriarche dans le Judaisme palestinien et hellénistique").

43. On the Patriarch Joseph in Josephus' interpretation, see D. Daube, "Typology in Josephus," *Journ. Jewish Stud.* 31 (1980), pp. 18–36. On Josephus and biblical narrative: L. H. Feldman, *Josephus and Modern Scholarship* (1984), and that same author's many articles on biblical figures in Josephus.

44. On the Ass Romance, see B. E. Perry, *The Ancient Romances, A Literary-Historical Account of Their Origins* (Berkeley, 1967), pp. 211–235; M. D. Macleod, *Lucian* 8 (Cambridge, Mass., 1967), pp. 52–144 (text and translation); J. L. Mason,

"Fabula Graecanica: Apuleius and his Greek Sources," in B. L. Hijmans, T. T. van der Paardt (eds.), *Aspects of Apuleius' Golden Ass* (Groningen, 1978), pp. 1–15; G. Anderson, *Ancient Fiction*, pp. 198–216. See also the translation and discussion by A. Angelini in Q. Cataudella (ed.), *Il romanzo antico greco e latino* (Florence, 1981), pp. 313–352.

45. On Apuleius' Ass Novel: *Metamorphoseon Libri* ed. D. S. Robertson with a translation by P. Vallette (Paris, 1956); *Apuleio, L'asino d'oro*, Italian translation by Massimo Buontempelli with R. Helm's Teubnerian Latin text (1907) and essays by V. Ciaffi and T. Alimenti (Turin, 1975); *Apuleio, Le Metamorfosi*, Italian translation, introduction and notes by F. Carlesi, and Q. Cataudella (ed.), *Il romanzo antico greco e latino* (quoted above, n. 44), pp. 1055–1308; A. Scobie, *Apuleius' Metamorphoses* I: *A Commentary* (Meisenheim-am-Glan, 1975); B. E. Perry, *The Ancient Romances* (quoted above, n. 44), pp. 236–282; P. G. Walsh, *The Roman Novel, the Satyricon of Petronius and the Metamorphoses of Apuleius* (Cambridge, 1970); G. Anderson, *Ancient Fiction*, pp. 198–216, and pp. 229–238, for further bibliography.

46. See H. J. Mason in B. P. Reardon (ed.), *Erotica Antiqua* (Bangor, 1977), pp. 146–148. To the "notorious triangle" of texts (so termed by G. Anderson, *Ancient Fiction*, p. 208) one should add the Milesian tale by Aristides of Miletus translated by Cornelius Sisenna in the first century B.C.E. and going back to the second century B.C.E. For a possible reconstruction of this tale see now G. Anderson, *Ancient Fiction*, pp. 200–204. The connection of Aristides' tale (which may be judged only on the basis of what we know of Sisenna's translation) with the Ass-Romance tradition seems strong, in spite of O. Weinreich, *Der Trug von Nectanebos* (Leipzig-Berlin, 1911), p. 37 n. 4. Anderson's hypothetical reconstruction is not relevant in the debate concerning the connection.

47. Connections between the Aesop Romance and the Ass Romance were seen already by F. R. Adrados, *Quad. Urb.* (quoted above, n. 20), pp. 93–94 and passim; they are described thus by G. Anderson, *Ancient Fiction*, pp. 211–212: " . . . we find Aesop introduced to Xanthus' household: they had been expecting a handsome man, and are horrified by his animal-like appearance. This time it is Apuleius who contributes to the parallel: the homosexual priests expect Philebus to introduce a man, and are horrified to find an ass. But the matter does not end here . . . Both Lucius and Aesop perform a minor favour for a goddess (Atargatis and Isis respectively). The latter deity restores Aesop's voice, just as she restores Lucius' whole human shape; while the succession of Aesop's sales is similar to Lucius changes of master. And the pornographic episode in which Aesop cannot quite meet the demands of the master's wife is similar to Lucius' eventual failure with the foreign voluptuary."

48. I Samuel 9. H. W. Hertzberg, *Die Samuelbücher* (*Das Alte Testament Deutsch*), Göttingen 1960, compares the passage discussed here (Gen. 43, 34) to the passage in the first Book of Samuel (I Sam. 9, 22–24) where Saul, a descendant of Benjamin, is given a special part of the victim as a sign of kingly election during a sacrificial banquet. On this passage and on its Ugaritic and Homeric parallels see C. Grottanelli, "L'ideologia del banchetto e l'ospite ambiguo," *Dialoghi archeol.* n.s. 3 (1981), pp. 128–141.

49. On Joseph's divination, see F. Cunen, "Les pratiques divinatoires attribuées à Joseph d'Egypte," *Rev. sciences relig.* 33 (1959), pp. 396–404.

50. This is probably connected with the "cavalry over the hill" motif of Greek

novels briefly examined by G. Anderson, *Ancient Fiction*, p. 89, and already by
B. P. Reardon, "Aspects of Greek Novel," *Greece and Rome* n.s. 23 (1976), p. 118.

51. IX 28, 5–6.

52. This important difference between Aesop and Joseph is paralleled by the
distinction between characters like Ahiqar and the "antihero" Aesop that we find in
F. R. Adrados, *Quad. Urb.* (quoted above, n. 20), pp. 101–106. Compare this to my
"twofold" Aesop in *Akten der XXV R.A.I.* (see above, n. 20), pp. 561–565: Aesop is a
trickster and an "antihero" in Greece, but a successful courtier, like Ahiqar and
Joseph, in Babylon. For Joseph as both a seductive and a chaste hero see Grottanelli, *Oriens Ant.* (quoted above, n. 23), pp. 138–139.

53. The hiding-place (a tomb, or reminiscent of a tomb) in Aesop's and
Ahiqar's *Scheintod* episode is not present in the Aramaic Ahiqar text. It is already
found, however, in the Book of Tobit (14, 10) where the text says "[Ahikar] was
forced to go underground, though still a living man. But God made the criminal
pay for his outrage before the eyes of his victim, since Ahikar came back to the
light of the day, while Nadab [=Nadin] went down to everlasting darkness for plot-
ting against Ahikar's life. Because of his good works, Ahikar escaped the deadly
snare Nadab had laid for him, and Nadab fell into his own ruin." Evidently, the author of Tobit knew Ahiqar in a form not identical with either the Elephantine text
or the later versions. For all this see J. M. Lindenberger in Charlesworth (ed.), *The
Old Testament Pseudepigrapha* 2 (quoted above, n. 21), p. 489.

54. C. Grottanelli, "Healers and Saviours of the Eastern Mediterranean in Pre-
Classical Times," in U. Bianchi, M. J. Vermaseren (eds), *La soteriologia dei culti
orientali nell'Impero Romano* (Brill: 1982), pp. 656–657 (republished in this book as
chapter 7). These are the motifs "The Wiseman as Saviour" and "Disgrace and
Rehabilitation of a Wise Minister" recognized in the Joseph story by D. B. Redford, *A Study of the Biblical Story of Joseph* (quoted above, n. 27), pp. 656–657.
One can quote the stories of Tobit, Daniel, Mordekhai in the Bible, the restoration of Jehoiakin, the imprisonment of Jeremiah, the unjust imprisonment of
Onkhsheshonky and of Hy-Hor in Egyptian literature, the story of Saul and David
(II Sam. 19, 9–10), the story of Cambyses and Croesus in Herodotus III 36. The
motifs continue into the literature of late antiquity and the Middle Ages: see Perry's
article quoted above, n. 26, *passim*. For the motif of the disgrace and rehabilitation
of a wise minister, see also comparative material in E. Reiner, "The Etiological
Myth of the 'Seven Sages,'" *Orientalia* n.s. 30 (1961), pp. 1–11; A. H. Krappe,
"Is the Story of Ahiqar the Wise of Indian Origin?" *Journ. Am. Orient. Soc.* 61
(1941), pp. 280–284. The motif is also recognized by J. M. Lindenberger, in J. H.
Charlesworth (ed.), *The Old Testament Pseudepigrapha* 2 (quoted above, n. 21),
pp. 490–491, who gives some of the bibliography quoted above. See also, for more
general folkloric parallels, S. Thompson, *Motif-Index of Folk Literature* (Blooming-
ton, 1932–1936), motifs K 2101, K 2214, 3, K 2214, 3, 1. Further material can be found
in B. E. Perry's article quoted above, n. 26. For the motif of the wise man as savior,
one should see the bibliography quoted above, in n. 34, especially the article by
Niditch and Doran: *Journ. Bibl. Lit.* 96/2 (1977), pp. 179–193, and the volume *The
Types of the Folktale*, by Aarne and Thompson (Type 922).

55. B. H. Stricker, "Prison de Joseph," *Acta Orientalia* 19 (1943), pp. 101–137.

56. On this episode see n. 22 above. Since I agree with G. W. Coats on the
unity of the biblical story of Joseph, I do not follow Redford, *A Study of the Biblical
Story of Joseph* (quoted above, n. 27), pp. 106–186, on the complex redaction his-

tory of Genesis 37; even less do I accept the traditional "source-critical" interpretation of the passage. On the meaning, origin and function of the episode, and on the importance of the recurring term *bôr* in the Joseph story, see C. Grottanelli, "Guiseppe nel pozzo I," *Oriens Ant.* 17, 1978, pp. 107–122 (mythical elements of the episode); idem, "Giuseppe nel pozzo II," *Oriens Ant.* 22, 1983, 267–290 (folkloric parallels). On the symbolic value of *bôr*: C. Grottanelli, "da Myrrha alla mirra: Adonis e il profumo dei re siriani," in the volume by various authors *Adonis. Relazioni del Colloquio in Roma (Maggio 1981) (Rome, 1983) (C.N.R.)* pp. 43–45; and very extensively, with special attention to *bôr* as Underworld, N. J. Tromp, *Primitive Conceptions of Death and the Netherworld in the Old Testament* (Rome, 1969), pp. 33, 57, 66–69. See also the old article by Ch. Clermont Ganneau, "La Citerne de Joseph," *Rec. archéol. orient.* 1 (Paris, 1888), pp. 332–333.

57. For such *Scheintod* scenes, with gruesome details of the killing of animals and the use of the blood or of parts of the victim, see G. Anderson, *Ancient Fiction*, pp. 123, 160–162 (details of the first *Scheintod* scene in Achilles Tatius' novel).

58. See Anderson's treatment of the problem in the passages just quoted and in his *Ancient Fiction*, passim. See also F. R. Adrados, *Quad. Urb.* (quoted above, n. 20), pp. 103–110, for the mythical overtones of the real or supposed deaths of Aesop and Ahiqar. This interpretation should be linked to the "mythical" interpretation of Joseph as a fertility figure, for which see note 28 above and my article in *Oriens Ant.* (quoted above n. 23), pp. 137–139 (section 4.3 Il rapporto con la fertilità).

59. The passage is III 3. For Chariton's novel see G. Molinié (ed.), *Chariton: Chaireas et Callirhoe* (Paris, 1982); B. E. Perry, "Chariton and his Romance from a Literary-Historical Point of View," *Am. Journ. Philol.* 51 (1930), pp. 93–134; B. P. Reardon, "Theme, Structure and Narrative in Chariton," *Yale Class. Stud.* 27 (1982), pp. 1–27; Perry, *The Ancient Romances* (quoted above, n. 44), pp. 96–148; "Caritone, Le avventure di Cherea e Calliroe," translated into Italian with an introduction by R. Nuti, in Q. Cataudella (ed.), *Il romanzo antico greco e latino* (quoted above, n. 44), pp. 15–179.

60. III 3.

61. For the "rationalization" of mythical plots and motifs in the Greek and Latin novel, see G. Anderson, *Ancient Fiction*, pp. 25–42 (chapter 2: "Narrative into Novel"), pp. 75–87 (chapter 5: "Myth and Mystery"), and *passim*. For the "realism" of the ancient novel, see that same volume, pp. 88–105 (chapter 6: "History and Society"), and such studies as A. M. Scarcella, "Les structures socio-économiques du Roman de Xénophon d'Ephèse," *Rev. Et. Gr.* 90 (1977), pp. 249–262, and idem, "Realtà e letteratura nel paesaggio sociale ed economico del romanzo di Longo sofista," *Maia* 22 (1970), pp. 103–131.

62. For this quality of biblical narrative, see the important contribution by R. Alter, *The Art of Biblical Narrative* (New York, 1981), especially pp. 23–46 (chapter 2: "Sacred History and the Beginnings of Prose Fiction").

63. See the acute remarks by A. Momigliano, *Alien Wisdom* (quoted above, n. 14), chapters 4 and 5. A good discussion of Greek influence upon Palestine is found in M. Smith, *Palestinian Parties and Politics that Shaped the Old Testament* (New York, 1971), chapter 3 ("Hellenization").

64. On the "mythical" quality of biblical narrative see the material collected and discussed by J. W. Rogerson, *Myth in Old Testament Interpretation* (Berlin, New York, 1974), and the structural studies of E. Leach, *Genesis as Myth and Other Essays*, (London, 1969); E. Leach, A. Aycock, *Structuralist Interpretations of Bibli-*

cal Myth (Cambridge, 1983). For a brief discussion of the quality and function of biblical narrative, see C. Grottanelli, *Oriens Ant.* (quoted above, n. 23), pp. 115–117.

65. This article was written during the winter of 1986–87. At the time, I had not read G. F. Gianotti's important book on the Ass Novel of Apuleius, *"Romanzo" e Ideologia. Studi sulle* Metamorfosi *di Apuleio* (Naples, 1986), nor did I consult T. Hägg, *The Novel in Antiquity* (Oxford, 1983; Swedish edition: Uppsala 1980). The new series of translations into Italian of many Greek and Latin novels (*Storie d'amore antiche* [Bari, 1987], with an introduction by L. Canfora, and *Antiche storie d'avventura* [Bari, 1987]) had not yet been published; and I have not yet seen the collection of new English translations edited by B. P. Reardon, University of California Press, announced in Hägg's book. In the meantime, much has been published (e.g. L. Canfora, *Ellenismo* [Rome-Bari, 1987]), or intelligently republished (e.g. A. Momigliano, *Pagine Ebraiche* [Turin, 1987]) that sheds light on the relationship between the Jews and the Greeks, and between the Bible and other literary *corpora* of the ancient Mediterranean.

9

PROPHECY AND WRITING IN
THE ANCIENT NEAR EAST

1. Prophecy: Divination, Message, Action

Near-Eastern prophecy is, above all, a form of divination, although not exclusively so. In the societies of the ancient Near East divination plays a central role, and is one of the basic ways of knowing. The available documents illustrate that divination presides over all operative choices, at least those of the state and court.[1]

As a form of divination, prophecy displays the same central importance that generally accrues to Near-Eastern divination. We must immediately add, however, that prophecy is a unique type of divination. If divination consists largely in the deciphering of messages (or of phenomena interpreted as messages), it can be called a form of "reading." Prophecy, on the other hand, as a form of exceptional divination, consists in direct communication of a message from the supernatural. The means of such direct communication include dreams and visions, in which supernatural beings communicate directly with a human being. They also include the possession of a human being by supernatural beings who speak through the human's mouth.

These considerations comprise two important corollaries. First of all, insofar as prophecy is directly inspired divination, it is opposed to the world of writing. For the cultures of the ancient Near East, according to a widespread mythic tradition, the destiny of the cosmos is written on certain tablets entrusted to the gods. These cultures view the world as a totality of signs to be read. One who practices divination (and is capable, therefore, of reading the mantic signs) is normally a palace scribe. The diviner is thus part of a limited category of individuals taught in specialized schools, who are capable of reading cuneiform signs. Prophecy breaks this system. In prophecy communication by the supernatural is not symbolized, but enunciated outright. Therefore, this communication can be enunciated by or through one who is not a scribe.

The second corollary pushes prophecy beyond divination. Direct communication of a message from the gods to a human being, and through that human being to a social group, opens the way for the discourse of the deities. In the case of divination the supernatural lets itself be read. It communicates if it is questioned. It communicates well if it is questioned properly. The divine sphere tells human beings what they wish to know. In the case of prophecy the supernatural can also speak without being addressed, and without fear of being misunderstood—even if it always runs the risk not being heeded. Above all, the supernatural can speak of things that human beings do not want to hear.

From this point of view, prophecy is much more than a form of divination. It transmits not only information but also a *will*, in ways that are quite explicit. The prophet is thus more than a diviner. He is entrusted with and carries out a supernatural will. The divinity who speaks to or through him also makes him act. At the very least, the divinity pushes him to move in order to communicate, in order to publicize that which has been told him.[2]

Prophecy goes beyond divination because, on the one hand, it transmits a broader message and, on the other hand, it comprises movement and action. Since the action of the prophet is an aspect of his prophetic mission, it presents itself as essentially a means to or extension of the enunciation of the message. The action of the prophets about whom we have texts (that is, those found in the texts of the Hebrew Bible) is fundamentally symbolic action. One could describe an entire typological spectrum with highly nuanced gradations of symbolic acts. To simplify matters, however, it is possible to isolate two overlapping types of symbolic action that between them comprise the full spectrum. These are: (1) symbolic actions that possess a value of signification or that support signification; and (2) symbolic actions that have a real efficacy, and an unmediated, operative value. This second type of symbolic action in other words consists of magical actions. I refer here to a type of magic that has a strong demonstrative value. Its miraculous efficacy constitutes, in turn, the "sign" that guarantees the validity of a divine message or the truthfulness and authority of the prophet.

Precisely at this double extradivinatory level, prophecy contradicts its own "oral" premises and brings writing into play. This double aspect includes: (1) the transmission of broad and complex messages which are actually whole systems of religious belief; and (2) symbolic action that signifies a message or is directly efficacious. First of all, writing (by this I mean consonantic writing) provides prophecy with a means of disseminating its message, a means which is more powerful than orality: this explains the relationship between the establishment of the Phoenician "alphabet" and the origins of the first founded religion, a relationship that has yet to be adequately studied.

Second, prophecy uses writing in symbolic action: to mark the objects of the symbolic act, to give material form to a message and use it as an object, or in other ways. One might say that writing is a function of telling, when prophecy makes use of writing to spread its message. When, however, prophecy makes uses of writing in symbolic action, writing mediates between telling and doing. In various ways, telling is materialized in writing in order to make something of it. We are concerned here with precisely that writing which mediates between prophetic telling and doing. To explore this, it is necessary to paint a broad picture of the relationship between prophecy and writing, in which prophetic writing is only one element among many. Without it, however, the picture remains incomprehensible.

Let us summarize and, at the same time, open a new discourse. In the chain of communication from the deity, through the prophet, to other human beings, prophecy (which is direct communication and divination without "reading") can either use writing or not use it at all, remaining completely oral. If it utilizes writing, prophecy will place it at a certain point in the chain of communications. It is possible to trace an outline of the relationship between Near-Eastern prophecy and writing—an outline which is *only partly* diachronic. This outline is made possible by observing the presence or absence of writing, and the position of writing in the chain of prophetic communications. Clearly, depending on its position in the chain writing will have different functions, meanings, and implications.

2. The Absence of Writing

The Hebrew Bible is our primary source of testimonies concerning purely oral prophecy. In the canon of texts that contains the works of the writer-prophets, the description of prophetic phenomena is, first and foremost, a description of oral communication. The mechanism is simple. Possessed by the divinity or visited by visions or dreams, the prophet receives the divine word and repeats it to the king or the people.

For example, in the first book of Kings (22:1–26) the kings Jehoshaphat of Judah and Ahab of Israel joined forces to reconquer the city of Ramoth-gilead. Before departing for war, the king of Israel gathered 400 prophets and asked them whether to undertake the expedition. The response was positive. The king of Judah, however, had no confidence in their judgment, and suggested consulting Micaiah, son of Imlah, whom Ahab had ignored, since he generally prophesied misfortune. The messenger who called Micaiah exhorted him to prophesy the success of the venture, as the other prophets had. Micaiah answered that he would prophesy that which Yahweh would tell him. Having come into the presence of the kings he initially prophesied the venture's success. But when he was asked by the king of Israel "the truth of Yahweh," he announced their defeat, speaking now in poetic verses. In his vision, Yahweh is seated on a throne and all the ranks of heaven are around him, to his right and to his left. Yahweh seeks out a spirit who will deceive Ahab so that he may rise and fall at Ramoth-gilead. Finally, a spirit rises up and places himself before Yahweh. He offers to do Yahweh's bidding, to "go forth" and become a lying spirit in the mouths of all the prophets of the king. This was Micaiah's report. At this point, one of the prophets who foretold good fortune slapped Micaiah on the cheek and Micaiah was imprisoned by order of the king. Naturally, the prophesied defeat came to pass. The scene presents a clear image of prophetic activity. It is composed of a double pyramid. On earth we see the thrones of the kings with the ranks of prophets and with the recalcitrant truth-telling prophet. In heaven we see the throne of Yahweh with the ranks of spirits, and the lying spirit volunteer. We will encounter this scenario again in the following pages, just as we will encounter the spiritual ascent of the prophet to the heavenly court.

By means of possession, dream or vision, the prophet is the bearer of a message sent from a heavenly court to an earthly court. As such, he is entrusted with a *dbr*, a word which is also an action. The prophetic books of the Bible are filled with the formula *dbr Yhwh*, which is repeated before each important oracle. In the most ancient Hebrew prophetic books, such as Amos and Hosea, the written text contains neither an ideology nor a terminology of writing. The world is one of pure orality. Rather different is the case of the "prophetic" texts of Mari from the eighteenth century B.C.E. These cuneiform texts are actually letters written to the central administration of the state and preserved in the palace archive of Mari, a city of the middle Euphrates.[3]

These texts present the following chain of communications: divinely inspired figures betake themselves to a (marginal) functionary of the palace administration; they declare that a certain god (often Dagan) has sent them; and they pronounce an oracle. The oracle is usually directed toward the king and refers to events of immediate interest to the internal or international politics of Mari. But the oracle is delivered in the form of specific divine orders, most frequently of a cultic character. At this point, the faithful functionary writes to the king of Mari, reporting this phenomenon just as he reports all other important facts. To the chain of communications there corresponds a chain of responsibility: the prophet, who in one case wavers and has to be pushed violently by the divinity to speak up, transmits the message to the functionary and thus, the text explicitly tells us, shifts the responsibility onto him.

At times, a piece of the prophet's garment and a lock of the prophet's hair are sent to the palace along with the letter. These are means of identification or, according to a more widespread interpretation, "signatures" of the prophet. In all probability, these tokens serve as a guarantee for the palace and protect against thoughtless or malevolent prophecies insofar as these are raw material of black magic that can be used against the bearer of the divine message.

Writing belongs only to the closing or final phase of the chain of communications, that is, to the phase that links the functionary to the king. Nevertheless, through a sort of feedback loop, writing enters the consciousness of the prophet who bears the oral message, at least insofar as he then dictates it to the functionary. In fact, in certain letters the transfer of responsibility from the prophet to the functionary is accomplished through the exhortation: "Write to your Lord."

3. The Prophet Writes

The Neo-Assyrian "prophetic" texts attributed to the reigns of Esarhaddon (680–669 B.C.E.) and Assurbanipal (668–629 B.C.E.) also hail from a palace archive and are written by palace scribes. These cuneiform texts are, however, extremely different, and bring us to a point where writing plays a far greater role in the chain of communications and in the ideology of prophecy.[4] The content and the type of these oracles is not so different from those found in the texts of Mari. They are told to the king and to the queen mother, and concern the politics, especially international politics, of Assyria. They proceed from the gods Ashur and Ishtar. But rather than being reports of a functionary to the king, the texts present themselves as the very words of the deity to the king, beginning with one of four canonical formulas: "Do not fear"; "I am the god x"; "Oracle of salvation"; "Word of the god y," and may be collected together in tablets containing several oracles. Often, but not always, a final note indicates the person from whose "lips" the prophecy derived. We must assume, given that in these texts the divinity speaks in the first person and without any mediation, that the persons in question were possessed prophets—"lips," so to speak, of the deity itself.

These oracles came to us not in the form of written reports of a preceding oral transmission, but as texts that simply reproduce the divine word leaving the lips of the prophet. In substance, things are probably not much different than they are at Mari. But the form has undergone a real qualitative transformation. The prophetic text has made its appearance. The oracular sanctuary must also be a means by which prophetic writing makes its appearance, especially in the areas where royal, courtly, and state organization is weaker and less rooted. Excavations of the Palestinian sanctuary of Tell Deir ʻAlla have brought to light an inscription in a northwest Semitic language in the eighth century B.C.E., most likely written in ink on a plastered wall, and about ten lines long. The inscription begins: ". . . . s]p̄r [.blʻ]m̄ [.brbʻ]r. ʼš ḥżh. ʼlhn̄.", that is "[this is the] book of Balaam son of Beor, seer of the gods . . . ." The inscription then consists of a series of prophecies for good and evil, attributed to the prototypical diviner Balaam, who is also mentioned in the Bible.[5] The coordination of the various brief oracular phrases is not clear. One could imagine a repertoire of prophetic expressions. The content of the text is entirely prophetic and completely autonomous, given that the oracular phrases are preceded only by the report of the prophet's dream, as happens in many prophetic books of the Bible.

We owe the prophetic biblical texts to the transition from a strictly oral prophecy to a written one. This process begins when oral prophecy is transcribed not as part of a report but in its own right. In the next step the prophet is no longer a voice recorded by the palace staff as part of their administrative routines. Rather, he would be able to speak directly to a scribe who works for him, or to write the text down himself. The text, which emanates from the deity through the prophet, remains in the prophet's hands (within his sphere of influence) and no longer in the hands of the powerful individuals to whom it is so frequently directed, even if polemically. This is the phase that interests us the most. It exemplifies the double valence of the prophetic text: a vehicle of broad diffusion and an instrument of symbolic action. Some aspects of this phase are illustrated by two accounts from the book of Jeremiah that concern the use of prophetic texts written by the prophet or dictated by him to "his" scribe.

In chapter 36 of the book of Jeremiah it is told that Jeremiah dictated to the scribe Baruch all of the words addressed to him by Yahweh. Baruch wrote these on a scroll. Jeremiah said to Baruch: "I cannot go to the house of Yahweh [that is, to the temple of Jerusalem]; I am prevented from doing so. Do you go on the fast day and read publicly in Yahweh's house Yahweh's words from the scroll you wrote at my dictation" (Jer. 36:5–7). Baruch did as he was told and read from the scroll in the house of Yahweh in the chamber of Gemariah son of Shaphan, the scribe, in the upper court at the entrance of the New Temple-Gate of the house of Yahweh. He read the scroll to all the people. But Micaiah, son of Gemariah, having heard "the words of Yahweh read from the book," took himself to the palace to the scribe's chamber where the dignitaries were in session. He reported to them what he had heard. The dignitaries sent for Baruch and enjoined him to read the text to them as well. Upon hearing it they were frightened and said: "We must certainly tell the king all these things" (Jer. 36:16). When they questioned Baruch about the redaction of the scroll, they learned that Jeremiah had dictated it. After advising Baruch to go into hiding with the prophet, they placed the scroll in safekeeping, and informed King Jehoiakim. The king sent for the scroll, which was read for the third time "to the king and to all the princes who were in attendance on the king" (Jer. 36:21). The king was seated in his winter lodgings since it was the ninth month. Before him blazed a brazier.

> Each time [the scribe] Jehudi finished reading three or four columns, the king would cut off a piece with a scribe's knife and cast it into the fire in the brazier, until the entire scroll was consumed in the fire. Hearing all these words did not frighten the king and his ministers or cause them to rend their garments. And though Elnathan, Delaiah, and Gemariah urged the king not to burn the scroll, he would not listen to them. (Jer. 36:23-25)

Hearing of this incident, Jeremiah took another scroll. "He gave it to his secretary, Baruch, son of Neriah; he wrote on it at Jeremiah's dictation all the words contained in the book which Jehoiakim, king of Judah, had burned in the fire, and many others of the same kind in addition" (Jer. 36:32). Soon afterward, Jeremiah was captured and imprisoned by Zedekiah, a successor of king Jehoiakim. The content of the burned and rewritten book seems to coincide with the text of the preceding chapters of Jeremiah, which constitute a series of prophecies of calamity in store for Judah and the king.

What interests us here is the ideal framework that the passage presents regarding writing. It is immediately clear that the twice-written scroll dictated by Jeremiah to Baruch is both *something less* and *something more* than what would be called a written text today.

It is *something less* because from the beginning it is clear that the text is written only because the prophet, persecuted by the royal authority, cannot go in person to speak to the people in the temple. The text is like a letter sent to those who cannot be reached by the prophet's own voice. The text contains the words of Yahweh, that *dabar* that, through the lips of the prophet, must reach others. The text is written to be orally recited before an audience, which, in contrast to the scribe, takes in only its orality. It is, in a manner of speaking, a prop for orality itself. Moreover, it is possible to rewrite the text just as it was (even if materials are added) precisely because it is divinely inspired. Further, the ideology of divine inspiration may be involved with archaic techniques of memorization. The text appears as a supplement to a memory which is no less "exact" than writing. Once the text is destroyed, it is remade because its content lies in the inspiration, not on the scroll.

The scroll is *something more* than what would constitute a text today because it is a vehicle for a divine word concerning destinies. It is thus endowed with a specific magico-symbolic power. Elsewhere, I have compared the destruction of this roll to the burning of Protagoras' works in Athens and to the attempted burning of Democritus's texts.[6] A more careful examination of the biblical passage shows, however, that the symbolic power of Baruch's scroll is a central theme. Clearly, the king is attempting to ward off that power by destroying the object. This is highlightened in the meticulous care with which Jehoiakim cuts up the scroll's columns with the tiny knife; and the fact that the rending of the monarch's garments is explicitly denied points to the importance of such a gesture, which is the correct behavior in similar circumstances (e.g., II Kings 22:11) if the text is recognized as inspired by Yahweh.

Beyond being an object imbued with magico-symbolic value, the scripture "dictated to Baruch" is, above all, the vehicle of a divine message destined for broad dissemination. This is attested to by the fact that its content seems to coincide with certain chapters of the prophetic book that has come down to us.

The magico-symbolic aspect is decidedly central in the case of another prophetic text described in the book of Jeremiah (51). Jeremiah recorded on one single scroll the whole story of the misfortune that he prophesied would befall Babylon. He entrusted this book to his emissary, who was a member of the entourage of King Zedekiah of Judah and en route for Babylon. Jeremiah ordered this emissary to "read aloud all these words" in Babylon (Jer. 63–64). At this point, Jeremiah adds a preamble that he communicates verbally to the emissary: "When you have finished reading this book, tie a stone to it and throw it in the Euphrates, and say: Thus shall Babylon sink. Never shall she rise, because of the evil I am bringing upon her" (Jer. 51:63–64).

This is no longer a simple text brimming with misfortune in its message, and therefore very dangerous, but a true episode of sympathetic magic. In the course of this episode the physical prop of the message of misfortune (that is, the scroll) is identified with that to which it is addressed (namely, Babylon). On the one hand, the prophetic word is "materialized" in the scroll, while on the other hand, it is made real through magical action. This action can be placed in the category of efficacious symbolic actions of which I spoke. Except for the singular object used in this case, the action is altogether similar to the shattering of the earthern flask that symbolizes Judah in Jeremiah 19, also to the decomposition of the loincloth and the smashing of the wine flasks in Jeremiah 13, and to the treatment of the clay tablet in Ezekiel 4 on which (the name of) Jerusalem is inscribed. The passage in question is an exemplary case of the materialization of the message in order to mediate between prophetic word and efficacious symbolic action.

4. God Gives the Text

The last step, and the decisive one in the process by which writing affects prophecy, is the myth of the presentation of the text written by the divine hand and transmitted to the prophet. In Exodus we are presented with an ambiguous situation. On the one hand, Moses is described as writing down the divine words. On the other hand, Moses provides the tablets on which Yahweh then traces the commandments with his finger. Nevertheless, it is precisely the Mosaic tradition that marks the turning point to the sacred written word, in which the ideology of the Torah as the sacred *written* word is rooted. True, the Mosaic story contains elements of a sacred process by now familiar: the tablets written on the mountain; the *incipit* "I am the god x" that recalls the Assyrian prophetic texts cited above; the smashing of the two tablets when the covenant is broken by the people; and the repetition of the whole procedure (from the ascent of the mountain to the redaction of two new identical tablets) when the covenant is renewed and definitively ratified. This familiar sacred process displays both of the nonmantic aspects of prophecy: the broad message transmitted by a prophet; and symbolic action. But the Mosaic story represents, above all, the point at which biblical religiosity most neatly detaches itself from its own premises and acquires its own peculiar physiognomy. In presenting the message as written directly by the divinity, the Mosaic story presents itself as the story of the origins of the Hebrew religion, pretending that the ethnic religion of Israel was a founded religion. The story of Moses establishes this religion as a religion both revealed and written, or, more properly, as a religion of prophecy transformed into scripture. The fact that the Ark of the Covenant—witness to the covenant of Israel with Yahweh, protector of the nation during war, focal point of the cult, object around which and for which the Temple of Jerusalem is built, and shining seat of the deity—is nothing more than a chest in which were placed "only the two tablets of the law given by Yahweh to Moses" demonstrates the powerful role of the written text in the Mosaic tradition. Through the centuries the brief text written by the national god remains the heart of the religion of the people, without which they would forget its inspired origin. Crystallized in writing, prophecy would henceforward constrain reality and force every subsequent prophecy to proceed from that revelation, written once and for all. The mechanisms of prophecy, with their direct communication between the divine sphere and humans, seemed to guarantee the possibility of continuous revelaton. Paradoxically, however, it is precisely that originating direct communication from the deity to a prototypical prophet which limits that fluidity of revelation.[7] The means by which this limitation occurs is the writing down of prophecy.

It is difficult to date Mosaic ideology and tradition. I would tend to place these toward the end, rather than toward the beginning, of the process that resulted in the biblical religion. It is easy, however, to identify in the prophetic books of the Bible the first appearance of the motif of the book transmitted from the deity to the prophet. The book of Ezekiel tells of a celestial vision comparable to the one (cited above) described by Micaiah, son of Imlah, to Ahab of Israel in the first book of Kings. In this case as well the divine throne is both at the summit and at the center of the divine courts. The divinity does not command "spirits," but enjoins the prophet to open his mouth and to eat that which he offers him.

> It was then I saw a hand stretched out to me, in which was a written scroll which he unrolled before me. It was covered with writing front and back and written on it was: Lamentation and wailing and woe! He said to me: Son of man, eat what is before you; eat this scroll, then go, speak to the house of Israel. So I opened my mouth and He gave me the scroll to eat. Son of man, He then said to me, feed your belly and fill your stomach with this scroll I am giving you. I ate it, and it was as sweet as honey in my mouth. He said: Son of man, go now to the house of Israel, and speak my words to them. Not to a people with difficult speech and barbarous language am I sending you, nor to the many peoples [with difficult speech and barbarous language] whose words you cannot understand. If I were to send you to these, they would listen to you; but the house of Israel will refuse to listen to you, since they will not listen to me. For the whole house of Israel is stubborn of brow and obstinate in heart. (Ezek. 2:9–10; 3:1–7)

In this passage also, a written message is destined to be recited orally before the people. As in the case of Moses on Mount Sinai, the words of Yahweh spoken by the prophet are Hebrew words. Although Israel will refuse to listen to them, these are words that Israel can comprehend. Rather than dictate this text, the divinity transmits an already written text. It is a scroll doubly filled with writing because it is covered with signs both front and back. The prophet must interiorize, even physically, a text which has already been recorded, and he must regurgitate it before the people.

The passage specifies quite intentionally that the text transmitted to Ezekiel is comprehensible to its addressees, who do not appreciate it only because they do not wish to do so. The same may not be said of other messages written by the divinity. Consider, for instance, the mysterious words traced on the wall by a divine hand in the banquet hall of Belshazzar, son of Nebuchadnezzar, which only the prophet Daniel could interpret.[8] In another prophetic passage, the scroll, in particular the sealed scroll, is a symbol of obscurity itself—the sort of obscurity that results from the blunting of mantic capacities, as described in Isaiah 29:11–12: "For you the revelation of all this has become like the words of a sealed scroll. When it is handed to one who can read, with the request, 'Read this,' he replies, 'I cannot; it is sealed.' When it is handed to one who cannot read, with the request, 'Read this,' he replies, 'I cannot read.' "

In the ways illustrated above, prophets assumed a prerogative previously held by royal courts; namely, the written redaction of prophetic communication. Here, written prophecy is treated as the privilege of another court: the heavenly court. The message is written in the heavens. It arrives already fixed in human hands and, moreover, it can be read. To the canonization and rigidity of the message, so characteristic of the Mosaic tradition, is added an increasing obscurity of the message, which is decipherable by only a few. These are the premises of apocalyptic thought. In fact, in the canonical Apocalypse of John, the scroll written on both sides and the book eaten by the prophet reappear in timely fashion, while the opening of the seals that secured the scroll is connected to the trumpets of the hierophany. In the book of Enoch as well, the destinies written in celestial words—as in the Mesopotamian tradition—will be revealed to human beings with the breaking of the seals.[9]

Truth now resides in the written text, which the divinity has infused with a total message. The interpretation of that text rests with those who are authorized to read it. As the religions of the Book organize their institutions, their new totalizing ambitions ultimately give rise to wars of religion which are, in effect, wars of books in which the good book struggles against a book that is bad. Among the new universal religions prophecy has triumphed, because direct contact with the divinity is now not only the means of knowing what will occur, but also of knowing how things are, once and for all. But prophecy has lost as well, because the truth communicated by God is once again written in books that only a few know how to read well.

NOTES

1. Concerning Near-Eastern divination seen from this perspective the fundamental work is the long essay by J. Bottéro, "Symptomes, signes, écritures en Mesopotamie ancienne," in J. P. Vernant et al, *Divination et rationalité* (Paris, 1974).

2. North discusses and radically reshapes the recent theory of the biblical prophet as "messenger" in "Angel-Prophet or Satan-Prophet," *Zeitschrift für die alttestamentliche Wissenschaft* 82 (1970), pp. 31–67. Nevertheless, the data that support the notion of biblical prophet as an emissary of the divinity are not negligible, if in a less specific sense than that proposed by H. B. Huffmon, "The Covenant Lawsuit in the Prophets," *Journal of Biblical Literature* 78 (1959), pp. 285–294.

3. Concerning Mari and prophecy: F. Ellermeier, *Prophetie in Mari und Israel*, Theologische und orientalische Arbeiten vol. 1. (Herzberg, 1970); W. L. Moran, "New Evidence from Mari on the History of Prophecy," *Biblica* 50 (1969), pp. 15–56; K. Koch, "Die Briefe profetischen Inhalt aus Mari: Bemerkungen zu Gattung und Sitz im Leben," *Ugarit-Forschungen* 4 (1972), pp. 53–77; E. Noort, *Untersuchungen zum Gottesbescheid in Mari: Die "Mariprophetie" in der alttestamentlichen Forshung*. AOAT series vol. 202 (Kevelaer-Neukirchen, 1977).

4. See M. Weippert, "Assyrische Prophetie der Zeit Asarhaddons und Assurbanipals," in M. Fales, ed., *Assyrian Royal Inscriptions: New Horizons in Literary, Ideological and Historical Analysis* (Rome, 1981), pp. 71–115.

5. On the Balaam Bar-Beor text see J. Hoftijzer, G. v.d. Kooij et al., *Aramaic Texts from Deir ʿAlla*, Documenta et Monumenta Orientis Antiqui series no. 19 (Leiden, 1976); A. Caquot and A. Lemaire, "Les textes araméens de Deir ʿAlla," *Syria* 54 (1977), pp. 189–208; E. Hammershaimb, "De Aramaiske indskrifter fra udgravigerne Deir ʿAlla," *Dansk Teologisk Tidsskrift* 40 (1977), pp. 217–242; J. Hoftijzer, *De ontcijfering van Deir ʿAlla-teksten*. Ooster Genootschap in Nederland series no. 5 (Leiden, 1973); idem, "The Prophet Balaam in a 6th Century Aramaic Inscription," *Biblical Archaeologist* 39 (1976), pp. 11–17; J. Lust, "Balaam an Ammonite," *Ephemeridae Theologicae Lovanienses* 54 (1978), pp. 60–62; H. P. Müller, "Einige alttestamentliche Probleme zur aramäischen Inschrift von Deir ʿAlla," *Zeitschrift des Deutschen Palästina–Vereins* 94 (1978), pp. 56–57; A. Rofè, "The Book of Balaam (numbers 22:2–24:25): A Study in Methods of Criticism and the History of Biblical Literature and Religion," *Jerusalem Biblical Studies* 1 (1979), pp. 59–70 (in Hebrew).

6. See my report to the round table concerning the book of J. Svenbro, *La parole et le marbre* (Lund, 1976) published in *Dialoghi di Archeologia* 2 (1981), pp. 55–67.

7. Concerning an analogous question in primitive Christianity, see E. Pagels, *The Gnostic Gospels* (New York, 1979), especially chapter 1; also by Pagels, "Visions, Appearances, and Apostolic Authority: Gnostic and Orthodox Traditions," in B. Aland (ed.), *Gnosis: Festschrift für Hans Jonas* (Göttingen, 1978), pp. 415–430. Concerning Shiite and Ishmaili prophetology and its relationship to the religion of the Book, see H. Corbin, *Histoire de la philosophie islamique* I (Paris, 1964), chapter 2.

8. For this passage see the book of Daniel, chapter 5.

9. Concerning this aspect of First Enoch see the famous book by G. Widengren, *The Ascension of the Apostle and the Heavenly Book* (Uppsala, 1950), pp. 36–49.

MAKING ROOM FOR
THE WRITTEN LAW

The Hebrew Bible (or the Old Testament, as some believers in a further testament like to call it) contains a written law (or, better, a written *tôrāh*, to use
the correct term, which is not identical in meaning to our term *law*).[1] That
tôrāh which is contained in some books of the Bible is clearly the very core
and pivot of the Bible itself. Now, the law contained in these books is considered to be, and presented as, inspired by the national god Yahweh, and the
term *tôrāh* is today also the name of the first part of the Bible, which contains
not only the laws but also the story of how those laws came to be given by the
deity to the people of Israel, as well as the earliest story of that people and of
its god.

In turn, this further part of the Bible is traditionally considered to have
been inspired by Yahweh through the great intermediary, Moses—a law-*taker*
and transmitter, rather than a law-*giver*—who had received the law from Yahweh.[2] And this belief in the inspired quality not only of the biblical laws, but
also of the narrative framework of those texts is central in at least two of the
world's great religions of today.

What I shall try to discuss here is the way in which the sacred text itself—the
Hebrew Bible in some of its most crucial passages—constructs the very quality I
have described—that is, its own inspired quality, its own divine origins, and,
thus, its own authority. In doing this, I shall turn to the biblical narratives that
tell us of the giving—or of the finding—of the *tôrāh* or of parts of the *tôrāh*.

Indeed, as soon as one is confronted with these texts, it becomes immediately clear that their concern about the divine inspiration of the sacred law is
in reality a concern about the ultimate source of authority and power. These
narratives are stories of authority contested, validated, guaranteed, and of conflict between, or of juxtaposition of, different authorities. In these texts, texts,
priests, prophets, and kings face one another and interact, often most violently,
but the outcome of such interactions must be—indeed it is, each time—the
founding of the authority of the text about which the story is told, as well as of
the authority of the text that is telling the story.

I

If we now turn to the Bible in search of narratives about the origin of the *tôrāh*
or of parts of the *tôrāh*, we shall find that there are two such stories: the story of

the finding of the "book of the *tôrah*" (*sēper hattôrāh*) that most modern critics identify with the book of Deuteronomy (II Kings 22–23) and the story of the giving of the tablets to Moses on Mount Sinai (Exodus 19–24).

We shall start with the first episode mentioned in the previous paragraph: King Josiah (639/638–609 B.C.E.) ordered the Jerusalem temple to be restored; during the process of restoring it a book was found, the *sēper hattôrāh*. This is a translation of the relevant text:

> Hilkiah the high priest said to Shaphan the scribe: I have found the book of the *tôrāh* in the house of Yahweh. And Hilkiah gave the book to Shaphan, and he read it. And Shaphan the scribe came to the king . . . and Shaphan the scribe said to the king, Hilkiah the priest has delivered to me a book, and Shaphan read it before the king. And, when the king had heard the words of the book of the *tôrāh*, he rent his clothes. And he gave orders to Hilkiah the priest, and to Ahikam the son of Shaphan, and to Achbor the son of Michaiah, and to Shaphan the scribe, saying: Go, inquire of Yahweh for me and for the people, and for all Judah, concerning the words of this book, for great is the wrath of Yahweh that is kindled against us, because our fathers have not obeyed the words of this book. . . . So they went to Hulda the prophetess, the wife of Shallum the son of Harbas, keeper of the wardrobe, and they talked to her. And she said to them: Thus says Yahweh god of Israel: Tell the man who sent you to me: Because they have forsaken me, and have burned incense to other gods, so as to provoke me to anger with all the works of their hands—therefore my wrath shall be kindled against this place, and shall not be quenched. But to the king of Judah who sent you to inquire of Yahweh, you shall say thus: Thus says Yahweh god of Israel: As for the words you have heard, because your heart was tender, and you have humbled yourself before Yahweh . . . and you have rent your clothes, and you have wept before me, I also have heard [you], says Yahweh. Therefore I shall gather you with your forefathers, and you shall be gathered in your grave in peace; and your eyes shall not see all the evil which I shall bring upon this place. And they [i.e., the men sent to Hulda by Josiah] brought this message to the king. [II Kings. 22:8–20]
>
> And the king had all the elders of Judah and of Jerusalem gathered about him, and he went into the house of Yahweh, and all the men of Judah and all the inhabitants of Jerusalem went with him, and so did the priests, and the prophets, and all the people, both small and great; and he read to their ears all the words of the book of the covenant [*sēper habberīt*] which was found in the house of Yahweh. And the king stood by a pillar and made a covenant [literally: cut (*krt*) a *berīt*] before Yahweh to walk after Yahweh, and to keep his commandments, and his testimonies and his statutes, with all heart and soul, to perform the words of this *berīt* that were written in this book. And all the people stood to the *berīt*. [II Kings 23:1–2]

What follows is the so-called reform of Josiah, consisting of a general destruction of all cultic places, objects and practices not pertaining to the strict Yahwistic cult, of the general massacre of all the cultic personnel devoted to such practices, and of a solemn celebration of the Passover (II Kings 23:4–24). The conclusion is a further declaration in praise of Josiah: "There was no king like him, who turned to Yahweh with all his heart,and with all his soul, and with all his might, according to all the laws [*twrt*] of Moses [*b^ekol tûrat mošeh*]; and after him none rose up like him" (23:25). In spite of this, we are told (23:26–27), Yahweh did not turn away from the fury of his great anger, provoked by Manasseh, Josiah's predecessor, and the destruction of Jerusalem was only delayed, not withdrawn from the deity's plans.

Many approaches to this important text may be—and have been—adopted. The problems most debated are the relationship between the "book of the *tôrāh*" discussed here and the biblical book of Deuteronomy (a relationship surely exists, but is it really an identity?); and so-called covenant involving the king, the deity, and the people described in 23:1–3 (is *b^erīt* really "a covenant," or does it simply mean "a solemn promise," as proposed by Perlitt and Kutch?).[3] As for the Josianic reform: did it really take place? Was it really a reform? Doubts are permitted.[4]

Here I shall leave aside all these problems that are both so difficult and so popular. I shall say nothing about what actually happened historically during the reign of King Josiah of Judah—a question that is impossible to answer because the only evidence we have is a couple of narratives (II Kings 22–23 and II Chronicles 34–35) from two sacred books—and instead of worrying about possible facts we shall deal with texts. In particular I shall deal with the connections between this biblical text and two other biblical texts.

The first connection is obvious, for it is made by the text itself. We have read in II Kings 23:25 that Josiah had turned to Yahweh according to all the laws of Moses (the MT has *kl twrt mšh*; the Septuagint has κατὰ πάντα τὸν νόμον Μωυσῆ). Does this mean that the *sēper hattôrāh* that was found in the temple is identified here with the laws of Moses followed by Josiah? Or is the meaning less specific—in which case the expression would simply refer to the Yahwistic, holy behavior of Josiah as a behavior in accordance with the laws established originally by Moses? We are not able to decide, but in any case the story of the recovery of the written law deposited in the temple of Yahweh in the time of Josiah refers back to the story of the written law given by Yahweh to Moses as recounted in Exodus 19–24. We shall consider these two stories together here; let it be declared once and for all that one of them contains a reference to the other, and thus entitles us officially, so to speak, to proceed as we shall.

The second connection is less obvious, for it is suggested by the similarity in form between the narrative in II Kings 22–23 (the finding of the book of the *tôrāh* in the temple of Jerusalem), and the narrative in II Kings 11 and II Chron. 22:9–23:21 (the finding of the heir to the throne, Joash, in the temple of Jerusalem). Let us turn briefly to a translation of the text in II Kings.

When King Ahaziah was killed (in 849 or 851 B.C.E.), his wicked mother Athaliah, the biblical story goes, arose and destroyed all the royal seed, in order to reign undisturbed. "But Jehosheba, the daughter of King Joram, sister of Ahaziah, took Joash the son of Ahaziah and stole him from among the king's sons who were slain, and they hid him, him and his nurse, in the bedchamber from Athaliah, so that he was not slain" (II Kings 11:2). After this, the child was hidden with his nurse "in the house of Yahweh for six years, while Athaliah reigned over the land." In the seventh year the priest Jehoiada "sent and fetched the rulers over hundreds with the captains and the guard, and brought them to the house of Yahweh, and cut a $b^e r\bar{\iota}\underline{t}$ with them, and made them swear an oath in the house of Yahweh, and showed them the king's son" (11:3–4). He then gave them precise instructions (11:5–8), "and the captains over the hundreds did according to all that Jehoiada the priest commanded, and they took . . . [their] men and came to Jehoiada, and the priest . . . gave [them] King David's spear and shields, that were in the temple of Yahweh. And the guard stood every man with his weapons in his hands, round about the king [i.e., Joash], from the left corner to the right corner of the temple, by the altar. . . . And Jehoiada brought forth the king's son, and put the $n\bar{e}zer$ upon him, and gave him the $\acute{e}\underline{d}\bar{u}\underline{t}$, and they made him king, and anointed him; and they clapped their hands, and said, 'Hurrah for the king!'" (11:9–12).

What follows resembles the events that follow the finding of the book of the $t\hat{o}r\bar{a}h$ in the time of Josiah. When Athaliah hears the noise of the guard and of the people, she comes to the people who are gathered in the temple of Yahweh, and when she looks, "behold, the king stood by the pillar [$\acute{a}l$-$h\bar{a}\acute{a}mm\bar{u}\underline{d}$; the Septuagint has επι τον στυλον] as the custom was, and the princes and the trumpeters stood by the king, and all the people of the land rejoiced, and blew trumpets; so that Athaliah rent her clothes and cried: Treason, Treason!" (II Kings 11:13–14). At an order from Jehoiada, the queen is killed by the guards; then "Jehoiada cut a $b^e r\bar{\iota}\underline{t}$ between Yahweh, and the king, and the people, that they should be Yahweh's people; also, [a $b^e r\bar{\iota}\underline{t}$] between the king and the people" (11:15–17). The house of Baal is then destroyed and its priest slain; then the new king is escorted to the throne room and sits on the throne. All the people of the land rejoice. Joash becomes a pious king and repairs the house of Yahweh (11:18–21 and 12:1–20).

Mario Liverani has shown that this narrative was highly conventional, if not actually falsified.[5] The fact that things probably did not go the way we are told is not particularly interesting here; what is more important, I think, is the conventional quality of the narrative. If we compare it to the story of the finding of the book of the $t\hat{o}r\bar{a}h$ in the house of Yahweh in the time of Josiah as told in II Kings 23–24, the stereotyped narrative discussed by Liverani can be shown to be one of a couple of stereotyped narratives that clearly, if implicitly, refer to each other. Each part of each story has its precise counterpart in the other story. The common scheme is the following; during a period in which Israel worships false gods and is ruled by bad monarchs, a true and just king, or a true inspired text, is hidden somewhere in the house of Yahweh. One day, the legitimate and true king or text is found, revealed, and accepted by the people (because it is warranted by a priest or by a prophet). The true king is given a sacred "text" (the $\acute{e}\underline{d}\bar{u}\underline{t}$); the true text is given to a king.[6] The two immediate consequences are the destroying of false gods or of bad and illegitimate monarchs; and the renewal of a covenant tying the people and the king to the true deity, and the people and the monarch to each other.

It would be possible, if it were necessary, for us to dwell at length on the details of this comparison. The correspondence is extremely precise (including minute aspets such as the pillar by which the king stands in both stories, or the use of an identical lexical repertoire in both passages), and if added together they could make my case irresistible. Yet I prefer to let my readers test it by themselves, and I hasten to draw from the comparison the consequences that seem to me important. To express things simply and directly, I shall observe that the lost king plays, in II Kings 11–12, almost the same role that the lost book plays in II Kings 22–23: both are hidden, found, presented as true, and acclaimed, and both become the center of a $b^e r \bar{\imath} t$ ceremony. The main difference between the king of II Kings 11–12 and the book of II Kings 22–23 lies in the fact that the book is in its turn accepted by a king who solemnly swears to "perform the words of the $b^e r \bar{\imath} t$ that were written in the book" (II Kings 23:3) and swears this before all the people. Even though something of the kind probably happens in both narratives—we are told that Joash is given the $\dot{\imath} ed \bar{u} t$, probably meaning a written text of some kind, but possibly also oral instructions—yet in II Kings 11–12, where the text is possibly present, but not central, the issue is the power of the legitimate king, while where the book of the $t \hat{o} r \bar{a} h$ is central, in II Kings 22–23, the book rules over the king and the "legitimacy" of the king is tested through his faithfulness to the book. The book is thus, in our pair of narratives, similar in meaning and function to the king, but more important—more powerful—than the king, because the book rules over the king.

Further differences can be perceived, and they seem to point in the same direction. First, the story of the finding of king Joash refers to a period that is older than that of the finding of the book of the $t \hat{o} r \bar{a} h$ (the first episode is dated, as we have seen, around 830; the second is dated around 620 B.C.E.): if we admit a hierarchy of importance and of power such as the one I have suggested above, the sequence Joash–book of the $t \hat{o} r \bar{a} h$ in the time of Josiah is also a crescendo in time, from the finding and installation of a powerful and righteous king to the finding and installation of a more powerful and sacred text. A crescendo is surely present, and easy to detect, in the efficacy of the new elements—king or text—introducing and warranting the "reform," for this efficacy is expressed directly by the thoroughness of the destruction of non-Yahwistic cults. Thus, during the reign of Joash the temple of Baal was destroyed and its priest killed (II Kings 11:18), and the house of Yahweh was restored (12:4–18), but "the $b \bar{a} m \bar{o} t$ were not taken away, and the people still sacrificed and burned incense on the $b \bar{a} m \bar{o} t$ (12:4). On the other hand, the destruction of non-Yahwistic cults was complete under Josiah, and the $b \bar{a} m \bar{o} t$ were duly destroyed (23:8, with the difficult v. 9). So we have, first, the installation of a pious king, found in the temple of Jerusalem, and a partial destruction of non-Yahwistic cults, and second, the installation of a sacred text, found in the same temple of Jerusalem, and a total destruction of non-Yahwistic cults. The crescendo, I think, is clear.[7]

While we must conclude, I think, that the $s \bar{e} p e r$ $h a t t \hat{o} r \bar{a} h$ is more powerful than the king, we must at the same time beware of considering the book in itself all-powerful. For in II Kings 22, the book has to be tested, and the testing is done, as we have seen, by questioning Yahweh through the prophetess Hulda. It is true that King Josiah tears his clothes as soon as the book is read to him, but it is also true that the *berīt* ceremony involving the book is not celebrated until after the prophetess has confirmed the words of the book by speaking the words of the deity in the course of a trance session. This testing of the book through the prophet—there is no such testing to be done in the case of the king—creates problems and opens up new vistas. The authority and the power of inspired writing faces the authority and the power of inspired speech: the book faces the prophet. Even though the religion of the Hebrew Bible is not strictly speaking a revealed religion, we are confronted here with the great dilemma of all revealed religions.

To understand more about the deity's written law in the Hebrew Bible, but also more about the dilemma of revealed religions and of god-given law in general, we shall now turn to our third episode, the giving of the tablets to Moses on the mountain (Exod. 19–24) and to its immediate context.

2

To deal with this story, which has provoked oceans of ink and is still provoking mountains of software, we must avoid the obvious, so I shall not quote a lengthy translation. In spite of Sigmund Freud's revised version, we all remember what is said to have happened: while the Israelites were fleeing from Egypt, toward the land of Canaan, many generations before the time of Joash and Josiah, their leader Moses received from Yahweh the original tablets of the *tôrāh*. He brought them down to the people, but he found the people and the priests involved in the cult of the golden calf; in fury he broke the tablets, and he destroyed the golden calf, punished the guilty, returned to the mountain, and received new tablets from Yahweh.

The narrative occupies half of the book of Exodus, extending from chapter 19 to chapter 40. In the Sinai area, we are told, a fiery hierophany of Yahweh is witnessed by Moses, by the priests, and by the people. Then Moses, alone, climbs up the mountain. Yahweh voices the decalogue and the other laws, Moses goes back down to the people, and a *berīt* is made between the deity and the people, involving a book of the *berīt* (*sēper habberīt*) that had been written by Moses and contained "all the words of Yahweh" (chaps. 19–24). Then Moses climbs back up to the mountain once more, and in a further fiery theophany the deity voices instructions and then gives Moses "the tablets of the testimony" (*luhōt hā'edūt*), "tables of stone, written with the finger of Yahweh" (chaps. 25–31).

In the meantime the people miss Moses ("that [man] Moses who brought us out of the land of Egypt, we do not know what has become of him") and ask the priest Aaron to make gods (note the plural) to go before them. Aaron makes the golden calf, and the people say: "These are your gods [again, note the plural], o Israel, who brought you up out of the land of Egypt!" Then they offer sacrifice and rejoice. On the mountain, Yahweh tells Moses what is happening; Moses intercedes for the people, goes down to them with the tablets, breaks the tablets in rage at what he sees, destroys the golden calf and begins the massacre of the idolatrous Israelites—a massacre executed by those who choose to side with Yahweh, and first of all by the Levites. Moses then asks Yahweh to let his divine presence be visible to the people and guide them toward the land of Canaan, and Yahweh accepts the task (Exod. 32–33:23).

After this, Moses is told by Yahweh to prepare two new tablets; he does so, goes up the mountain for a third time, hears more commandments from the mouth of Yahweh, writes them on the tablets himself, and goes back down to the people. The new words, written on the new tablets, constitute a new $b^e r \bar{\imath} \underline{t}$: they are repeated by Moses to the priests and to the people (chap. 34). The $b^e r \bar{\imath} \underline{t}$ is thus renewed; the tent and the ark to go inside it are built, according to the instructions given before the golden calf episode (in chaps. 25–31); the testimony ($h \bar{a}^c e \underline{d} \bar{u} t$) is placed in the ark; and the glory of Yahweh, a visible sign of his presence, fills the tent (chaps. 35–40). From that day, we are told in the last verse of the book of Exodus, the cloud of Yahweh was upon the tent by day, and fire was on it by night, in the sight of all the house of Israel, throughout all their journeys (Exod. 40:38).

Let us look at this narrative with our eyes open (i.e., let us leave aside all preconceived views and, in particular, all preconceived subdivisions of the *Vorlage* into presupposed "sources"),[8] and let us compare it to the two narratives we have discussed so far, which deal with a lost king and with a lost book. It shall be clear at first sight that the things that happen both to Moses and to the tablets of testimony in Exodus 19–40 resemble the things that happen to the good king in II Kings 11 and to the true text in II Kings 22–23. To use the formula I have invented to express the sequence in the two episodes of II Kings, in Exodus 19–40 also a leader, Moses, and a text, the tablets of the $^c e \underline{d} \bar{u} t$, are lost and then found, or remade, presented as true, and acclaimed, and finally become the center of a $b^e r \bar{\imath} \underline{t}$ ceremony. In Exodus 19–40, just as in II Kings 11 and II Kings 22–23, the period during which the leader or the text are lost or destroyed is also a period during which the Israelites follow bad leaders and worship false gods, and the period of the restoration of the correct order after the return or reconstruction of the leader of the text begins, in Exodus 19–40 and in II Kings 11 and II Kings 22–23, with the killing of the guilty. The pattern is simple and is consistently followed.

Precisely because a simple pattern is always followed, it is easy to spot the existence of three important peculiarities that differentiate the Exodus narrative from the two stories (II Kings 11 and II Kings 22–23) I have discussed in the first part of this essay. First of all, the text is directly dictated, or even written, by the deity in the book of Exodus and then prepared and transmitted by an intermediary figure to the people, while in II Kings 22–23 we are not shown the production of the inspired text, but merely told that it was found, tested, and found true. Second, in the book of Exodus both an inspired person and an inspired text are central in the narrative and subjected to the same vicissitudes: the person here is no less inspired than the text, for it is a prophet, and not a king. Third, though one text (the second pair of tablets, which are finally placed in the ark) is the most important one, and the pivot of the whole narrative sequence, Exodus 19–40 mentions at least two texts, because the first text given to Moses is destroyed in Exodus 32, and another one is remade in Exodus 34 and placed in the ark in Exodus 40.

Now, it should be noted that the three peculiarities of Exodus 19–40 we have noticed in comparing it to II Kings 11 and to II Kings 22–23 are connected to one another: the fact that there are several texts mentioned in the Exodus narrative, and that one text is written twice, is made possible precisely by the existence, in that narrative, of an important "prophetic" figure functioning as an intermediator between the deity and the Israelites, and thus able to reobtain the sacred testimony containing the divine words. Because Moses is present, the tablets can be written again, so that the testimony exists once more and can be placed inside the ark.

This coexistence of a man (of a prophet, at least according to the classification we find in Deuteronomy)[9] and of a revealed text playing similar roles and endowed with similar functions is what makes Exodus 19–40 especially important to us in our specific perspective. To understand this coexistence, the key text is the narrative in Exodus 32, where the conflict between Moses and the tablets on the one hand, and the golden calf on the other, is expressed. The turning point in the narrative is the moment when Moses breaks the original tablets written by Yahweh. This gesture should be compared, in view of the position it occupies in the narrative structure of Exodus 19–40, to the violent gestures—to the rending of the kingly robes—made by Josiah and by Athaliah when confronted with the new situations in II Kings 22:11 and in II Kings 11:14, respectively. At the same time, the gesture is unique, and marks a total break: not only the breaking of the covenant, but also the destruction, by Moses, of the (only possiblity of a) heavenly text written by the deity's hand. Henceforth, the "original sin" of idolatry commited by the Israelites makes it impossible for them (according to the Exodus narrative) to have the real, original tablets. They have worshiped a manmade object, the golden calf, and they shall thereafter have only the second pair of tablets, with laws dictated to a mortal man. Thus, the coexistence of man and text becomes a structural element in the very giving of texts by the deity. Israel and Yahweh must communicate by way of prophet and scribe.

In spite of the necessity of the coexistence, marked as inevitable by the narrative in Exodus 32, the whole of Exodus 19–40 is the story of a difficult relationship between the holy man and the revealed text—between Moses and the ʿeḏūṯ. This difficult relationship, this alternative that is discussed in spite of the coexistence, is already clear in the very chapter in which Moses, so to speak, ostensibly sides with the tablets against the golden calf. For the solution of the conflict between Moses and the golden calf in that chapter is the choice of the tablets in the ark—rather than of Moses—as the pivot of the life of the people and as the leader of the Israelites toward the land of Canaan.

The logic of the narrative speaks for itself. When Moses takes long to come down from the mountain, the people miss their guide ("that Moses who brought us up out of the land of Egypt"), and ask for another guide ("Come, make us gods to go before us"). There is thus a direct relationship between the temporary disappearance of the human, inspired leader of the people and the people's request for man-made leaders, the non-Yahwistic gods. Clearly, in the eyes of the people, Moses and the golden calf have the same function: they must show the way. Since Moses may have to disappear again—and must, someday, "disappear" forever—the crisis that gave rise to the worship of the golden calf is bound to repeat itself. An object as solid—and as permanent—as the golden calf must then take the place of the golden calf, but also of Moses. That object is the ark containing the ʿeḏūṯ. After destroying the golden calf, Moses makes new tablets, follows Yahweh's instructions in building the ark, and places the tablets in the ark. He then prays to Yahweh, asking the deity to place a sign of his presence in and above the tent containing the ark. Yahweh does so, and the ark becomes the guide of the Israelites. Even after Moses' final disappearance, the ark continues to guide Israel.

The inspired man is thus an unsatisfactory guide, for in his absence the people may (indeed, are inclined to) turn to false gods. So, after the false gods have been destroyed, the lead is taken by the text, protected by the ark, and topped by the glory of Yahweh. It is the inspired man himself, the intermediary between the people and the deity and the leader in the journey toward the land, who prepares the text, gives orders to build its containers, and obtains from the deity the sign that consecrates the text as well as its containers. As a priest, Aaron made the golden calf as a guide for the people, thus the "prophet" Moses makes the text into a guide. The confrontation is over, the text has won, and its superiority is admitted, indeed, construed, by the very human leader it has replaced.

3

I have spoken of an open conflict between man-made gods, on the one hand, and the tôrāh and Moses, on the other. I have also suggested the existence of a problematic relationship between Moses and the ʿeḏūṯ contained in the ark, concluded by the victory, and by the established primacy, of the written text. We have traced this conflict and this relationship in the narrative of Exodus 19–40. But there are other important traces, both biblical and extrabiblical, of this complex interplay. The impression one receives if one considers the Exodus narrative and the other relevant traditions together is that, during and after the formulation of our biblical Vorlage, both the conflict between man-made gods and the Yahwistic cult and the problematic coexistence of written tôrāh and human intermediators were central issues. The process of making room for the the written tôrāh involved a fight on both fronts, and narrative traditions were among the weapons. Let us quote some examples, and consider (a) the golden calf, (b) Moses, and, finally (c) the ark.

a) First of all, let us consider the golden calf. The tradition in Exod. 32:1 that the people asked Aaron to make "gods to go before us" because "that Moses who brought us out of the land of Egypt" had been absent for a long time and nobody knew where he was, is echoed precisely by I Kings 12:28–29: Jeroboam, we are told, made two calves of gold, placed them in two sanctuaries of his kingdom, "and said to the people: It is too much for you to go up to Jerusalem: behold your gods, o Israel, which brought you up out of the land of Egypt." The calves are presented as the gods who guided Israel from Egypt to the land of Canaan: the whole expression used here is identical to that used in Exod. 32:1 for Moses, and the fact that there were, according to I Kings 12, *two* golden calves explains the strange use of the plural we have noticed in Exodus 31. Is the story of Jeroboam more "historical" than the story of Aaron's golden calf? I am afraid no one can really answer this question, but surely the existence of identical formulae in two different biblical texts referring to the cult of golden calves as guides in the desert journey points to a tradition different from the prevailing one, and substituting the golden calf or calves for Moses or for the ark, or both. The conflict was thus possibly not just a narrative device to express the struggle of Yahwism (or a type of Yahwism) against other gods (or against other types) but a real conflict between two versions of the story of Israel's journey from Egypt to Canaan, each of which may have been tied to specific religious beliefs and cultic behaviors.[10]

b) Second, let us consider Moses. In the complex biblical narrative traditions about Moses, and in the huge amount of midrashic and other material relating to that figure, it is possible to trace elements that point to an implicit—or even to an explicit—discussion of the centrality of Moses as the leader and founder of Yahwistic Israel, as a prefiguration of the prophets, as the intermediator of the Torah. In the perspective adopted here, some difficult or ambiguous aspects of the Moses tradition may be understood in the light of the dialectical relationship between Moses and the written *tôrāh* as represented by the *'edūt* in the ark. Thus, Moses' speech difficulty presented in various passages of the book of Exodus and discussed by Jeffrey H. Tigay may be interpreted as referring to the limitations of the oral transmission as opposed to the written.[11] The strange repetition in Exod. 19:9b of Moses' reporting of the people's answer to Yahweh and other similar textual problems, however one may solve them, point to an issue that is not Moses' office in general, as Brevard S. Childs suggests, [12] but more specifically the oral communication of Yahweh with Israel through Moses. But the aspect of the Moses tradition that seems most important in the present perspective is the story of Moses' death before the entry into the promised land that we find in Deuteronomy 32–34, in Numbers 27, and in Joshua 1.

Moses may not enter the promised land, because of the sin he has committed in the wilderness of Zin (Deut. 32:48–52; Num. 27:12–15). His successor, Joshua, is chosen, and consecrated by him (Deut. 34:9; Nu. 27:18–23); then Moses dies in sight of the promised land (Deuteronomy 34) and is mourned and buried (Deut. 34:5–8), but "no man knows [the location of] his sepulchre unto this day" (Deut. 34:6). From the point of view of the necessary but difficult coexistence between Moses and the *' edūt*, this means that there is no trace of the presence of Moses in the land of Canaan, and that the intermediator stopped functioning before Israel's existence in its historical setting began. More important still, it means that not even outside Canaan does a place exist where the memory of Moses may be rooted and give way to something resembling a cult. On the other hand, the *tôrāh* enters the land most forcefully, in two different ways. First of all, the ark enters Canaan and leads the victorious Israelites: the first conquest, the taking of Jericho, is a miracle of the ark. Second, the Israelites are led by Joshua, and Yahweh says to Joshua: "The book of the *tôrāh* shall not depart out of your mouth, and you shall meditate on it day and night, and be careful to do all that is written in it—for then shall you make your way be prosperous, and then shall you have great success" (Josh. 1:8). And, while Moses had no known burial place, the ark remains the center of all cultic and political life throughout the history of Israel in Canaan, and the Jerusalem temple itself is built to house the ark.

c) If we now turn to the ark, to consider the narrative traditions that concern it, we shall have to add that not even the victory of the ark we have just described is sufficient to guarantee a lasting triumph of the written *tôrāh* over the handmade objects and over the human intermediators and ancestors. For there seem to have been problems with the contents of the ark.

The first book of Kings describes the construction of Solomon's temple and solemnly concludes the description with the installation of the ark (I Kings 8:1–11). In this narrative, a strange passage stands out: "There was nothing in the ark," verse 9 reads, "except the two stone tablets which Moses laid up there at Horeb [the tablets of the *bᵉrīt*], which Yahweh cut with the children of Israel when they came out of the land of Egypt." As John Gray notes in his commentary to the books of Kings, "The statement that nothing was in the Ark but the tablets of stone (*luḥōt hā᾽ᵃbānīm*) obviously comes from a time when other objects were believed to have been in them, e.g., Aaron's rod and a pot of manna, the source of the tradition in Heb. 9.4."[13] It is true that such a tradition "is not specifically attested in the statement of the deposit of Aaron's rod in Numbers 17" (the rod is placed "before the *'edūt*") "and the pot of manna in Exodus 16.33" (in Exod. 16:34 the pot is placed "before the *'edūt*"), but this is not a good reason to see it necessarily as a late tradition: indeed, the installation of the rod and pot *before* the testimony rather than *in* the ark may well be a later correction of a relatively old tradition, to which I Kings 8:9 may be seen as a further reaction.

In the ark, too, not only in the biblical narrative, it thus seems to have been necessary to make room for the written *tôrāh*. But things seem even more complex if we consider that a midrashic tradition that was also popular in the literatures of Arabia and Iran[14] spoke of two arks accompanying Israel in the wilderness: "the ark of Joseph who was mortal, and the Ark of Him who lives for ever," that is, the coffin containing Joseph's bones and the ark containing the testimony. The biblical passages that gave rise to this tradition are Gen. 50:25–26 (Joseph makes the children of Israel swear an oath that they shall carry his bones with them; then he is embalmed and buried in a coffin in Egypt), Exod. 13:19 (Moses takes Joseph's bones with him on leaving Egypt with the Israelites), and Josh. 24:32 (the children of Israel bury Joseph's bones in Shechem). Since the term used for Joseph's coffin in Genesis is *'arôn*, the same term used for the ark, it is necessary only to add an *'arôn* to Joseph's bones as they already appeared in the biblical narrative, and to tell a story about how Moses found the bones and the coffin, in order to have two arks, one containing the written law and the other, lesser one containing a man's bones. The advantage resulting for the *'edūt*-centered tradition from the lack of a burial place for Moses was thus endangered. But, unlike the tradition about various objects in the ark, this tradition about two arks does not seem to surface clearly, not even in order to be denied, in the biblical text itself, and so we may consider it with more probability a late, secondary tradition.

If taken together and considered synchronically, however, the tradition about other sacred objects in the ark and the tradition about another ark may be seen as a couple of alternatives to the winning version, upheld by all relevant biblical texts, and most explicitly by I Kings 8:9, featuring an ark that contained only the tablets of the testimony. The existence of these traditions (one of which at least was probably well known when I Kings 8:9 was written) points to an ongoing discussion about the meaning of the ark and about its contents — in other words, to different solutions of the problem of what was central in Israel and what sacred object led the Israelites during the desert trek that constituted the prototype of all subsequent religious and social life. The winning answer to this question was the tablets with the text dictated by Yahweh and written by Moses, but, as I Kings 8:9 seems to show, it was not, and probably was never, the only answer. If not at all times, at least from time to time, it was necessary to reshape the traditions in order to make room once more for the written law.[15]

4

The problem of what or who must lead Israel in its journey in space to the promised land is the narrative expression of another problem: the problem of who or what shall rule Israel in its journey through time. The alternatives that are possible in the Exodus story are, as we have shown, similar to the alternatives that confront the kingdom of Judah in the time of Josiah and of Joash (II Kings 22–23 and 11). We have seen the answer to this problem to be both similar to, and distinct from, the answer to the problem of leading Israel in the desert: a pious monarch rules well, but an inspired text, tested by a prophetess and followed obediently by a pious monarch, rules better. And even in the first case, the pious monarch is given the *'edūt* — whatever that is in this case — during the ceremony of his consecration.

I have already connected the account of Israel's choice in the desert to the narratives about Israel's and Judah's attitude to the written *tôrāh* in later times, and we have noticed that the written *tôrāh* that has to be followed in later times is that same written *tôrāh* that has been dictated to Moses on Sinai, so that the written law is given in the narrative of Exodus 19–40 and found, restored, followed, or merely recalled in the other narratives. Indeed, continuity and faithfulness to the *bᵉrīt* require the upholding of the original sacred law, contained in the *ʿedūt*, that was placed in the ark.

Were innovations possible? How did one confer validity on *tôrāh*? I know nothing of the precise connections between *sēper hattôrāh*, found in the time of Josiah according to the narrative of II Kings 22–23, and the book of Deuteronomy. But I do know that the presentation of a book of *tôrāh* must necessarily have followed the consistent strategy illustrated by the narrative of II Kings 22–23 and by the book of Deuteronomy itself, in order not to contradict the general principle that all written *tôrāh* books were written by Moses when inspired by Yahweh.

A first version of this strategy—the version followed by the narrative in II Kings 22–23—consisted of presenting the book of the *tôrāh* as found, and thus as kept until it was found, in the holy place that was the receptacle of the ark and of the laws the ark contained. If validated by the inspired word of a prophetic person—such as Hulda in II Kings 22:12–20—the book could then (implicitly) be considered as ancient, Mosaic, and inspired, and thus possibly identified with the *sēper habbᵉrīt* written by Moses according to Exod. 24:4 or with the *tôrāh* of Moses written down by Joshua on the twelve stones and read aloud by him in Shechem during the renewal of the *bᵉrīt* there (Josh. 8:31–35; cf. Deut. 27).

A second version of the same strategy is the simpler one followed by Deuteronomy in presenting itself as the text written by Moses and given by him to the Levites who carry the ark, as well as to all the elders of Israel, with orders to read it aloud every seventh year to all Israel. By order of Moses, we are told, the book (called *sēper hattôrāh* here) was placed near the ark, "that it may be there as a witness against" Israel for Moses knew the Israelites would rebel against Yahweh (Deut. 31:9–29).

So, whether or not Deuteronomy is the *sēper hattôrāh* found in the temple of Jerusalem in the time of Josiah, the same strategy of convalidation is at work both in the narrative of II Kings 22–23 and in the book of Deuteronomy itself. But what is more important to us in the present context is the role played in each of the two texts by inspired persons. This role is the specific form that the confrontation between the revealed text and the inspired person takes on in the specific strategy for the convalidation of a written text. I shall turn to this role in order to shed more light on our general problem of the relationship between written law and divine inspiration in the Bible.

In Deuteronomy, the inspired man is Moses, who is in direct contact with the Deity and thus writes the revealed text. After he has disappeared, the text shall survive in the way we have seen: near the ark, guarded, and periodically recited, by the Levites. But two categories of Israelites are, so to speak, prophetically imagined by the text in connection with the future life of the *sēper hattôrāh*. The first such category (Deut. 17:14–20) is that of kings: the king must uphold the written law. "And, when [the king] sits on the throne of his kingdom, he shall write a copy of this *tôrāh* in a book in front of the Levite priests, and [this book] shall be with him, and he shall read it all the days of his life, that he may learn to fear Yahweh, his god, to keep all the words of this teachings and these statutes, and that he may put them into practice" (17:18–19). Joash and Josiah are already contained in this program. The second category is that of prophets (18:9–22): the prophets are the intermediaries asked for by the Israelites in the context of the desert journey. "As for you, Yahweh your god shall raise up for you a prophet from among your brothers, like me, and you will listen to them" (18:15). The prophets are like Moses, and what this similarity means is clear from the following verses, which quote the experience on Horeb: "It is according to what you asked of Yahweh your god in Horeb, in the day of the assembly, when you said: Let me not hear again the voice of Yahweh my god, and let me see this great fire no more! I do not want to die! And Yahweh said to me [i.e., to Moses]: They have spoken well. I shall raise a prophet for them from among their brethren, like you, and I will put my words in his mouth and he shall speak in my name all that I shall order them to say. If one shall not listen to the words that the prophet shall say in my name, I will have him account for this; but the prophet who shall presume to say a word in my name that I have not commanded him to say, or shall speak in the name of other gods, that prophet shall die" (18:16–20). The prophets exist because the people have refused the horrors and the fears of a direct contact with the deity, after experiencing it by the mountain of Horeb. And the existence of prophets immediately implies the possible existence of false prophets. While the true prophets must be obeyed, the false prophets must die. But how can one tell a true from a false prophet? Since there are two types of false prophets, there are two different ways to distinguish them. The first type of false prophet, as we have seen, is the prophet who speaks in the name of false gods: it is easy to identify this type. But the second type of false prophet, the prophet "who shall presume to say a word in Yahweh's name that Yahweh has not commanded him to say," is obviously more difficult to spot. A simple way of identifying him is suggested in Deuteronomy in the verse that follows: "And if you ask, in your hearts, How shall we know the words which Yahweh has not spoken? [the answer is:] When a prophet speaks in the name of Yahweh, if the thing he has said does not happen, and does not come to pass, that is the thing Yahweh has not spoken, and the prophet has said it presumptuously: do not fear him" (18:21–22).

The coexistence of prophet and written *tôrāh* is codified thus by the written *torah* itself. But one should note that in the passages of Deuteronomy I have quoted so far the written law is presented as always valid, while the prophets may be false. Indeed, the prophets must be tested, while the written *tôrāh* is the test of the king's righteousness and piety. If we compare this to the story of Hulda in II Kings 22:12–20, we shall note a reversal, for in this last passage it is through a prophetic figure that the authenticity of a book presenting itself as the *sēper hattôrāh* is tested. Yet the written law and the inspired persons do not cease to exist as complementary, and the centrality of the written law is never questioned by the true prophets of the canon. Indeed, the canonical prophets in their very action as testers of the written law are presented as firm upholders of the *tôrāh* that was once written by their predecessor Moses.[16]

5

I shall close on this triumphant tone. But before I conclude, I shall note that all the texts we have discussed so far—the two passages of the second book of Kings, the narratives about Moses and the ark, and now the words of the deity in Deuteronomy—feature three detainers of authority and play with them as in a chess game. Since the priest apparently plays a relatively minor role as up-holder of the right king, as custodian or chance discoverer of the holy text, or as helper of the inspired intermediary, these three detainers and sources of authority are the king, the inspired text, and the inspired intermediary or prophet. Of these three, it is the king who regularly gives way. He has power over the people, but, paradoxically indeed for a Near Eastern monarch, he is no lawgiver; on the contrary, he must follow the rules set by the text and the commands of the deity communicated to him by the prophet.[17] The laws are thus not kingly laws, but rules dictated directly by the deity; crimes are sins; pardon may not be granted by the kingly authority, nor may it be given by the injured party. Authority and power belong to Yahweh and are transmitted through prophet and text. Prophet and text may validate—or invalidate—each other, and I have described some aspects of this complex interplay. But it is through them that the real authority is conveyed, and, to judge by the Bible's later success, it would seem that the text has won—just as happened in our biblical stories.

I shall repeat once more that it is precisely the strategy of the text in pre-senting itself so ably and forcefully as divinely inspired that accounts for its success. But this time, as I conclude this series of disembodied speculations, I shall at least mention the vulgar fact that the strategy of a text does not exist in and of itself: it is the strategy of those who write it. I hasten to add that the his-tory of the formation of the Bible is not only complex, but practically un-known and in large part impossible to know—in spite of, and in some cases be-cause of, the millions of books published on the subject by *Alttestamentlern*.[18] So I have no answer—especially no answer in extremis—to the question of the authorship of the texts we have discussed. In general, one would be justified in identifying their authors with an elite group not too different from the groups of officials, priests, scribes, or temple "prophets" we met in our first two stories. More in particular, since at least the final redaction of our texts should be as-cribed to the postexilic age, it seems probable that the texts we have read here were profoundly reshaped, if not actually written, by the scribal elite of (exilic and) postexilic Israel,[19] which cemented the national unity not around a na-tional monarchy that existed no more, but around common beliefs, common laws, common texts.[20]

NOTES

1. An interesting discussion of *tôrāh* and of the corresponding Greek terms in the Septuagint translations is L. Monssengwo Pasinya, *La Notion de Nomos dans le Pentateuque Grec* (Rome: Biblical Institute Press, 1973), esp. pp. 62–100. A turning point in the study of this term was constituted by S. Schechter, *Some Aspects of Rabbinic Theology* (New York, 1910), pp. 116–141.

2. For a "Greek" view of Moses as a lawgiver in the work of Flavius Josephus, see A. Momigliano, "Un'apologia del giudaismo: il 'Contro Apione' di Flavio Giuseppe," in *Terzo Contributo alla storia degli studi classici e del mondo antico*, vol. 1 (1931; Rome, 1966).

3. L. Perlitt, *Bundestheologie des Alten Testament* (Neukirchen, 1969); E. Kutch, *Verheissung und Gesetz* (Berlin, 1973).

4. Some doubts are expressed in my "Specialisti del soprannaturale e potere nella Bibbia ebraica: appunti e spunti," in *Soprannaturale e potere nel mondo antico e nelle società tradizionali*, ed. M. Fales and C. Grottanelli (Milan: Angeli, 1985) (chapter 6 in this volume).

5. M. Liverani, "L'histoire de Joas," *Vetus Testamentum* 24 (1974): 438–53.

6. On the two objects given to Joash see J. Gray, *I and II Kings: A Commentary*, 3d ed., Old Testament Library (London: SCM, 1977), pp. 573–74.

7. Indeed, there is more here than a mere crescendo, for, as Jonathan Paradise points out to me, Josiah is the very type of the Yahwistic king and thus the standard against which every monarch of Israel and Judah is judged.

8. For good information on the perversions of this traditional approach, which is now defended by those same clerical circles that fought against it savagely when it was innovative and thought provoking, see B. S. Childs, *Exodus: A Commentary*, Old Testament Library (London: SCM, 1974), passim.

9. Deuteronomy 18:15, where Moses declares that Yahweh will raise up "to you a prophet, from your brothers, *like me.*"

10. On the golden calf see J. M. Sasson, "Bovine Symbolism in the Exodus Narrative," *Vetus Testamentum* 18 (1968): 380–387, an article that is still useful, and the bibliography quoted there. For the religion of Jeroboam, G. W. Ahlström, *Royal Administration and National Religion in Ancient Israel* (Leiden: Brill, 1982), pp. 56–62, is important. For a different approach to the golden calf episode in Exodus see S. E. Loewenstamm, "The Making and Destruction of the Golden Calf," *Biblica* 48 (1967): 481–490, and "The Making and Destruction of the Golden Calf: A Rejoinder," *Biblica* 56 (1975): 330–343. Along the same lines see C. Grottanelli, "The Enemy King Is a Monster: A Biblical Equation," *Studi Storico-Religiosi* 3 (1979): 39–63 (chapter 3 in this volume). On the meaning of the golden calf theme in later literature see P. C. Bori, *Il vitello d'oro: Le radici della controversia antigiudaica* (Turin: Boringhieri, 1983).

11. J. H. Tigay, "'Heavy of Mouth' and 'Heavy of Tongue': On Moses' Speech Difficulty," *Bulletin of the American Schools of Oriental Research* 231 (1978): 57–67.

12. Childs, pp. 374–375.

13. Gray, p. 210.

14. Traditions and sources are quoted in L. Ginzberg, *The Legends of the Jews* (Philadelphia: 1946), 2:180–183, 5:374–377 (vol. 5 contains notes to vols. 1 and 2). See also E. Zolli, *Israele: Studi storico-religiosi* (Udine, 1935), p. 139, quoting A. Marmorstein, "Beiträge für Religionsgeschichte und Volkskunde," *Jahrbuch für*

jüdische Volkskunde (1923), pp. 285–286; and *Pesikta de-Rab Kahana: R. Kahana's Compilation of Discourses for Sabbaths and Festal Days,* trans. W. G. Braude and I. J. Kapstein (Philadelphia: Jewish Publication Society of America, 1975), pp. 211–212 (*Piska* 11.12).

15. The problems I have discussed so far were not the only ones, for to the golden calf made by Aaron and destroyed by Moses (and "remade" by Jeroboam) one must add the bronze serpent *made* by Moses and destroyed by the pious king Hezekiah (!) according to II Kings 18:4. There is no space here to dedicate to this further contradiction; on the serpent see G. Garbini, "Le serpent d'arain et Moïse," *Zeitschrift für alttestamentliche Wissenschaft* 100 (1988): 264–267; and, for the traditions about Moses, see G. W. Ahlström, "Another Moses Tradition," *Journal of Near Eastern Studies* 39 (1980): 65–69.

16. For a view of the prophets as upholders of Yahwistic monotheism see B. Lang, *Monotheism and the Prophetic Minority* (Sheffield: Almond, 1983). But historically Moses was modeled on the prophets rather than vice versa: see C. Grottanelli, "Profezia e scrittura nel Vicino Oriente," *La Ricerca Folklorica* 5 (1982): 103–116 (chapter 9 in this volume).

17. I have discussed this point with Jonathan Paradise, and I wish to thank him for his suggestions.

18. A good starting point for a critical study of the formation of the biblical texts is M. Smith, *Palestinian Parties and Politics That Shaped the Old Testament* (New York: Columbia University Press, 1971), but the author still follows the biblical narrative too closely. G. Garbini, *History and Ideology in Ancient Israel* (New York: Crossroad, 1988), is important.

19. On the dating of the "historical" books of the Bible see J. Van Seters, *In Search of History* (New Haven, Conn.: Yale University Press, 1983).

20. On the function of canon as a pivot of identity, see J. A. Sanders, "Adaptable for Life: The Nature and Function of Canon" in *Magnalia Dei: The Mighty Acts of God: Essays on the Bible and Archaeology in Memory of G. E. Wright,* ed. F. M. Cross, W. E. Lemke, and P. D. Miller, Jr. (Garden City, N.Y.: Doubleday, 1976), pp. 531–560.

INDEX

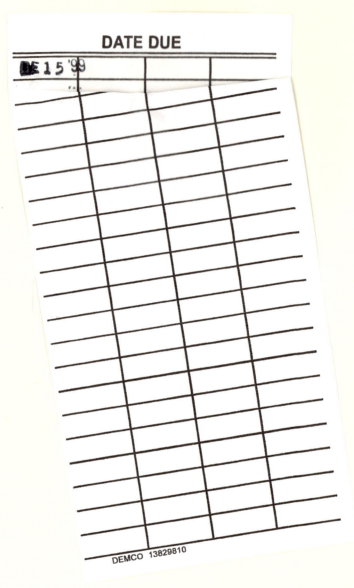

DATE DUE

DE 15 '99

DEMCO 13829810